The Penns' Manor of Spread Eagle

&

The Grist Mills of the Upper Mahantongo Valley

Including the African American Simmy Family Heritage

STEVE E. TROUTMAN

Mechanicsburg, PA USA

Published by Sunbury Press, Inc.
105 South Market Street
Mechanicsburg, Pennsylvania 17055

www.sunburypress.com

Copyright © 2015, 2016 by Steve E. Troutman.
Cover Copyright © 2015 by Sunbury Press, Inc.

Sunbury Press supports copyright. Copyright fuels creativity, encourages diverse voices, promotes free speech, and creates a vibrant culture. Thank you for buying an authorized edition of this book and for complying with copyright laws by not reproducing, scanning, or distributing any part of it in any form without permission. You are supporting writers and allowing Sunbury Press to continue to publish books for every reader. For information contact Sunbury Press, Inc., Subsidiary Rights Dept., 105 South Market St., Mechanicsburg, PA 17011 USA or legal@sunburypress.com.

For information about special discounts for bulk purchases, please contact Sunbury Press Orders Dept. at (855) 338-8359 or orders@sunburypress.com.

To request one of our authors for speaking engagements or book signings, please contact Sunbury Press Publicity Dept. at publicity@sunburypress.com.

ISBN: 978-1-62006-715-4 (Trade Paperback)

Library of Congress Control Number: 2015953320

THIRD SUNBURY PRESS EDITION: January 2016

Product of the United States of America
0 1 1 2 3 5 8 13 21 34 55

Set in Bookman Old Style
Designed by Crystal Devine
Cover by Lawrence Knorr
Edited by Lawrence Knorr

Continue the Enlightenment!

Cover Photo courtesy of Ronald Maurer, Halifax, PA.
Ron lived in Klingerstown during his youth.

Earl & Marion Troutman in 1985, during a visit to Rough and Ready for a Summer Picnic

This book is dedicated to my mother, Marion Anna (Romberger) Troutman
(December 26, 1929 – May 13, 2005), and
my father, Earl George Troutman (born April 21, 1928).

Acknowledgments

A very special thank you is in order for my dear wife Joan Elizabeth (Masser) Troutman. Joan typed most of this manuscript for publication. She edited my page preparations, sometimes repeatedly, putting aside her frustration with my writing skills. She made countless corrections of spelling and grammar, forcing me to write intelligently.

    A special thank you to my daughter Valerie Specht who designed every page doing manuscript preparation, working with me when she had time available and when she did not have time available. I think she enjoyed doing the book preparation although sometimes it became burdensome considering she had a young family to take care of.

    Thank you to all the others who contributed to the book, every story and photo provided for publication made the effort worthwhile. I thank you all for what you have done for me.

Table of Contents

Preface vii

Introduction ix

Part I: Spread Eagle Manor and the Establishment of
           Klingerstown and the Klingerstown Grist Mill 1

Part II: The Klingerstown Mill 153

Part III: The Mills of the Upper Mahantongo Valley 203

Part IV: The Simmy Family—An African American Pioneer
           Family in the Mahantongo Valley 257

Appendix 299

Preface

My mother learned to speak English when she attended first grade at the one room Noble School. The Pennsylvania German dialect was spoken in her home. My father Earl likewise had an appreciation of his heritage and often spoke of his Germanic ancestry.

Their interest in family genealogy prompted my own pursuit of local history. In 1992 Marion and Earl G. Troutman, my parents, published a local history book entitled, "Klingerstown, Reflections of Yesterday". The reason for this collection of early photographs and accompanying narrative was Hurricane Agnes. In 1972 Hurricane Agnes caused a terrible flood covering most of the houses in Klingerstown. Many were filled with water up to the second story of the buildings. Precious photographs, thought to be one of a kind, were destroyed by the muddy waters. My mother and a few of her close friends determined they would replace these family pictures for those whose loss was great. And so her book of photos was printed, sold out, and reprinted again. It is presently no longer available.

Some of the photos and narrative from this first book were incorporated into "The Klingerstown Bi-Centennial Album, 1807-2007." This was compiled in 2007 by an anniversary committee with the Klingerstown Fire Police. This book continues to be available for $20 and is being sold by a fund raiser. Several hundred copies have been sold. It is a wonderful resource for genealogists and anyone who has a connection to "Klingerstettle."

Continued interest in local heritage, and new information available, prompted the consideration of another book. The loss of the Klingerstown Mill also provided impetus to further tell its story. The Klingerstown Mill's presence for over 200 years, made it a landmark for the area.

In my mother's latter days, she expressed interest that a book should be compiled about the mills along the Mahantongo. With this request still unfulfilled, I determined to commemorate the Klingerstown Mill as well as the other mills my mother fondly recalled from her youth. She was a born Romberger with family tree roots including Klinger, Stiely, and Knorr. All four of these families were associated with the operation of grist mills dating back to the immigrant families from Germany. The milling tradition existed within the generations in Germany as well.

So it is with humble gratitude that I present this book in memory of my mother who suggested the topic over 10 years ago.

Steve E. Troutman, 2015

Introduction

Thirty years ago, I retrieved a book from a deteriorating one room school house near Klingerstown. The building was very weathered with a leaking roof. The book had been water soaked many times but appeared to be salvable. It was entitled, "United States, Its Past and Present", by Henry W. Elson, published in 1926. Pages 1-72 are the source of much of the following:

> It is a notable fact of history that 400 years ago nearly half the land area of the world was unknown to the inhabitants of the other half. In 1492 this one sided view of the world changed when Columbus left a Spanish seaport of Palos on a great voyage across the sea of darkness. For many years Columbus had tried to enlist the interest for his voyage from Portugal, France, and England before Queen Isabella of Spain raised the money to fit him out for the voyage. After discovering the islands of Cuba and Haiti, he returned to tell the news of his wonderful discovery.
>
> Five years later John Cabot was the first to discover the mainland of America. He was a citizen of England. He and his son, Sebastian, were sent out by the English King, Henry VII, in 1497. He reached Labrador and explored the Atlantic coast as far south as Cape Cod. It was this voyage and a later one by Sebastian Cabot that formed the basis of the English claim to North America.
>
> The Americas had been inhabited by human populations for thousands of years before European contact. The American Indians were a diverse group of people, with varied beliefs, but one thing they did not have in common with the European explorers was the concept of land ownership.
>
> The father of English colonization in America was Sir Walter Raleigh. In 1585 Raleigh sent out a colony of men who settled on Roanoke Island off the coast of North Carolina. His efforts awakened a desire to colonize the new lands of the west. He named the new land Virginia. The colony of Maryland was the second colony established by Lord Baltimore, George Calvert, in 1634. In 1663 King Charles II of England gave a charter to the vast region known as the Carolinas. The colonies of Massachusetts, Rode Island, Connecticut, New Hampshire, New York, New Jersey, and Delaware were all founded before Pennsylvania.
>
> In 1682 William Penn crossed the Atlantic on the ship, Welcome, to join three shiploads he had sent the year before. William Penn would establish a new colony named Pennsylvania. It was a vast domain of 40,000 square miles extending from the Delaware River, over the Alleghenies, into the Ohio Valley.

Part I:

Spread Eagle Manor and the Establishment of Klingerstown and the Klingerstown Grist Mill

On March 4, 1681, King Charles II of England signed the Royal Charter establishing the new colony of Pennsylvania. The colony established by William Penn was based upon the concept of religious freedom. John Carter in his book, "Early Events in the Susquehanna Valley," page 149, describes this event.

"Although William Penn's grant from King Charles II gave him legal claim to practically all of what is now Pennsylvania, nevertheless no lands were to be surveyed or settled upon until said lands were deeded by the Indians.

Another practice inaugurated by William Penn was the setting aside of a tenth or less of all newly acquired territory before any of it were thrown open for purchase and subsequent settlement. Such lands reserved for the use of personal disposal of the Proprietors were known as Proprietary Manors. The most desirable lands and those occupying the best strategic positions were of course selected.

The purchase of Indian lands in 1736 extended the northern boundary of the Province to the Blue Mountain. The Treaty of 1749, when Line Mountain became part of the new northern boundary of the Province, the Penns located their Manor at the forks of the Mahantongo and Pine Creeks, where the Onondaga–Shackamaxon Trail passed through the gap in Mahantongo Mountain, within sight of Line Mountain, the newly established boundary. The Proprietors very appropriately named their newest reservation Spread Eagle Manor."

In 2015, Steve and Joan Troutman visited the city of London and Great Britain. One of our points of interest was the Tower of London. A Yeoman of high military rank gave a tour of the vast castle. When the Yeoman tour guide learned we were from Pennsylvania, he told us some interesting history pertaining to William Penn. It is recorded that William Penn criticized King Charles II of England, pertaining to the King's persecution of people of religion other than what the King professed. William Penn was put on trial and found guilty of this crime and imprisoned in the Tower of London. This large castle was originally built as a fortress. Over many centuries of its existence, it was utilized for many purposes, one of which was a prison for persons of the Aristocracy being a higher class of people. William Penn was able to pay the necessary fines and was released upon the condition set forth by King Charles II of England. The conditions were that William Penn must leave the country and so he came to Pennsylvania to the land he had inherited.

The English King, Charles II, on March 4, 1681, granted Pennsylvania to William Penn. The King named the land Pennsylvania in honor of Sir William Penn, the father of William Penn. This put him in possession of more than 28 million acres of land in the new world.

History of the Spread Eagle Tree
As taken from "History of the Mahantongo Valley" printed in the
Pottsville Republican Morning Paper, February 21-26, 1935
Original source <u>The Joseph H. Zerby History of Pottsville and
Schuylkill County, Pa</u> p. 1290-1291

Mahantongo is an Indian name and means "the place where we had plenty of venison to eat." The low land at the Junction of the Pine and Mahantongo Creeks was a favorite spot of the Indians, if not an Indian village, then at least a noted camping place. The maps of the Sculls (cartographers) of 1750 have this place noted. It is known as Spread Eagle. In the dim and distant colonial days, an Indian carved the figure of a spread eagle on a giant sycamore tree…It may have commemorated some feat of an Indian runner, or marked some tribal boundary, or it may have been the emblem of some Indian tribe.

In 1745 Moravian missionary Bishop Spangenberg, speaking of this region, says, "Here we found encamped the family of an Indian, who on learning from whence we came, and realizing that we must be hungry, said to his wife, 'Give them some spits full of venison.' In return for this kindness, Brother Spangenberg gave them knives and thimbles."

Above drawing is page 10 from the Klingerstown Bicentennial Album 1807-2007. "Joseph H. Zerby History, Pottsville and Schuylkill County, Penna.," p. 1290, 1291 Upper Mahntongo Twp.

Part I: Spread Eagle Manor and the Establishment of Klingerstown and the Klingerstown Grist Mill

---

Mahantongo is an Indian name, and means "The place where we had plenty of venison to eat." We have no definite record of who the first settlers in the western portion of Mahantongo Township were. They no doubt came from beyond the Blue Mountains through the Klingerstown Gap. The lowland at the junction of the Pine and Mahantongo Creeks was a favorite spot of the Indians; if not an Indian village, then at least a noted camping place. The maps of the Scull's of 1750 have this place noted. It is known as Spread Eagle. In the dim and distant past colonial days, an Indian carved the figure of a spread eagle on a giant sycamore tree that has stood on the banks of the Pine Creek, almost in the center of the present village of Klingerstown. The tree was a landmark for the entire region, even in colonial times, for it is noted by the traveling missionaries as early as 1745 on their trips to Shamokin (Sunbury) over the Tulpehocken Trail, which passed through the Gap. Rev. David Zeisberger, Bishop Spangenberg, Rev. Frederick Conrad Muhlenberg and Conrad Weiser were among the men who hallowed this spot by their presence. Bishop Spangenberg, speaking of this region, says, "Here we found encamped the family of an Indian, who on learning from whence we came and realizing that we must be hungry, said to his wife, 'give them some spits full of venison.'" In return for this kindness, Brother Spangenberg gave them knives and thimbles.

Spread Eagle Tree Replica carved by Butch Kieffer of Leck Kill for the Klingerstown Bicentennial Celebration—Summer 2007

Gary Schreckengost, an educator from Lancaster, PA, is a Lenni Lenape descendant. "Len" means people and "api" means as or like. "Nee" means me or I. He is familiar with the Indian language and gives us the origin of the word Mahantongo. "Mahan Ing" means eat place, and Mahantongo is an English corruption of "May-ho Ah –to Go" which means eat deer place.

Mr. Joseph Zerby, page 1291, "Referring again to the Spread Eagle symbol, it may have commemorated some feat of an Indian runner, or marked some tribal boundary, or may have been the emblem of some Indian tribe. The "spread eagle" sycamore tree was blown down during a severe storm in the early 70's (1870's). The name remained for some time as the name of the hotel, "Spread Eagle Tavern . . ."

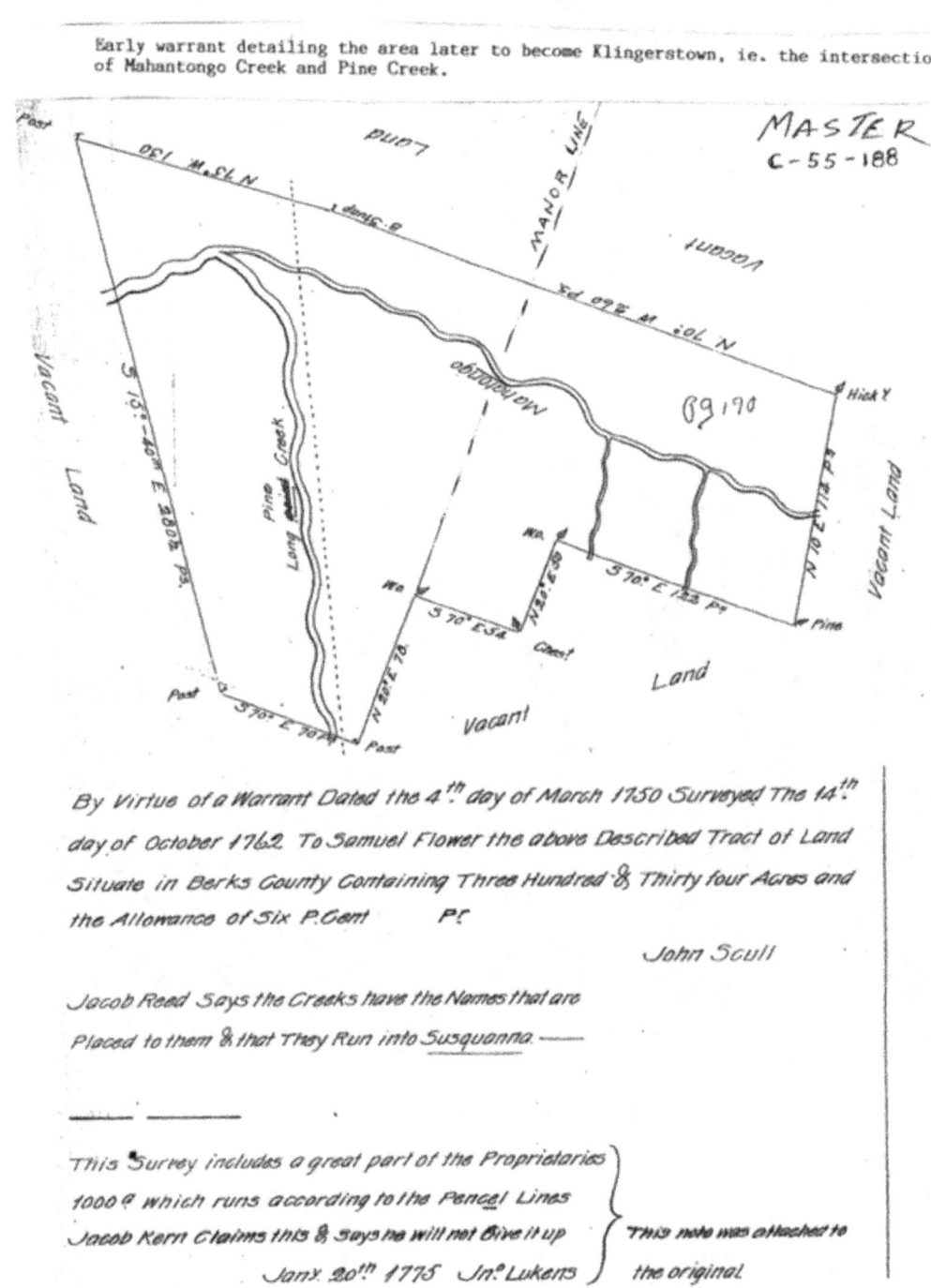

Early warrant detailing the area later to become Klingerstown, ie. The intersection of Mahantongo Creek and Pine Creek.

Part I: Spread Eagle Manor and the Establishment of Klingerstown and the Klingerstown Grist Mill

Johannes Klinger, Founder of Klingerstown

Johannes is the son of Alexander Klinger. Johannes, by tradition, is identified as the probable founder of Klingerstown. Please take note of the date of his death in the year 1800. His wife, Elizabeth, died only 4 years later in 1804.

Johannes Klinger (April 3, 1753) – (April 3, 1800), married Elizabeth (Henninger) Klinger (June 15, 1763) – (Aug. 20, 1804). These dates are recorded in "Zion (Klinger's) Church History" by Irvin Klinger. Johannes and Elizabeth are buried in Erdman, PA in the Klinger's Church Cemetery, row 2, stones 13 and 14. Johannes was 47 years old and Elizabeth was 41 years 2 month, and 4 days.

Mary Klinger, in her book, "The Klingers 1610-1989," published in 1989, p. 497, refers to "The Zerby History of Schuylkill County". Mary states that "John Klinger was gone before the town was established. John Klinger had purchased the Double Eagle from the Penns, it being the center of present day Klingerstown." Mary writes that the town was named Elizabethtown, after John Klinger's wife. She outlived her husband for 4 more years, her death recorded in 1804.

Phillip Klinger and Alexander Klinger emigrated as brothers from Pfaffenbeerfurth, Odenwald (Hessen-Darmstadt) Germany. They came from a long tradition of mill operators. They had previously purchased lots in the earliest years of the settlement of the City of Reading, PA. These Klingers were familiar with the concept of buying and selling lots for residents and business men. They themselves had residences and a hotel named the Butcher's Tavern. They had purchased some of the first lots sold in 1753 located on the hill in the south portion of the city. Phillip and Alexander served in the Berks County Militia during the Revolutionary War at various times between 1777 and 1781. See page 10 of Max E. Klinger's book, "The Descendants of John Peter Klinger and Catharina Steinbruch," published by Sunbury Press, 2005.

"The Joseph H. Zerby History of Pottsville and Schuylkill County" on page 1291 also states "Alexander Klinger and his four sons bought land and settled in the vicinity of Klingerstown in 1780, and John Klinger, no doubt, gave the place its present name in 1807, when he laid out lots and sold them, but it was originally called Waynetown, no doubt, named for General Anthony Wayne of Revolutionary fame, and later Elizabethtown." A very important date is given here by Mr. Zerby. He records the year 1807 as the founding date of Klingerstown. "So the extreme western corner of Schuylkill County was known as Spread Eagle, Waynetown, Elizabethtown, but it is now Klingerstown, to all intent and purpose, but no Klinger originally settled it. Jacob Baum, Robert Clark, Solomon Shumann, Andrew Osman, Peter Klock, Mr. Heim, John Reed, Jacob Wiest, George Maurer, Jacob Stenner and Mr. Renninger were among the early settlers of the township."

Johannes Klinger seems to be the likely builder of the log grist mill in Klingerstown before the year 1800. Since he died in 1800, at age 47, it may be assumed he built the mill shortly before an unexpected death. Perhaps his wife Elizabeth (Henninger) Klinger (June 15, 1763-August 20, 1804) continued her husband's efforts. Perhaps Elizabeth operated the mill until her death in 1804, dying at the young age of 41 years, 2 months and 2 days. John and Elizabeth are buried at Zion Lutheran Cemetery, in Erdman, PA. (Author's note: There is a conflict between the death dates of Johannes in 1800 and Elizabeth Klinger's death in 1804 and the proposed Klingerstown founding date of 1807.)

Alexander Klinger and his wife Anna Elizabeth (Geiss) came to America on the ship ALBANY, with his second cousin once removed, arriving at Philadelphia on 2 Sept 1749. They settled at Reading, Pa. He acquired about 1000 acres of land in the Mahantongo Valley east of Klingerstown and came to that area with four of his sons in 1780. He himself returned to Reading where he remained until his death, leaving the administration of his land to his sons. The children of Alexander and Elizabeth are as taken from research done by Richard Whittington Clifton:

1. Johann Michael, who was born in Pfaffen-beerfurth, Germany, where it is said he remained with the grandparents when the parents came to America.
2. Johannes who married Maria Elizabeth Henninger. According to Orphans Court records from Northumberland County, they had the following four children:
  1 Jeremiah who married Anna Maria Kreys or Krebs. 2 Mariah who married John Clark. 3 Catharine who married John Schreckengast. 4 John
3. Eva Elizabeth who married Gideon Williamson and lived on what is now the John Mausser farm in the Mahantango Valley according to Steve Troutman's book on the Troutman's. There were 10 children, according to information supplied by Carolyn Schwalm: 1 James who married a Catharine 2 Thomas 3 Maria who married Jacob Troutman 4 Hannah who married Jacob Leitner 5 Rachel who married Andreas Erdman 6 Catharine who married (1) John Witman (2) John Strohecker 7 William 8 Alexander 9 George who was living in Stark County in 1841 10 Emma who married William Heath.

Eva Elizabeth had a daughter prior to her marriage to Gideon Williamson, Elizabeth van der Sluiss who married Abraham Haffa. They lived in a tavern, still standing, between Fearnot and Sacramento. According to information supplied by Carolyn Schwalm they had 11 children. 1 Philip who married Elizabeth Henninger 2 Elizabeth who married Johannes Kunzelmann 3 Jacob who married (1) Elizabeth Schwalm (2) Machdalena Saber 4 Catharine who married Daniel Tobias 5 John 6 Maria who married David Shadel 7 Alexander who married Rebecca Kimmel 8 Hannah who married John Shade 9 Henry who married (1) Elizabeth Wiest (2) Anna Elizabeth Hartman 10 Sarah who married Michael Adams 11 Barbara married Solomon Bressler.
According to Mary Klinger's book on the Klingers, Rachel and Andreas Erdman had the following 5 children: 1 Hannah 2 George W. 3 Elizabeth 4 Salome 5 John

4 George Henry who was born 14 July 1758
5. George Adam who married Eva Zeller and spent most of his adult life working the 200 acres of land he acquired from his father in the Mahantango Valley. According to research done by Mr. Clifton mentioned above, they had the following ten children: 1 Elizabeth who married John Kline 2 Mary who married William Sydal 3 Susanna who married Daniel Maurer 4 George Adam Jr. who married Elizabeth and moved to Sugarloaf Township 5 John Peter 6 John Philip 7 Johannes 8 Alexander who married Anna Maria 9 Catharine who married William Lightner 10 Henry
6 Jacob who was born 21 January 1765 and died 22 September 1765
7 John Michael who was born 21 January 1765 and died 10 October 1765
8 John Jacob who was born 15 April 1768 and died 1 February 1774
9 Elizabeth who married William Shenes

Alexander and Eva Elizabeth Klinger are buried in Reading. Elizabeth and Abraham Haffa are buried on Klinger's Cemetery as are Rachel and Andreas Erdman and Hannah and John Shade. Eva Elizabeth and Gideon Williamson and Eva and George Adam Klinger are also probably buried on Klinger's Cemetery although there are no markers for them.

by Irwin R. Klinger

Part I: Spread Eagle Manor and the Establishment of Klingerstown and the Klingerstown Grist Mill

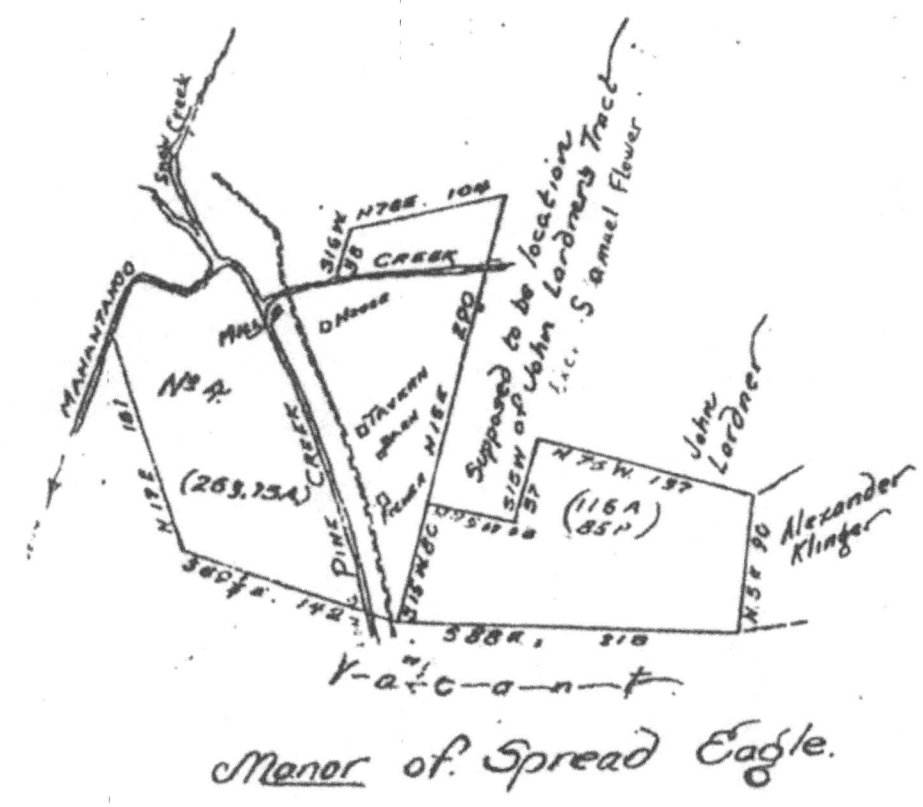

The Berks County Historical Society has provided an early draft of the Manor of Spread Eagle

Early draft of Spread Eagle Manor, Parcel No. 4. Early land owners include Samuel Flower, John Reed, and John Klinger, son of Alexander. In this very early draft there are only two houses, the mill and a tavern with a barn. The house nearest the mill would be the miller's residence. Later records including the 1850 and 1860 Census and the 1875 map of Schuylkill County indicate the first miller's dwelling was across the road, opposite the mill. The tavern would be the Spread Eagle Tavern. It stood north of the present Klingerstown Hotel, across the intersection.

There is mention of an early Mahantongo Valley school in the Klingerstown Bi-Centennial Album, page 48. Perhaps the other house on this early draft is the school identified with Rev. Victor George Charles Stock. In a letter to the ministerium from the Machadunky, dated May 26, 1803, Rev. Stock, who was also the school teacher, complained about a miserable school house he and his family were living in. It was located 22 miles from Sunbury. (Klingerstown is 22 miles from Sunbury.)

"Property Transfer from John Klinger to Henry Baum," Book C – 122-134.

"The Klingestown Bi-Centennial Album, 1807-2007" p. 100, shows a large tract of land, 130 acres, previously warranted by Johannes Klinger on August 3, 1793. This 130 acre tract was surveyed in April of 1842 and transferred to Henry Baum in July of 1842. This tract is located near the southern portion of Klingerstown. No buildings are shown on the map. Here we see that Johannes Klinger in 1793 warranted some of the land where Klingerstown would be eventually located. This is according to the map of land sold to Henry Baum in 1842.

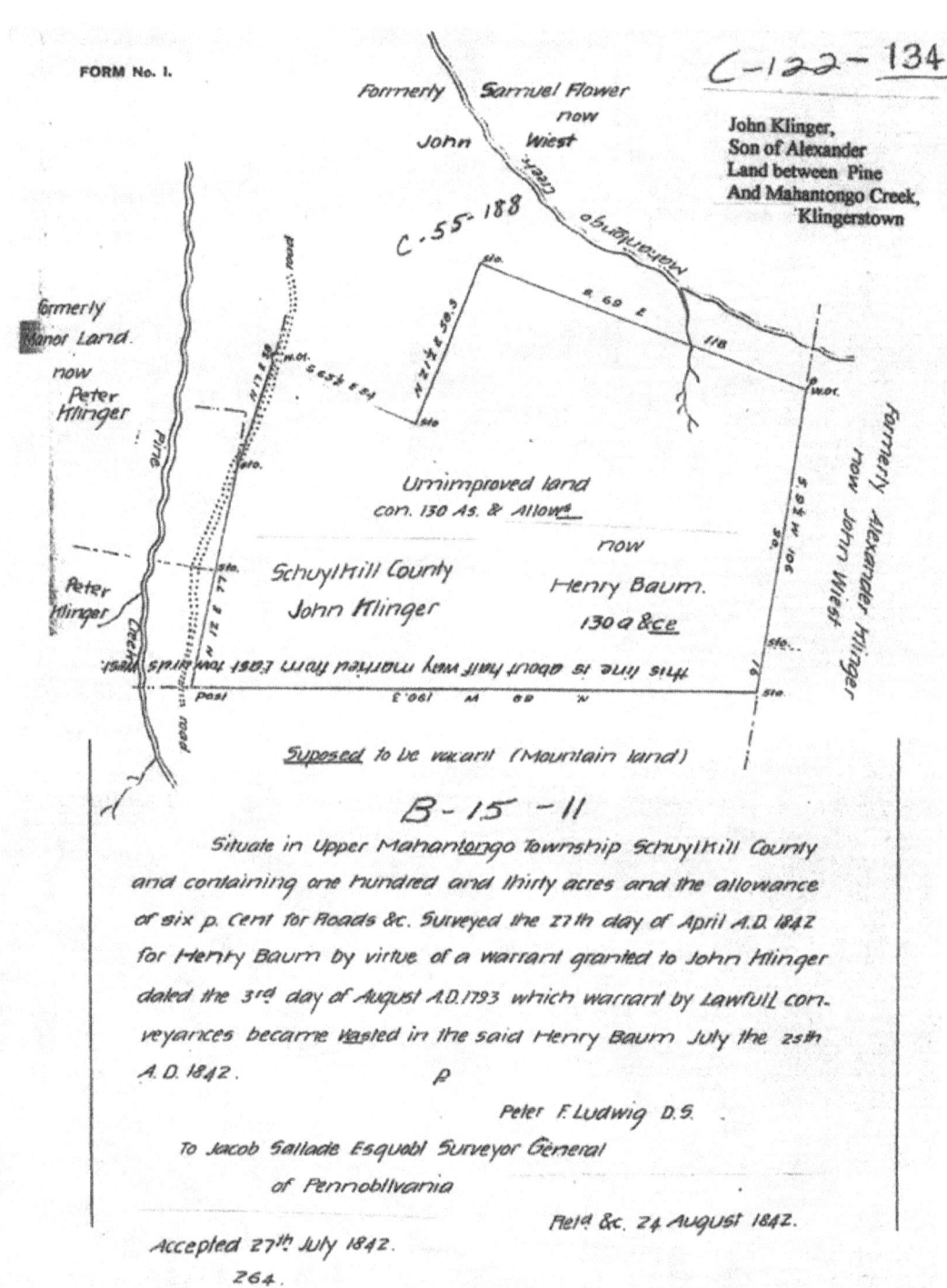

Part I: Spread Eagle Manor and the Establishment of Klingerstown and the Klingerstown Grist Mill

Ownership of Lands Within the Manor and Outside the Manor

George Wheeler, Pd.D., described the Penn Family and their ownership of the land of Pennsylvania, in "The Pennsylvania Magazine," Vol. LVIII, 1934, No. 8. "When Charles II, on March 4, 1681, granted Pennsylvania to William Penn, (1644-1718), he put him in possession of more than 28 million acres of land in the new world." William Penn set forth "certain conditions" agreed upon between the Proprietary (Penn Family) and the purchaser. These conditions as described in the above named source had the purpose of restricting purchasers of land to encourage settlement and discourage land speculation.

Lands surrounding the Manor were available for purchase at an earlier date than the land within the Manor. By March 4, 1750, the proprietary survey of Spread Eagle Manor "at the North-West Passage" had been completed and the land surrounding the Manor was thrown open for purchase.

William Penn was deceased at the time of this survey of manor land in the wilderness. According to "World Book Encyclopedia," 1965, Vol. 15, page 217 states, "At his death, Penn left his interests in Pennsylvania to his four sons. Thomas Penn, (1702-1775), managed the interests until 1741. John Penn, (1729-1795), a grandson, was Lieutenant Governor of Pennsylvania from 1763 to 1771 and from 1773 to 1776. Another grandson, Richard Penn, (1735-1811), was Lieutenant Governor from 1771-1773." The grandsons of William Penn sold the lands in the Mahantongo Valley outside and within the Manor.

After the Revolutionary War began, The Divesting Act of 1779, allowed land transfer of ownership from the Penn Family. The lands within Spread Eagle Manor were now made available for sale. Lands in the Mahantongo Valley outside the Manor had been available for purchase for several decades prior to the land within the Manor.

When originally surveyed by Thomas and Richard Penn, Spread Eagle Manor lay entirely within Lancaster County. When Berks County was erected in 1752, the greater part of the Manor fell within Berks County, but the western-most part was still within the limits of Lancaster County. Schuylkill County was formed out of Berks County in 1811 and the eastern portions of the Manor are now in Schuylkill County.

The book will now continue with an examination of the parcels within the Manor of Spread Eagle.

Draft of Spread Eagle Manor from the collections of the Berks County Historical Society showing land ownership and transfer of ownership

8 Parcels Within Spread Eagle Manor

This draft is largely the work of Mr. George Wheeler of Philadelphia, a native of Pine Grove. Mr. Wheeler published many articles for historical societies and was associated with the Philadelphia public school system. He was deceased before 1955.

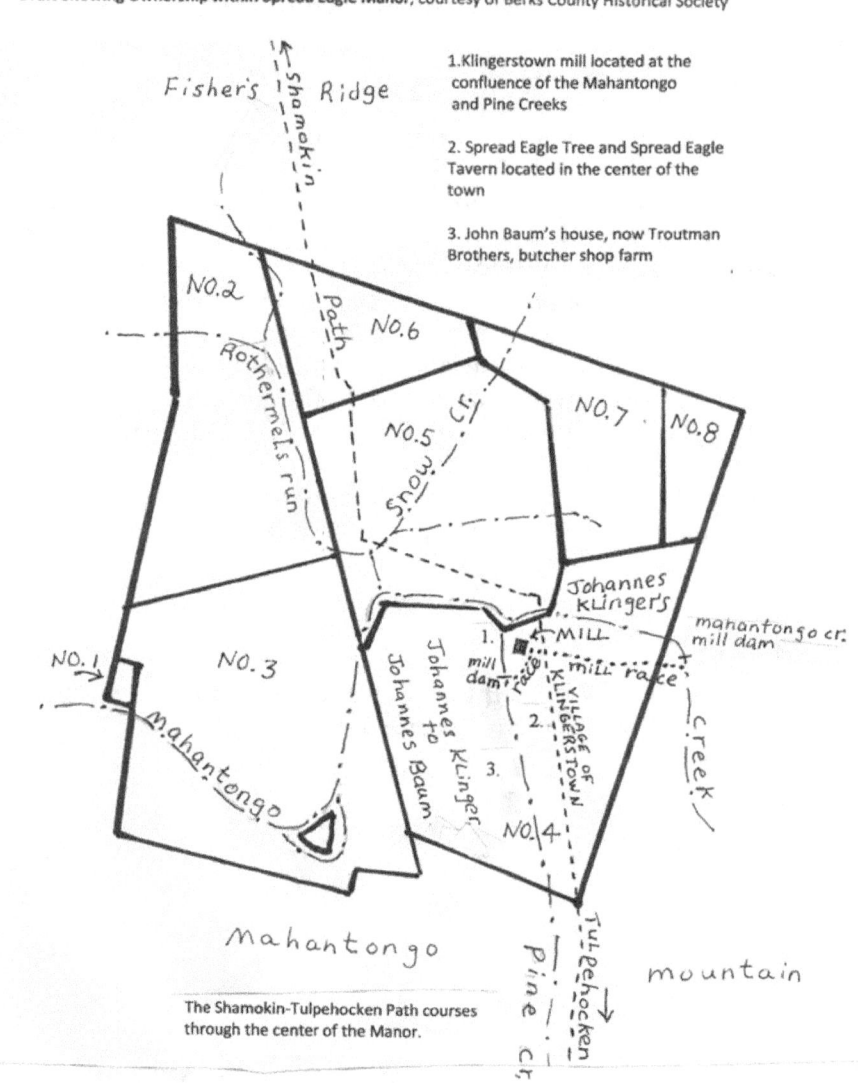

Draft Showing Ownership within Spread Eagle Manor, courtesy of Berks County Historical Society

1. Klingerstown mill located at the confluence of the Mahantongo and Pine Creeks

2. Spread Eagle Tree and Spread Eagle Tavern located in the center of the town

3. John Baum's house, now Troutman Brothers, butcher shop farm

The Shamokin-Tulpehocken Path courses through the center of the Manor.

Part I: Spread Eagle Manor and the Establishment of Klingerstown and the Klingerstown Grist Mill

8 Parcels within Spread Eagle Manor

Draft of Spread Eagle Manor by John Carter, page 150-151 in his book, "Early Events in the Susquehanna Valley," Spread Eagle at the northwest passage

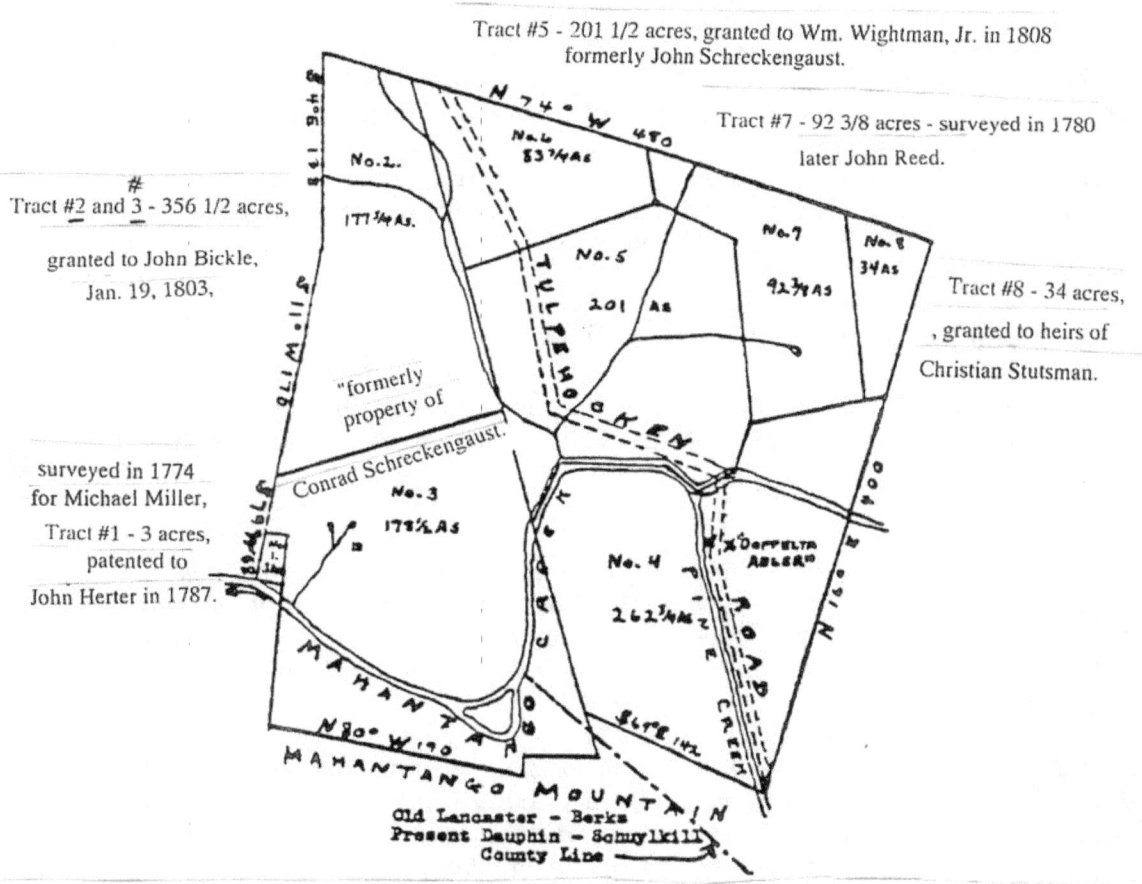

Tract #6 - 83 3/4 acres - part of larger tract surveyed 1778 for Peter Troutman and Philip Spoon. Granted in 1804 to Mr. Wightman, Jr. by John and Richard Penn.

Tract #5 - 201 1/2 acres, granted to Wm. Wightman, Jr. in 1808 formerly John Schreckengaust.

Tract #7 - 92 3/8 acres - surveyed in 1780 later John Reed.

Tract #2 and 3 - 356 1/2 acres, granted to John Bickle, Jan. 19, 1803,

Tract #8 - 34 acres, granted to heirs of Christian Stutsman.

surveyed in 1774 for Michael Miller, Tract #1 - 3 acres, patented to John Herter in 1787.

Tract #4 - 262 3/4 acres, warranted Mar. 4, 1750 to Samuel Flower, and surveyed for him in 1762. Later owned by John Reed, then by John Klinger. The site of Klingerstown.

At present, about three-fourths of the original Manor lies within the bounds of Northumberland County, the remainder being in Schuylkill and Dauphin Counties.

Some time after the passage of the Divestment Act, the Manor was re-surveyed, and at that time contained 1292 acres. The Penns eventually partitioned Spread Eagle Manor into (8) eight tracts, ranging from (3) three acres to 262 3/4) acres each.

Parcel No. 1, 3A.

John Jacob Harter. This could be Jacob born 9 August, 1757, died 12 July, 1837, in Northumberland County, married Elizabeth Heim, born 17 October, 1766, died 7 March, 1844, Married ca.1782-1784. Buried David's Cementery, Hebe, PA.

The oldest Harter grave marker is in David's Cemetery located just outside the Manor boundary. Johannes Hartter, born in Wurtemberg, 25 December, 1725, married 47 years, with 5 children, died 22 December, 1800, age 75 years, 3 days. He married Anna Maria (Witzemann?). Her grave marker is adjacent. It states Anna Maria born 5 April, 1726, in Germany, married 1753, died 22 November, 1800, in Mahanoy Township, Northumberland County, PA.

John Harter Jr., born ca. 1754 is recorded as dwelling on the land north of his brother Jacob, where the farm of George and Mary Troutman is located in Jordan Township, Northumberland County. John's improvement was the first made to this property which borders the Manor on the west side.

The Harter family became quite numerous in the Hebe area where Andrew, Jacob, Mathias, and John were early land owners, having surveys completed by 1774. See "Trautman-Troutman Family History," page 596, by Steve E. Troutman. See homestead photos on later pages.

Parcels No. 2 and No. 3, 177 ¾ A. and 178 ½ A.

Conrad Shreckengaust. Parcel No. 2 would be the John Rothermel farm now owned by the Eugene Erdman family, and the William Rothermel farm now owned by Joe and Ruby Michetti.

Benjamin Schrecengost

Benjamin Shreckengaust is the son of Conrad Shreckengaust. Benjamin was born on the John Rothermel Farm north of Joe and Ruby Michetti. Benjamin became a grist mill owner and operator near Red Bank, Clarion County, PA. Benjamin has many descendants.

Parcel No. 2 also includes the William and Tim Landis Farm, and the Charlie Erdman Farm located on the Tulpehocken Path highway north of Klingerstown. Conrad Schreckengaust has earlier warranted parcels number 2 and 3 but did not patent the land. The Schreckengaust brothers chose to move further westward in Pennsylvania where unsettled lands were available to purchase.

Part I: Spread Eagle Manor and the Establishment of Klingerstown and the Klingerstown Grist Mill

The Rothermel Family of Parcel No. 2

"Genealogical and Biographical Annals of Northumberland County," published in 1911, by Floyd, pages 923 -927 include extensive family history of the Rothermel Family. Other sources of information are cited as well.

The Rothermel family is well represented in Jordan Township, where William W., Lazarus W., Manasses W., and Monroe W. Rothermel, all sons of the late Isaac Rothermel reside. The Rothermels have been identified with this section of Northumberland from the beginning of the last century, when Abraham Rothermel, grandfather of the 4 brothers mentioned, came hither from Berks County, where his ancestors located in an early day.

The Rothermel family traces its genealogy back some 400 years to one Johannes Rothermel, who won both fame and a name in the early wars of Germany. He was a brave soldier, and so frequently dyed his arm in the blood of his enemies that his comrades designated him as "der Roth Ermel" (red sleeve), and in this way he acquired the name Rothermel.

According to the family history, "Rothermel Heritage and Genealogy in America," by the Rothermel Family Association, published in 2011, Johann Leonard Rothermel is the ancestor of the Mahantongo Rothermels. Johann Leonard Rothermel's name is recorded in the Lutheran Church records from Hassloch, within the Palatinate of the Rhine, Germany. His confirmation in 1703, his marriage to Margaretha Zimmerman in 1709, and all his children are listed prior to 1727. He and his family emigrated to Pennsylvania in 1727.

J. Leonard Rothermel's only daughter, Anna Margaretha (b. Feb. 12, 1712) married Peter Fetterolf. Peter was born March 20, 1699, in Wachbach, Germany. Wachbach is 60 miles due east of Manheim and 3 miles south of Mergentheim, Germany. Peter emigrated to Pennsylvania. He arrived in America on the ship, "The Thistle of Glasgow," and located near Seisholtzville, Herford Township, Berks County, PA. Peter and Anna Maria are buried in Seisholtzville in the Bittenbender Cemetery. For more extensive information on the Fetterolf and Rothermel families see the book, "The German and Welsh Origins of the Charles and Lottie Fetterolf Family," by Steve and Joan Troutman, available from Sunbury Press.

Peter Z. Rothermel (1715-1782) was one of the sons of Johann Leonard Rothermel. Peter H. Rothermel (1742-1792) was one of the sons of Peter Z. and Sybilla Hoch Rothermel. Abraham D. Rothermel, son of Peter H. Rothermel and Mary Dreibelbis was born in Oley Township and died in Washington Township, Northumberland County, PA.

Abraham Rothermel (1777-1861) was a blacksmith who was a man of great strength and practiced his profession until late in life. He and his wife, Catherine Yeager, are buried at the Himmel's Church Cemetery. Isaac Rothermel is their son.

Isaac Rothermel(1820-1896) married Hannah Wiest, daughter of Samuel and granddaughter of Jacob Wiest. Isaac was also a blacksmith but later turned to farming. The sons of Isaac are named above by Mr. Floyd. Isaac Rothermel lived on Parcel No. 2 of the Spread Eagle Manor. His farm today is owned by the Eugene Erdman family and is referred to as the "back farm". Isaac, in his old years, lived with his son Monroe, although he did not die at Monroe's house. Monroe W. Rothermel lived where the William Landis farm is today. Isaac died at the home of his son Manasses W. Rothermel who lived on the homestead.

William W. Rothermel, son of Isaac, was born in 1842 and remained at home on the farm until he went to the army during the Civil War, as a member of Company A, 50th Regiment, Pennsylvania Volunteer Infantry. He became a third sergeant and right general guide. His experience of trial and hardship were unusual. He returned at the close of his service to his home on a tract of 22 acres as a farmer and carpenter. William built his home on the same location which his father had established a blacksmith shop. It is of interest of the author to note that he lived in the house that William W. Rothermel built which is now the residence of

Joseph and Ruby Michetti.

Lazarus W. Rothermel, son of Isaac, was a farmer in Jordan Township on land which is a portion of Parcel No. 2. He was born in 1855 and worked for his parents, eventually purchasing a tract of 70 acres adjoining his father's homestead. It was formerly the Israel Geise place. He made a specialty of poultry raising. He married Emma Bush and 13 children were born to this union. Samuel Rothermel, son of Lazarus, lived here as well.

Manasses W. Rothermel, son of Isaac, was born September 24, 1857, on the homestead "back farm" in Jordan Township. After working for his parents until he reached the age of 18 years he followed the blacksmith's trade for 7 years in Uniontown (Pillow) and at Klingerstown. He was next engaged in huckstering for about 15 years. In 1898 he began farming on his father's homestead which contained 101 ½ acres. This farm is part of a tract of 500 acres which long ago was purchased by Samuel Wiest from the Bickels, who lived in Berks County. It is now divided into several farms, including the Erdman family "back farm," the William Landis farm, the Joseph Michetti farm, and the Charles Erdman farm. Manasses first married Eliza Wentzel, and to them were born 8 children all deceased at a very young age. His second marriage was to Susan Bixler, and they are the parents of 5 children. On April 20, 1908, Mr. Rothermel had the misfortune to lose his house by fire, which totally destroyed it with all its contents including valuable documents of historic worth. The summer of that year he erected the nice frame house which he and his family now occupy. The barn on the farm is a landmark of the region, having been built by Isaac Rothermel in 1852, when he came to Jordan Township and built the house (the one that burned in 1908) the same year; at that time only 10 acres were cleared. Another fire which occurred sometime in the 1930's destroyed this house. It was the residence of John E. Rothermel, son of Manasses. Today the barn is in good condition, but only the house foundation remains.

Monroe W. Rothermel, son of Isaac, was born March 6, 1862, and lived with his parents until they died, working with his father until 1888. All his life had been passed in his native township. His farm is an attractive place of 100 acres, well located, on the road between Hebe and Klingerstown. This is the William Landis farm today. It was once the homestead of Peter Rebuck and was later bought by Frederick Schwalm, from whom Mr. Rothermel purchased it. In 1886 Mr. Rothermel married Lizzie Schmeltz, and they had 3 children including Allen S. Rothermel who lived on this farm 50 years ago.

Part I: Spread Eagle Manor and the Establishment of Klingerstown and the Klingerstown Grist Mill

Family picture 1907. Manasses (1870-1947) and wife Katie (Kissinger) Rothermel (1871-1954),sons, Edmond and Austin, daughter, Florence (Rothermel) Hoffman.

Conversation with Dale Erdman, the son of Eugene Erdman, confirmed the story that Isaac Rothermel was a blacksmith. Dale remembers an old farm building on the "back farm," previously the Isaac Rothermel pioneer farm, which contained many blacksmith tools. They had been in storage for two generations and had become very rusted and were sold for scrap. Dale suggests that Isaac Rothermel's blacksmith would have been built along Klingerstown road between the residence of Joe Michetti and his barn. Dale also stated the barn on the pinoeer Isaac Rothermel homestead is dated 1857 and is of log construction. The barn is well preserved and marked with a plaque denoting the year it was built. He confirmed the story that two different dwellings burned on this farm. The Isaac Rothermel pioneer log home was destroyed by fire. The John Rothermel home was destroyed by fire in 1949, according to Earl Troutman.

Civil War Veteran of Klingerstown - William W. Rothermel, son of Isaac Rothermel, and wife Sarah (Shaffer) Rothermel. Children were: Emma (m) Mrs. John Saltzer, Mannasses (m) Kattie Kissinger, Monroe (m) Rachel Engle, (m) Bessie Gottshall, Polly (m) Mrs. Charles Brown, Jennie (m) Mrs. Gordon Klinger, Minnie (m) Mrs. Harvey Smith. Civil War Record: Enlisted in Pottsville with Co. A - August 19, 1861. Promoted from Corporal to Sergeant March 18, 1865, Mustered out with Co. A July 20, 1865.

Photo by George Troutman. The William Rothermel homestead later owned by George Troutman, now the Michetti Residence.

Part I: Spread Eagle Manor and the Establishment of Klingerstown and the Klingerstown Grist Mill

Nobel School, located between Hebe and Klingerstown. Your photographer, Steve E. Troutman, lived next to this one room school house as a boy. His parents, Earl G. Troutman, md. Marion A. Romberger, attended here through elementary grades.
Michael and Valerie Troutman pose, 1983.

The following story related to Steve E. Troutman, by John D. Troutman, s/o Victor Troutman, who attended "Pig Town" school. It seems William Troutman was the school master at this school many years. In his later years, he allowed the children to be quite noisy, so that there was little difference between school time and recess time. During William's last years as teacher, some of the local farm boys appeared to have had the upper hand with the teacher, as when Manassis Rothermal and Al Williard drilled a hole through the floor beside their desks in order to spit tobacco juice during school hours!

This page from the Trautman-Troutman Family History by Steve E. Troutman

Nobel School 1938
Locally known as Rothermel's School

```
NOBEL SCHOOL    1938    Teacher - Warren Leitzel
West of Klingerstown

        Left to right - Front to back

Row 1                   Row 2                   Row 3

Bryant Rothermel        Rosie Boyer             Miriam Shadel
Bruce Troutman          Roxie Leitzel           Roxie Rothermel
Earl Troutman           Anna Rothermel          Racheal Deitz
Bobby Hoffman           Lee Romberger           Warren Leitzel - Teacher
Glenn Leitzel           Shirley Rothermel       John Romberger
                        Marion Romberger        Ray Leitzel
                        Jean Rothermel          Kenneth Boyer
                        Bryant Troutman


                    Total 19 pupils
```

John Romberger Recalls his Early School Days at the Noble (Rothermel's) School
Jordan Township, Northumberland County, PA
by Steve E. Troutman, July 2, 2015

Several years ago the Gratz Historical Society held a summertime meeting at the Kessler's one room school house in the village of Erdman. John A. Romberger was the speaker on the topic of one room schools. John attended Noble School in Jordan Township, about one mile west of Klingerstown. He lived next door to this school in a house built by Civil War veteran, William Rothermel. This was locally known as Rothermel's school on Rothermel's Run. John's presentation included a few memorable occurrences from his days at this one room school.

One day while class was in session at Noble School, there was an urgent knock on the door. Andy Schwalm, a farmer nearby the school, on the east toward Klingerstown, was calling loudly in Pennsylvania German dialect, "Kumme raus. Kumme raus. Sis ebbes zu sehna." Come out. Come out. There is something to see. Andy was wearing his barn coat and boots as he had come running straight from his barn chores. He pointed toward the heavens where a large motorized blimp was slowly making its way westward across the sky. The children exited the school. They saw something they had never seen before. As I recall John telling the story, he later learned that this was the Navy airship Macon. The Macon met its end in 1935 when it plunged into the Pacific Ocean. It was the last of the giant rigid constructed air ships owned by the Navy. It was 785 feet long, being built in 1933.

Another event that John Romberger recalled was the occasion when the farmer's water pipe froze. Noble School was built near Rothermel's Run. This stream crossed under the highway on the west side of the school. A pasture for the Schwalm's dairy cows was located north of the school. The watering trough was located along the main road. Sometimes cattle from the Schwalm's barn were led up the road to the trough to drink. The summer had been dry and water was scarce. To make things worse, the fall continued to be dry. The small amount of water in Rothermel's Run was ponded up to fill a pipe which led to the road side water trough. Cold nights with temperature below freezing, froze the slow flowing water in the fill pipe. Water was needed for the livestock. It was decided to wrap the iron pipe with burlap bags. Coal oil was poured on the burlap and it was lit on fire. The long line of flames burned brightly and furiously. The hot metal pipe thawed open, water flowed, and the cows could drink once more at the trough.

John recalled the dirt road in front of the school. It was covered with macadam while school was in session. The school children were allowed to watch the road construction as crushed stone and tar was put in place and rolled to form a paved road surface. The boys re-enacted this road building at recess in the sandy soil behind the school. They built their own roads.

Teacher, Vern Leitzel, was the instructor for all subjects, one of which was science. There was a solar eclipse of the sun forecast in the newspaper by astronomers. The students were told they could view the eclipse by looking through smoked glass. Instructions were given as to how to prepare smoked glass. Those who could do this, should bring their glass to school on the day of the eclipse. John's father, Ralph Romberger, was an early photographer. He had dark glass from developing photographs. He gave this glass to his son John, to use to view the eclipse. The John Rothermel boys and girls who lived further up Rothermel's Run, had a different idea. There was an abandoned automobile on the farm. Or perhaps it was an old truck. The boy removed the windshield, built a fire, and successfully smoked the glass. The Rothermel children showed up at school with the largest piece of smoked glass! It was so big that they could actually sit behind the windshield as they viewed the eclipse.

Some additional information that I can add about the Noble School, concerns my mother. Some of the children in the school could not speak English when they arrived for first grade. My mother, Marion Romberger, lived ¼ mile east of the school. She spoke the Pennsylvania German dialect at home with her parents and older brothers. This was the language used by everyone in the area. Marion soon learned to speak English at the Noble School where the English vocabulary was much preferred. Despite the fact that she knew no English when she entered school, she became one of the best spellers. Ray Davis and my mother were often in spelling bees. Ray told me he would have often been in the first place, if Marion wouldn't have been in the contest. Ray settled for second best speller. Later in her life Marion travelled to Germany to research her Romberger family roots. The ancestral German dialect allowed her to communicate very well with the people of Bavaria and Austria. Here she made many Romberger acquaintances. As a youth, my father, Earl, learned to speak both languages at home. He could speak English when he went to school and Pennsylvania Dutch home on the farm and at work.

Earl and Marion (Romberger) Troutman Residence
April 1948 – October 1962

Photo by Roland Romberger, age 12 or 13 in 1936. Allen Rothermel pulled a white pine log with his team of black horses to clear a pathway for students to walk to school. Steve, Glenn, and Ruby grew up on this farm.

Part I: Spread Eagle Manor and the Establishment of Klingerstown and the Klingerstown Grist Mill

---

A new Amish one room school is being built in 2015 near where I live in Rough and Ready. The David Ray Stoltzfus family is the first Amish family to live in what I term to be Rough and Ready. The Amish folks have arrived in the valley with their children. They as well will learn to speak English in the new one room school.

"Dinner Time Ball Game," painting by Deanna Wiseman
At Nobel (Rothermel's) School. The school was built in Jordan Township in 1865.
It was a typical little red school house that measured 30x30 feet.

Allen Rothermel – William Landis Farm now Tim Landis
Photo by Earl Troutman 1957

Part I: Spread Eagle Manor and the Establishment of Klingerstown and the Klingerstown Grist Mill

---

Rothermel- Fetterolf Reunion
Kutztown, Pa.
September 12, 2009

Conversation with Jean M. Rothermel Hummel, 5344 Burn Point, Honeoye, New York 14471. Telephone 585-229-4772

Bryan A. Rothermel, P.O Box 437, Wiconisco, Pa. 17097

Jean and Bryan Rothermel attended Noble School with Marion Romberger, Earl, Bruce and Bryant Troutman. Jean and Bryan lived north of Nobel School along Rothermel Run on the John Rothermel farm now owned by Eugene Erdman's descendants. Jean recalled in her school days the Ralph Romberger family lived next to the school.

Jean told me she knew my parents Earl and Marion well. She knew mom's birthday was December 26. Jean is one year younger than my mother, who was born in 1929. She then told me she had premonitions as to future events, and that she knew there would be a fire at her homestead many years before it happened. She had a dream 8 times that the fire would start under the porch. Each dream was progressive and more detailed than the previous. She repeatedly warned her family about the impending fire. When the fire occurred she and her mother were not home. Her 2 brothers were home alone, one being in a wheelchair. The one brother, Bryan, pushed the other brother in the wheelchair out of the burning house, barely escaping with their lives. The fire as described by the boys was just as Jean saw it in her dreams.

Another premonition that she had was that of her immediate family (husband and children) walking in the woods. The next dream of this series showed her family walking except her daughter and husband were not with the group. She dreamed this dream several times, each more progressively detailed. Her daughter died an untimely death and after one year later her husband left Jean. She raised the remaining 3 children. Jean had warned her daughter that she felt some calamity would happen to her and shortly after she was gone. Her daughter of course discounted her mother's warning at that time.

Jean also had an out of body experience. She felt herself floating above her body and looked down on herself. A Christ like figure was in the room with her and motioned her to come to him. She refused 3 times and rubbed her eyes and stamped her feet to make sure she was awake. The Christ like figure slowly rose and departed through a veil which had surrounded the divine being and herself. There was a brightness about the room.

I only had 15 minutes to talk with Jean but I told her I was glad she told me of her extra-ordinary experiences, as it affirmed our belief in the afterlife. She agreed and said she felt she was given these dreams to help her become prepared for changes in her life. She told me she had these dreams her entire life. Jean appears to be very healthy. She told Joan that she was a mechanical electrician, schooled in Oklahoma, to specifically repair postal electrical equipment. She attends a Bally's Health Gym for many years, (20 years?), and still lifts weights. She maintains her high school weight of 113 pounds! Also she added that her height remains unchanged, whiled many of her school mates have become shorter!

Joan's stepmother Leah Rothermel Masser took care of Jean's father, John Rothermel, who was Leah's cousin. She stayed with John in his later years, at his residence in Lykens, Pa. Leah was a widow at this time, and worked as a cook at the Lykens Hotel. After his death, she was able to remain in the house and did so until she married Joan's father, Clement Masser.

Earl Troutman recalls the John Rothermel house fire occurred the same year Earl and Marion were married in 1949. Earl and Marion began house keeping in the Wm. Rothermel house to the south along the main road between Klingerstown and Hebe.

Parcel No. 3, present land owners include Troutmans with names Earl, Amelia, Richard, Shirley, and Troutman Brothers. A large portion of this acreage was previously the Hoffman Dairy Farm. Florence Rothermel married Ira "Pit" Hoffman. The access road is Hoffman Farm Road.

The Schreckengausts were early settlers in this local including John, Conrad, Henry, and George. One family historian is Gary Schreckengaust, schreck@ptd.net. He writes, "I have Johann Jost Schreckengast (John Sr.) coming into the valley about 1772, with his 3 sons Henry, George, and Conrad. Henry just completed his indenture with a Philadelphia gunsmith. It was along the present Rothemel Run where George and then Conrad chop out 10 acres of land. We're out of the valley by 1804 as this is my last record of them: "Henry's twins, Sarah and Henry were born January 1, 1803 and baptized at Klinger's Church on March 18, 1803. Sometime between 1800 and 1803, Henry, Conrad, and John decided not to convert their land warrants into land patents and resolved to move west to Armstrong County, PA, where the newly opened land there was being sold for less. They sold their warrants to the land speculator John Bickle, who sold them to Samuel M. Wiest. Tract No. 2 and Tract No. 3; 356 ½, granted to John Bickle, by attorney for John and Richard Penn, January 19, 1803. Formerly property of Conrad Schreckengast."

Photo by Ralph Romberger Summer of 1915
Ira "Pitt" Hoffman Family and son Bobby Hoffman Family lived here for two generations.
The Benjamin Leitzel farm in the background now owned by Troutman Brothers.

Part I: Spread Eagle Manor and the Establishment of Klingerstown and the Klingerstown Grist Mill

Parcel No. 4, 264 ¾ A, Eastern Portion

This parcel was first owned by Samuel Flower, surveyed for him in 1762, later owned by John Reed and by Johannes Klinger. It includes the site of Klingerstown. Johannes Klinger divided the property with the Pine Creek being the dividing boundary. The eastern portion included various owners, including John Reed, Jacob Wust III, and John Wiest, his son.

Klingerstown Bicentennial book cover artwork by Deanne Wiseman of Wiseman Graphics. Book is available from Steve E. Troutman, benefit the Klingerstown Fire Police.

The Wiest Family originated in Oley Township, Berks County, and followed the Tulpehocken Path to the Mahantongo Valley. The Wiest family homestead is identified near the "O" in Oley.

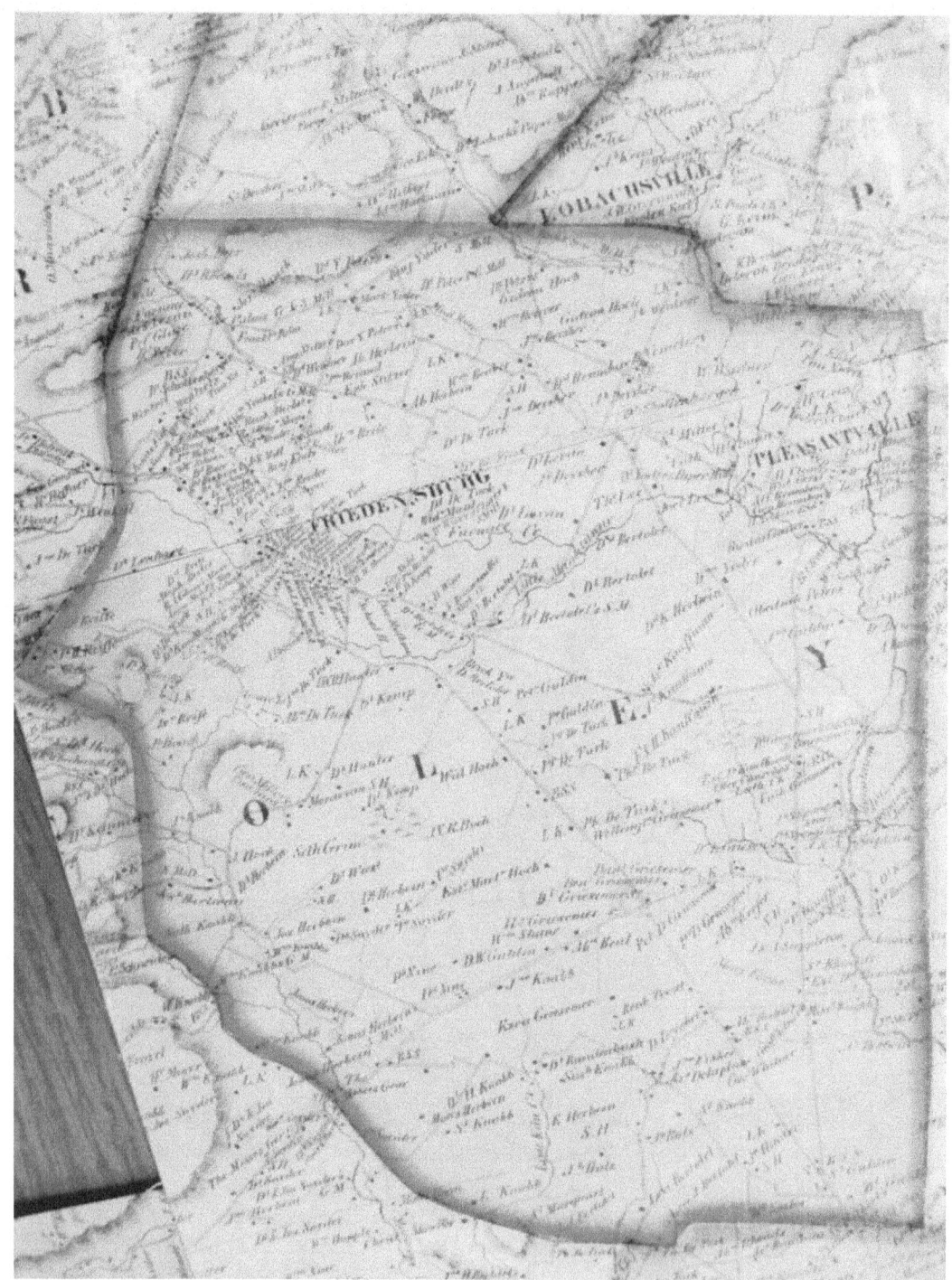
1860 Oley Township Map naming Wiest district, courtesy of Allan Wiest

Oley Wiest home photo, courtesy of Sally B. Wiest Troutman.

Parcel No. 4, containing 264 ¾ acres is shown as the property of Johannes Klinger. A portion of this tract is the site of Klingerstown. The land ownership progression, as this tract was divided, identifies John Baum as receiving the western portion and John Reed as receiving the eastern portion where the Village of Klingerstown was eventually located. John Reed's tract of land was soon transferred to Jacob Wust III (Wiest) who later transferred this tract to John Wust (Wiest) his son. The Klingerstown mill is situated upon this tract of land.

Parcel No. 4: Eastern Portion- Future Wiest Family Settlement

At the time of his death Jacob Wiest III (1775-1811) owned the land where the Klingerstown mill was located. There are no facts or legend to connect Jacob Wiest III or his oldest son, John Wiest, (1794-1881) to the milling profession, although they owned the land where the mill existed. It would seem that Johannes Klinger's mill was in the hands of the Wiests a few years after it was built. Johannes Klinger died in 1800. We can assume that the log grist mill was completed at the time of his death. Jacob Wiest III and his son John Wiest owned the Klingerstown grist mill but it is unlikely that they established the mill.

A view of Klingerstown from the farm land owned by Jacob Wust III, later Emmanuel Klinger's Farm

Cement Arch bridge over Mahantongo Creek boarding the old Jacob Wiest, III, Farm. Photo July 2015 shortly before its removal.

Part I: Spread Eagle Manor and the Establishment of Klingerstown and the Klingerstown Grist Mill

The "Spread Eagle Tavern" was owned and operated by Jacob Wiest III. It was located a bit further north of the homestead at the center of the town. Jacob Wiest III died at the age of 36 in 1811. By this time, just before the Village of Klingerstown was established, the Wiest family had become quite prolific.

Spread Eagle Tavern
Tentative Identification of People:

Daniel M. Wiest, standing at telegraph pole, his father John Wiest next to him. Mrs. John Wiest (Katharina Merkel) sitting with Phoebe Thomas (the 4th wife of Daniel M. Wiest), holding a baby standing behind Katharina. The children of Daniel M. Wiest are the rest of this group except for the younger man sitting on the chair who may be Moses M. Wiest, a younger son of old John Wiest.

When old Kate Wiest from Klingerstown allowed Earl G. Troutman to make a photograph of her original, Kate called the dwelling "The Spotties Nest". This was in references to the many Wiest offspring in comparison to the flocks of English Sparrows so prevalent in our area.

The Wiests owned large areas of land within Spread Eagle Manor and nearby the Manor boundaries. The homestead of Jacob Wiest III was eventually sold to Emanuel Klinger. Today we know it as the Ivan Klinger farm. The Klingerstown Lutheran Church was built in 1895 on a portion of land originating from this farm.

Wiest historians have contributed to the recording of Wiest family history.
1. Robert (Bob) Viguers, 109 Wayne Drive, Harrisburg, PA 17112-2962.
2. Bruce Hall, 843 Harbor View Terrace, Annapolis, MD 21401-4674.
3. Allan Wiest, P.O. Box 70, Shippensburg, PA 17257.

The Will of Jacob Wiest III, Berks County Court House, Reading, PA

Schuylkill County was formed out of Berks County in 1811

In the name of God, Amen. I give and becuethe unto my wife the power of having possession of all the property that we own until the children have there own age. And also that my wife must have a room in one of the houses that I own as long as she lives. After the children have there age, my wife, Barbara Wiest, is to have her third of the whole property as the law directs. Also she is entitled with the room, three acres of land where she choses and likewise one quarter of an acre of the garden wich belongs to the house in wich she choses to live in. Rails and firewood must be delivered at the door or where she choses. In the house that she likes best she is to have her rooms likewise she is to receive six pounds of money Pennsylvania currency, yearly, out of the estate, and with the seller and kitchen of the house she lives in she has a right to do with what she choses. Likewise, she must have a quarter of an acres of flax yearly, and six bushels of wheat yearly, and stabling for two cows as long as she lives the whole of this to be fulfiled by my heirs and executors. This the twenty second of July, one thousand eight hundred and eleven. Signed in the presence of Jacob ? and ? Signature, Jacob Wust

Addition: My wife is to have yearly 50 pounds of good pork. Signed Jacob Wiest

Addition: My wife, Barbara West, is to have 2 beds and bedsteads, one chest, 2 of the cows wich two she choses, likewise all kitchen furniture wich is nessary to have, likewise a tennplate stove and four chairs. Witness, Jacob ? (eye witness) and ? (eye witness)

Eleven lines of German script, signed by John M. Hyneman, signed by Barbara Wust

"Zion (Klingers) Church History," compiled by Irvin R. Klinger, page 319. Cemetery record.

Row 7, No. 10, Jacob Wust, b. in Oley Township, Berks County, b. January 5, 1775, d. August 4, 1811, age 36 years, 6 m.

Row 10, No. 13, Barbara Wust,(b. Fick)
(1) wf. of Jacob Wust , (2) wf. of Michael Sallende
b. Jan. 29. 1774, d. Sep.11, 1855 age 79y 7m 13d

Part I: Spread Eagle Manor and the Establishment of Klingerstown and the Klingerstown Grist Mill

"The Joseph Zerby History of Schuylkill County", page 1291 names John Wiest is as a pioneer business man. Mr. Zerby continues with some Wiest history. "One of the leading business men of Klingerstown in the pioneer days was old John Wiest. He used to hitch four horses to a covered wagon, loaded with dried apples, snitz, dried cherries, eggs, butter and other products of the farmers, and take them to Phila. in exchange for merchandise for his store. The round trip would take a week."

In the early years of the settlement, the barter system was used. There was little money and farm produce was exchanged for store goods. The Wiest merchants did embrace the concept of monetary exchange as time passed. The Wiest storekeepers printed their own money for exchange.

Victor Wiest's Store
Main Street Klingerstown
Victor standing in back at doorway with coat

Old John Wiest standing photo center with high top boots

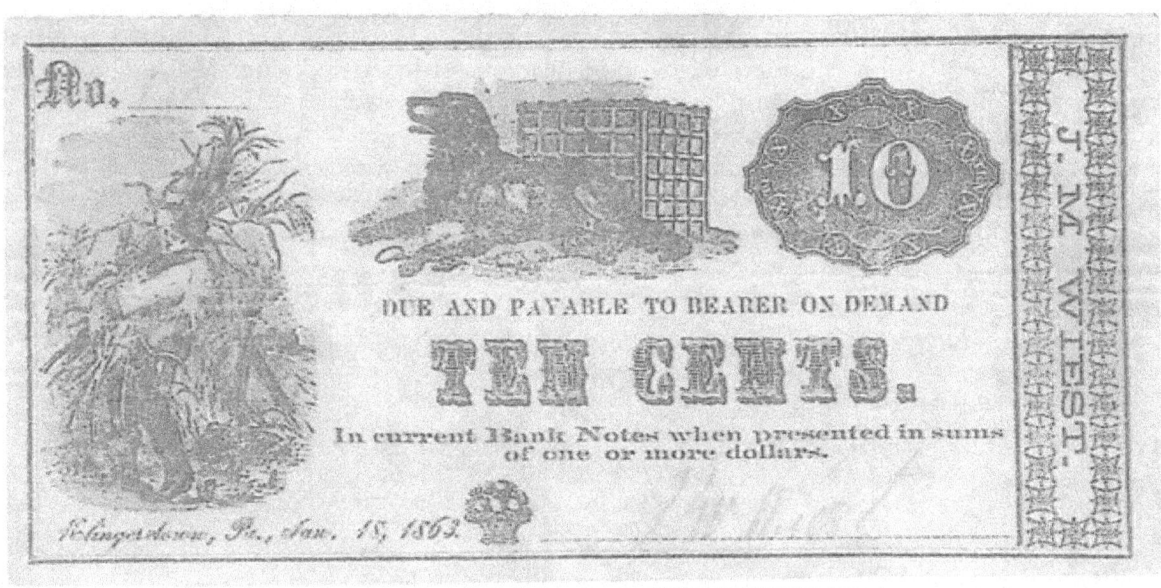

Notes of 10 cents and 50 cents signed by John Wiest

This currency was printed by John Wiest for use in his store on Main Street, Klingerstown, PA, later this store was operated by Victor Wiest. The paper money is dated January 1, 1863, and January 18, 1863. Signed J.M. Wiest.

Part I: Spread Eagle Manor and the Establishment of Klingerstown and the Klingerstown Grist Mill

**Connection showing the Prop. Manor of Spread Eagle, Dauphin and Northumberland and Berks Counties
by E. Terry PA Historical and Museum Commission.
12/27/1984**

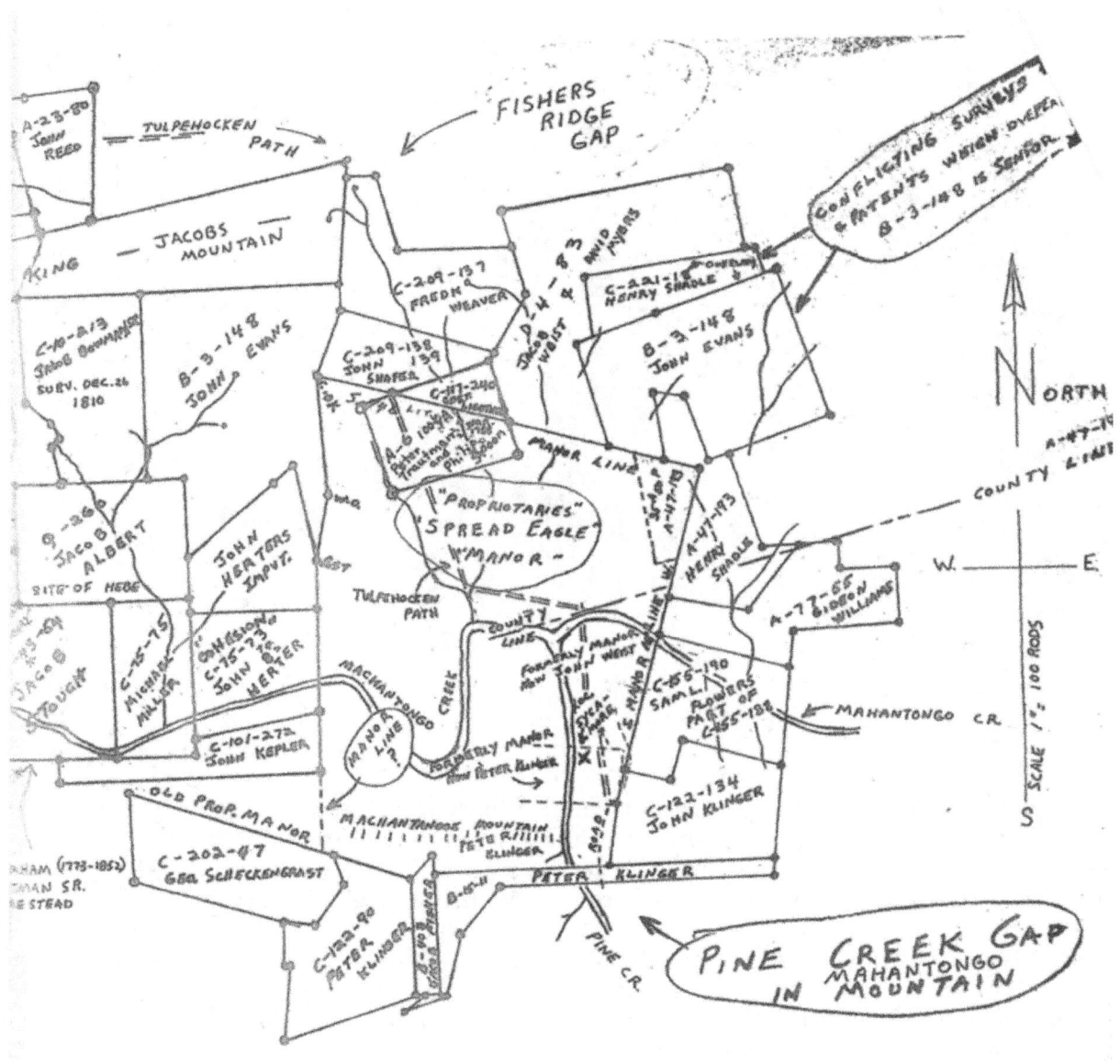

This connected land map shows John Wiest owning the site of Klingerstown and the location of the Spread Eagle sycamore tree. Mr. Terry also shows the location of the sycamore tree as being on the land of Peter Klinger, prior to John Wiest. Note Mr. Terry's handwriting which states "formerly Manor—now John Weist."

The early Wiests were merchants, post office operators, and bankers. Later generations of Wiests, who did operate the mill, are the sons of John Wiest (1794-1881). They are Daniel Merkel Wiest (1822-1901) and Moses Merkel Wiest (1826-1902). Daniel is recorded in the 1850 Census records having the profession of miller. See page 192 and 193 of the "Klingerstown Bi-Centennial Album". Oral history recalls Moses Wiest as operating the mill also.

Moses M. Wiest Homestead, lately recalled as the Billy Wiest residence. Currently the Stoltzfus farm house

The name of Daniel Wiest has been recently found in 2015 written on a floor board. The floor board of this house is located between Hebe and Klingerstown. Brandon Boyer uncovered the name during a renovation of the Sterlin Boyer residence. Sterlin was his great grandfather. Daniel Wiest was married 4 times and is credited with the largest Wiest family on record, 26 children.

Daniel is buried in Klingerstown at St. Michael's Cemetery. Some records state that he is buried at Zion's in Erdman, but this is incorrect. He has a tall obelisk in the south east corner of St. Michael's Cemetery. It records "Father, Daniel M. Wiest, died 16 September, 1901, 79y 6m 9d." (7 March 1822-16 September 1901).

Part I: Spread Eagle Manor and the Establishment of Klingerstown and the Klingerstown Grist Mill

Schuylkill County Deed Book, Vol. 97, page 70, states Daniel Wiest sells farm in Upper Mahantongo Township to Samuel Klinger of Lykens Township, Dauphin County for $4750.00, dated 19th March 1864. Daniel Wiest is noted as living in Upper Mahantongo Township. The 1875 Map of Schuylkill County shows S. Klinger as identified living in the mill house in Klingerstown, which is now the residence of Leonard and Nancy Shaffer.

The Mill House and the Mill
Photo by Ronald Maurer
October 1989

Schuylkill County Deed Book, Vol. 97, page 70, lists Daniel Wiest's new address, as part of his estate settlement. Daniel Wiest has moved to Ellem Township, Caldwell County, Missouri.

Jim Schlegel, Rob Lesher and Robert Viguers have researched and recorded the following: Circuit Court Proceedings, Tuesday, June 29, 1875, State of Missouri, against Daniel M. Wiest. For on this 29th Day of June 1875, the Grand Jury return into court a true bill against the above named defendant Daniel M. Wiest for murder in the first degree.

The sheriff makes the following return to here by certify that I executed this by delivering a copy of this indictment to Daniel M. Wiest the within named defendant this afternoon. Signed, L.B. Clivenger, sheriff. Gallatin, North Missourian, May 20, 1875

A Fatal Shooting Affray at Breckinridge
Last Friday night, James B. Rogers, a clerk in the employ of McWilliam & Crooke of Breckinridge was at a sociable or party in that place. After the party, about 11 o'clock he went out about a mile and a half from town to the residence of Mrs. Wiest. Daniel Wiest and his wife do not live together but near each other. Daniel Wiest shot him, two buckshot entering

his bowles. His cries for help attracted the attention of neighbors and he was carried to town where Drs. Dewey and Dent did all in their power to relieve his sufferings. He died on Sunday morning and was buried by the Masonic fraternity. He was an excellent business man and highly respected in Breckenridge. Wiest has a rather hard name. He was arrested and is now in jail at Kingston.

Daniel M. Wiest was married to Emma Troutman at this time. Some of their children were born in Missouri. Daniel M. Wiest, Emma and family, returned to Klingerstown where Daniel is buried at St. Michael's Church Cemetery in Klingerstown. He died 9-16-1901, age 79y 6m 9d, father. Charles T. Wiest, who lived in the Leck Bush near Rough and Ready, often stated that "he was born out west". He is buried at Salem Cemetery, Rough and Ready, PA. He is the son of Daniel and Emma (Troutman) Wiest and carries the name Troutman as his middle name.

Daniel M. Wiest's first wife was Angelina Klinger, died 1854 in Klingerstown. His second wife was Sarah Rickert, third wife was Emi Troutman, fourth wife Phoebe Thomas.

Interview with Ray Davis of Rough and Ready, March 14, 2015. Uncle Albert Davis worked for Daniel Wiest at the mill. Later on Albert took over the mill operations for some time. While Albert was operating the mill, a cow kept coming to visit the corn field at the mill. The cow was from the Hoke family which lived across the creek where Terry Williard lives today. Albert got tired of seeing the cow eating in his corn field at the mill. Albert and his hired hand tied a sheave of corn stalks to her horns and chased her back home across the creek with something to eat. Hay was not as plentiful years ago, and corn was more abundant.

Currently the residence of Terry and Marla Williard. An old log house was removed when this large farm house was built. John Klinger Wiest, and Lucetta Beisel Wiestwere earlier farm residents. Their son John Beisel Wiest also lived here before migrating west in 1878. John Beisel Wiest, while working with the Wiest Lumber Company, drowned in the Columbia River as a log handler.

Part I: Spread Eagle Manor and the Establishment of Klingerstown and the Klingerstown Grist Mill

Albert and Bulah Wiest went to Canada in 1901 and homesteaded in Alberta. They came back home again in 1919. It was very dry in Canada for farming. Albert's wife left him and he returned with 3 sons to Klingerstown.

Ray Davis spoke of Daniel M. Wiest's reputation. Every time an unwed woman became pregnant, father unknown, the townspeople claimed it to be Daniel M. Wiest's! (He was the father of 24 children).

Klingerstown Post Office and Koppy's Store in 1986.

Klingerstown Post Office

Research Administrator/Historian
Office of the Postmaster General
United States Postal Service
June 8, 1992

KLINGERSTOWN POST OFFICE

SCHUYLKILL COUNTY, PENNSYLVANIA

NAME	TITLE	DATE APPOINTED
John Weist/Wiest	Postmaster	06/30/1851

    Discontinued on July 2, 1874
    Reestablished on February 10, 1875

NAME	TITLE	DATE APPOINTED
Edmund L. Umholtz	Postmaster	02/10/1875
Tobias M. Wiest	Postmaster	05/09/1881
Samuel W. Clark	Postmaster	07/18/1884
Isaac R. Trautman	Postmaster	03/01/1898
Harry S. Schadel	Postmaster	03/05/1915
Walter H. Davis	Postmaster	02/15/1917
Mrs. Helen S. Erdman	Acting Postmaster	06/30/1953
Kelvin L. Bowman	Postmaster	08/16/1954
Daniel E. Mulroy	Officer-In-Charge	12/12/1980
Robert W. Bloch	Officer-In-Charge	02/13/1981
Harry C. Brocious	Postmaster	03/07/1981
Patricia R. Schaeffer	Officer-In-Charge	11/27/1981
Ann H. Bettinger	Postmaster	05/29/1982
Janet M. Smith	Officer-In-Charge	09/30/1986
Richard W. Wagner	Postmaster	02/28/1987
Rosemary A. Wensus	Officer-In-Charge	05/15/1990
Myron J. Hardock	Officer-In-Charge	09/10/1990
Janet M. Smith	Postmaster	01/26/1991

*Medal Arch Bridge before an 8 ton weight limit.
In 1972 the flood waters were up to the top of the bridge arch.*

Newly constructed Klingerstown Bank located next to the metal arch bridge

Blacksmith Shop in Klingerstown located where Paul Shiffer Well Drilling business is now.

Some of the blacksmiths were named Smith and Hoffman.

This photograph courtesy of the Kenneth Fetterolf postcard collection.

Decoration Day in Klingerstown, ca. 1905

The Civil War ended in 1865. Patriotic events such as this scene in Klingerstown became common in local communities as a day to honor the men who died in this war. Memorial Day was officially established in 1868 when May the 30th was designated as a special day to honor the graves of soldiers.

It appears that two well dressed ladies in the crowd are walking to the foreground open area to address the group. One lady carries a booklet and wears a ceremonial pouch around her neck. Both women wear the same style decorated waist belt. More ladies, similarly attired, can be seen in the background center photo. Although presently unidentified, these ladies no doubt belong to the Daughters of America, Spread Eagle Chapter of Klingerstown. This group first met for meetings above the factory in town, lately known as the Klingerstown Market store building. Older residents recall that later chapter meetings were held at Katerman's School near Hepler. The Daughters of America was formed in 1891 and still exists to promote religion, patriotism, and charity.

Notice the flag flying over the square. Patriotic decorations are on the big yellow house and on Benjamin Leitzel's candy store, the building on the left edge of the photo.

Address comments to Steve E. Troutman, 1442 Ridge Road, Klingerstown, Pa. 17941.

Eckler's Hotel

Local historian Ray Davis recalls this building was built by Harry Wise from Gratz. He was known by the nickname "June" probably because he was Harry Junior. He was married to Della. Della's parents were Anna Maria (Wiest (1801-1891) and Joseph Tobias (1798-1844). They are buried at Zion's Cemetery in Erdman. They operated Wise's Restaurant for many years as a popular eating place and hotel. Della died young and Harry remarried Beulah Drumheller of Rebuck, PA. Ray remembers his mother speaking of dances held in the upstairs ballroom.

The Odd Fellow's Lodge as well as the Spread Eagle Chapter of the Daughters of America Lodge also met upstairs in the large hall. When Harry became ill in his old age, some members of the Odd Fellow's Lodge helped Beulah take care of Harry. These men included Marlin Baum and Belton Davis. George M. Troutman spoke of the history of this building. In the early years the mill dam created a pond behind the restaurant which was a source of entertainment for the patrons. George built a wooden paddle wheel boat for rides on the milldam. Ada Klinger Troutman recalled that the first silent moving picture show she saw as a young girl was held in the upstairs banquet hall. The light for the projector was provided by a kerosene lamp as this was before electricity.

The next owner/operator was Andy Morgan for a short time around 1944. Meals were served but the barroom was under utilized.

In 1945 Ernest and Florence Eckler took over the restaurant business and reopened the barroom. Many local ladies were employed in the kitchen and a large wait staff served the public. Music and dances continued to be popular. The Eckler Family included three children, a set of twins and one son. The twins were a boy and a girl. After several decades the hotel was purchased by Leroy and Shirley Schwalm. The basement lower level was utilized with an outside public entrance, near the metal arched bridge. Ronald L. Maurer recalls that the first Klingerstown Fire Company meetings were held in the basement, and that many Saturday night customers patronized both hotels in Klingerstown. The Klingerstown Hotel was just a few steps away across the main street and there was a constant coming and going of people.

Mention must be made of the well known Saturday night fights which were regular occurrences in the barrooms and in the street. Many people came to town on Saturday to shop at the stores and visit socially. They sat on the store benches. Almost always there was a fist fight. Some who were known as rough necks included Wiests, Laudenslagers, and Stielys. This was before Leroy Schwalm was the proprietor.

Leroy and Shirley Schwalm continued the old tradition of serving meals and beverage. During this time Percy Walborn had a barber shop in the lower level until the 1972 flood. After the flood, Leroy remodeled a street level shop for Percy, the barber. Ronald recalls the time that Leroy Schwalm went bear hunting. He was successful and brought the bear back to Klingerstown and hung it up on the hotel porch. The bear was cooked and Leroy served free meals for the community to any who would eat bear meat. The business ended with the passing of Leroy and Shirley. Schwalm family lived there for several years. It is presently unoccupied.

The oldest photograph of Klingerstown, Jacob Wiest house on the right. Looking north. The Wiest Homestead remains in 2015, adjacent to the open space where Koppy's Store was located (burned January, 2014).

Klingerstown Hotel built by John Reid. Proprietors, Wiest, Lewis, Umholtz, Wesley Erdman, Harry and Lydia Schadle, Charles Lark, Perriman, Allan Romgerger Jr., Marge Romberger, Catherine Herb, Randy Rothermel Sr., Randy Rothermel Jr.

An early automobile in front of the Klingerstown Hotel.

Marion (Romberger) Troutman often told the story about Nathan "Naty" Fetterolf from Snow Dale. He lived several miles north of Klingerstown in a remote area with poor roads but he had one of the first automobiles. He was mechanically inclined and stored his automobile on the attic of his house for the winter months. In late fall he was able to disassemble the automobile and carry it piece by piece up the stairs to the third floor. In spring, he would bring the parts of the automobile back down and put it together again. People recall he had an unusual horn on the vehicle. Perhaps this is his automobile.

This photograph courtesy of Wallace Knorr's photo collection

Rough and Ready Band, 1906

The Rough and Ready Cornet Band poses in Klingerstown at the red brick hotel on the square in 1906. The handsome uniformed men all have brass instruments, cymbals, or drums. Today this red brick hotel is owned and operated by the Rothermel Family. (2009)

First Row, (L-R) Elsworth Klinger, Jacob Ramberger, Samuel Erdman, Red Miller, John Starr, Wilson Paul.
Second Row, (L-R) Perry Stiely, Calvin Klinger, Oscar Starr?, ??, Oscar Erdman, William Reiner, Francis Schadel, David Engel.
Back Row, (L-R) Harvey Stiely, William Maurer?, Harvey Wolfgang, Monroe Dietz, William Emmon Knorr, Wellington Mattern, George Snyder.

Address comments to Steve E. Troutman, 1442 Ridge Road, Klingerstown, Pa. 17941

The Klingerstown Church was built in 1895. The church is center photo.

*This painting courtesy of Deanna Wiseman entitled "If My People."
The church in the painting is styled after the Klingerstown Church built in 1895.
The painting was commissioned by Bryant A. Troutman.*

Part I: Spread Eagle Manor and the Establishment of Klingerstown and the Klingerstown Grist Mill

The verse states: ***"If my people which are called by my name, shall humble themselves and pray, and seek my face, and turn from their wicked ways, then will I hear from heaven, and forgive their sin, and heal their land."***
II Chronicles 7:14

Klingerstown looking East. Note the covered bridge in the background.

Klingerstown looking North.

Very early view of Hotel. Spread Eagle Tavern seen on left.

A new Leitzel house is built where the old Spread Eagle Tavern stood.

*This photograph courtesy of the Kenneth Fetterolf postcard collection.
September 30, 1908, Klingerstown, PA, postmarked in Klingerstown. Rich Leitzel on carriage.
Samuel and Johanna Clark, Dr. Luther Havice, Victor Wiest.*

This photograph courtesy of the Kenneth Fetterolf postcard collection. September 30, 1908, Klingerstown, Pa., postmarked in Klingerstown.

Klingerstown Square, 1908

The big yellow house on the square in Klingerstown, was built by Wm. Oscar Leitzel, (1866-1938). He was the son of Benjamin B. Leitzel, (1839-1916) and Eva Elizabeth (Tobias) Leitzel. Mr. W. O. Leitzel became president of the Klingerstown Bank. His first wife was Emma S. Wiest, (1867-1896). Their children included: Della, Rich, Frank, and John.

Della Leitzel married Jun. Wise. They operated Wise's Restaurant and Hotel, across the street from the red brick Klingerstown Hotel. This restaurant was very popular for Sunday dinners. In later years this establishment was known as Eckler's Hotel and Leroy Schwalm's Hotel.

Rich Leitzel married Lillian Romberger. He is seen here on the horse and buggy. He established Klingerstown Ford Motor Company. Roy Leitzel, his son, became the manager. Rich also established the well known Leitzel's farmers' markets later managed by his sons, Ford and Paul. Today these markets are the Crossroads Market near Gratz and the Lewisburg Market.

Frank Leitzel moved out west where he lived with his family.

John Leitzel established a factory building at the south end of town which later became a general store. In recent years, this store was operated by Paul Wolfe, William Klinger, and Leonard Phillips. John Leitzel also worked at the Klingerstown Bank.

William Oscar Leitzel was married second to Cora Jennette Hollenbach, (1874-1938), from Herndon. Their children included Paul, Eva, and Fred.

Paul Leitzel worked with the Klingerstown Motor Company.

Eva Leitzel married Andy Morgan who worked at the Klingerstown Mill and Klingerstown Motor Company. Eva and Andy lived in her homestead, the big yellow house.

Fred Leitzel operated the Klingerstown Milling Company.

The Klingerstown Hotel seen here was operated by the Lewis Family at this time. The hotel staff poses proudly.

Others on the photo may include Isaiah Romberger (storekeeper), Victor Wiest, (storekeeper), and Dr. Luther Havice.

Some Leitzel information courtesy of Mrs. Lee (Jean) Phillips of Elizabethville, Pa., in 2009, and the St. Michael's Church 1894-1994 Anniversary Book.

Address comments to Steve E. Troutman, 1442 Ridge Road, Klingerstown, Pa. 17941.

Part I: Spread Eagle Manor and the Establishment of Klingerstown and the Klingerstown Grist Mill

The following recorded with sympathy
Adeline Klinger of Erdman spoke of four people who committed suicide by drowning in the Mahantongo Creek. They are remembered as:

Mrs. John Leiztel
Joel Strohecker
Harry Shadel
Lottie Erdman

Godfried Leitzel b.(1770) came from Berks Co. to North'd. Co. locating in Mahanoy Twp. where he married Magdalena Wagner b. (1769). He was a farmer and stock raiser. Benj. Leitzel, son of Godfried, was born 1803 and owned his father's farm. He was also a weaver in the winter time. He married Elizabeth Byerly. Benj. B. Leitzel, son of Benj. and Elizabeth (Byerly) Leitzel was born 1839 in Jordan Twp. During the greater part of his independent business career he was engaged in hotel keeping in which line he was very well known in his day, keeping the hotel at Klingerstown for fully 30 years. He still lives in Klingerstown where he now conducts a restaurant. Mr. Leitzel owns a 30 acre tract in Lykens Twp., Dauphin Co., upon which he lived for one year. (Now part of Troutman Brother's farm. Mr. Leitzel married Eva Elizabeth Tobias, daughter of Joseph and Mary (Wiest) Tobias. She died 1889 at the age of 47. The survivors include children, W.Oscar, Cyrus, Mary and John. (See Klingerstown Square narrative previously) W.O. Leitzel, son of Benj. B. Leitzel, was a business man engaged in selling farm machinery and general merchandise in Klingerstown. He also sold furniture and the well known Swab Wagons and was considered the leading representative of the company which makes these wagons. He was married first to Emma S. Wiest, daughter of Moses M. and Mary (Schadel) Wiest. Married second to Cora Hollenbach, daughter of George and Elizabeth (Schaffer) Hollenbach.

(Source: Page 916, Genealogical and Biographical Annals of Northumberland County," by Floyd)

Early Davis family in Klingerstown. Back Row: Albert, Belton, Charles, Carlos (Ike), Walter, Harry (Austin). Front Row: Eva (Davis) Artz, Wm. Davis (father), Lola (Davis) Artz, Precilla (Klinger) Davis (mother), Emma (Davis) Engle.

Samuel Clark (Jr.) and Johanna (Wiest) Clark's Store, 1885-1888. Samuel Clark, Jr. with hat aside of door, holding horse and Johanna in front of door.

Samuel Clark, Jr. and Johanne (Wiest) Clark storekeepers in Klingerstown in year 1885 - to early 1900's one daughter Elmira (Clark) Romberger. Samuel being the son of Samuel Clark, Sr. and Johanna being the daughter of Moses (Merkel) Wiest and Maria (Schadel) Wiest, Johanna one of eighteen children (reared at Klingerstown Mill). These people were very early pioneers in Klingerstown.

Part I: Spread Eagle Manor and the Establishment of Klingerstown and the Klingerstown Grist Mill

The old covered bridge over Mahantongo Creek at the mill.

Walter Reitz poses in 1946 before the bridge was torn down.

Klingerstown apartment house fire in 1941. Early owner, Willmer Deibert.

Early Klinger Family - Emmanuel Klinger married Christian (Schadel) Klinger. Children listed: Mary married Harvey Schwalm; Charles married Jane Bowman; James married Jemima Klinger; Henry married Carrie Bowman; Abraham married Lillian Troutman; Kate married Theodore Rabuck; Clara married James Scheib; Alda married 1. Harvey Seiler, 2. Scheib, 3. Harvey Bensinger; Fred married Jennie Paul; Ira married 1. Eva Rothermel, 2. Dorothy Wessner; Eston married Esther Radel; Meda married Edwin Knorr.

Part I: Spread Eagle Manor and the Establishment of Klingerstown and the Klingerstown Grist Mill

Interior of Isaiah K. Romberger Store - Early 1900's
Isaiah Romberger behind counter, Shoe Salesman and a Romberger son

Isaiah K. Romberger and Elmira (Clark) Romberger Store - 1922
Left to Right: Mrs. Harry (Myrtle) Romberger holding daughter, Helen (Romberger) Koppnhauer, Mrs. Isaiah (Elmira) (Clark) Romberger, Harry C. Romberger, Bertha (Romberger) Havice, Mazie Zerbe, Stanley C. Romberger, Dr. Luther Havice. Note Salted Fish Buckets.

Victor Wiest, owner; Harry K. Romberger (clerk) and W. O. Leitzel on front porch of Store, now Boyer's Hardware Store. 1900 - 1902

(Old) Harry K. Romberger. Clerk in store for Victor Wiest (Now Boyer's Hardware Strore) 1900 - 1902

James A. Reed's Store—"Al" and Phronie Reed were in business selling hardware, food and clothing. Later son Raymond Reed and wife Mary operated the business, building removed.

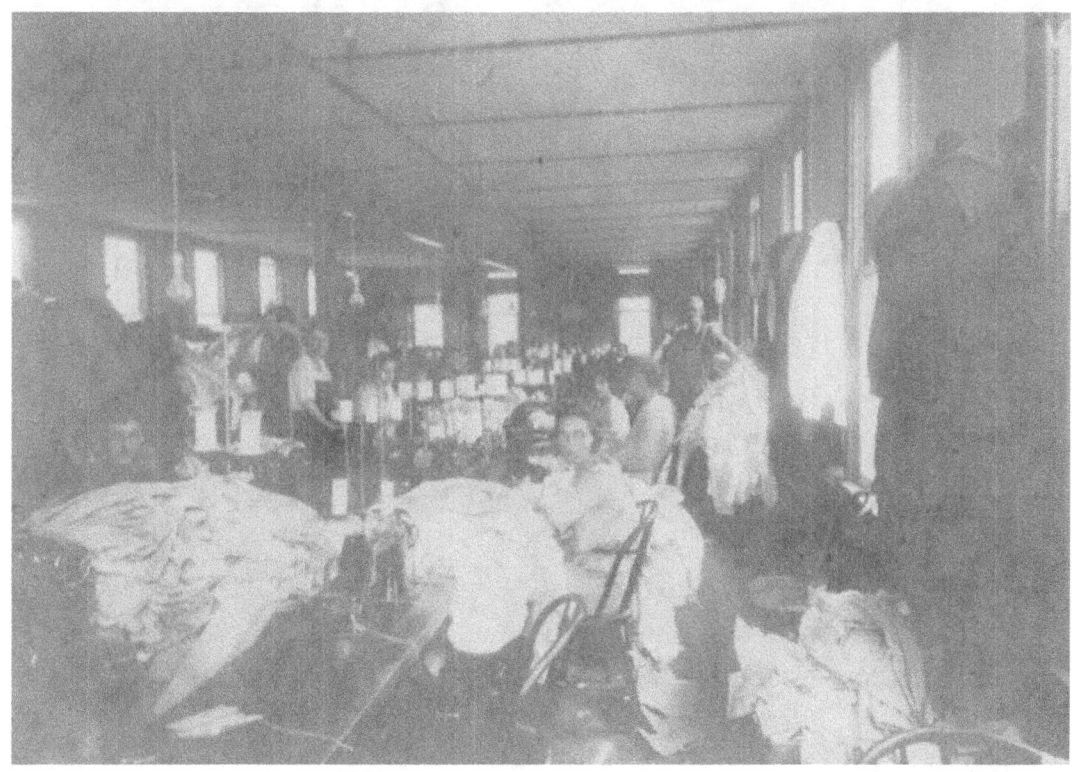

Klingerstown Sewing Factory- now Creek Side Café W.O Leitzel, Owner of factory

Ray "Eps" and Helen Knorr opened store business in 1932.
Later built home and garage, operating store - plumbing - and trailer business till retirement

Klingerstown Garage very early. Later on was called "Klingerstown Motors".
Owners in early days, Richard Leitzel then son - Roy Leitzel

1922- 1926 William A. and (wife) Katherine (Wiest) Romberger family left to right: Mary (R.) Deibert, Father Wm. Romberger, Gerturde (R.) Shaffer, Mother Katherine (Wiest) Romberger, Annie (R.) (Kessler), William Romberger (Billy), Lillian (R.) Leitzel.

Klingerstown, ca. 2010. A parade of antique cars on an outing, stopped in Klingerstown for lunch. The post office and Koppy's store - apartment house make a nice backdrop for this scene. The big building is gone now in 2015.

The Day Koppy's Store and Apartments Burned, January 28, 2014

The winter of 2014 began with a cold wave. The meterologists called it a Polar vortex, forcing the jet stream to dip further south than usual. The usual path of the jet stream crosses the central United States. It is a major controlling factor in our weather. The people of Pennsylvania were using all options for heat in their homes during this extreme cold period of weather.

Koppy's store occupied the central part of Klingerstown. The building was converted into 3 apartments for rent. The post office was attached to the north end toward the Hotel. This building began as the Samuel Clark Store in the early days of the village settlement. The original Clark Store formed the southern portion of the large building. Many generations continued merchandise sales at this location, and later became known as Romberger's Store. Large additions were added. The store was named Koppy's Store, at last, with Helen and Carolos Kopenhaver operating it as a grocery store. In 1989 it was closed as a grocery store. Several apartments were always occupied in the upstairs second floor level. They continued to be occupied above the store and post office at the time of the fire.

On Tuesday, January 28, 2014, about 2:45 P.M., the fire siren sounded. Steve and Joan Troutman were at work at the Troutman Brother's butcher shop. Michael, their son, came in the shop and reported smoke from Klingerstown could be easily seen by looking across the lowland from the Troutman Brother's farm. Brett Kahler was delivering fuel oil. His pager went off alerting him of a Klingerstown Fire Company fire call. He immediately called Michael Troutman to visibly check for smoke. The smoke was heavy and flames began to appear at the south end of the building. The flames and smoke continued and increased as the fire worked its way toward the north end where the post office was located. The following information is from fireman, Brett Kahler of the Klingerstown Fire Company as he recalls the event. The fire moved slowly and postal employees were able to remove all mail from the building. All of the residents were able to get out of the burning building. The children were in school and some adults at their work place. Some of the post office furniture was lost in the fire. Fireman from Klingerstown called for help. Six companies arrived. Gratz was the second on the scene, and set up a portable water dam on the road in front of the burning building. They began to fill it with water pumped directly from the creek. Temperatures were way below freezing, perhaps as low as 10 degrees. Ice began to form everywhere. The firemen kept their trucks running and pumping so the pumps would not freeze. Firemen were on the porch roof in front of the store building with hand lines pouring water through windows. Hickory Corners firemen set up their truck to pump water from the creek at the Spain Road bridge near by the fire location. These men filled tank truck to haul the water downtown to the portable dam. Pitman Fire Company concentrated on protecting the nearby Klingerstown Hotel, using hand lines to keep the roof of the red brick building wet. Klingerstown Fire Company fighters concentrated on the east and south side of the burning building. Lykens sent a ladder truck. Pillow Fire Company and Sacramento Fire Company all assisted. The main road through town was closed to all traffic except fire fighting apparatus. Hoses of all sizes criss- crossed the roadway. Water froze into ice everywhere. Ice formed dams over a foot deep which would have covered the fire fighter's boots. As night time came, the temperature dropped more and the men were very cold. Hickory Corner's fire engine's water pump froze and stopped working. Hand lines and air packs were freezing. The clothing the men wore, termed their "gear" became ice coated as well. This made it difficult for the men to move their arms in the frozen coats. The Hotel provided a much needed warm place where coats could be thawed out, and provided hot food and drink as well. The fire was put out during the night time darkness. Even PA Dept. of Highways provided assistance by spreading salt on the icy roadway. Michael Troutman delivered diesel fuel to the working fire company engines during the fire fight. Three or four men reported the following day to put more water on a few hot spots.

The burned out building stood for several months until Roy Adams was hired to demolish the ruins with a large excavator. The debris was taken in dumpsters to a landfill. The Adams' crew did a fine job. A much needed parking lot in the center of town was created where the store building once stood.

A view of the Klingerstown Post Office and Apartments (ca. 2010), previously the General Store operated by the Clarks, Rombergers, and Koppenhavers. Last known as Koppy's Store. A parade of antique cars passing through.

Klingerstown looking south in 2011.

A replica of the Klingerstown Grist Mill built by Art Wert of Mifflinburg for Steve Troutman. Art was well known for the many precise reproductions he created as replicas.

Early Grist Mill and Saw Mill in the Klingerstown Gap.

The up and down sawmill, photo by Earl Troutman ca. 1957.

Photos courtesy of Ms. Arlene Deibert

Turbine for the sawmill pulled out of the mill race by George Deibert after the 1972 flood.

Pulley and fly wheels that were beneath the up and down saw mill. Lower left of photo shows where push rod was fastened to operate the saw. Background is turbine shaft and gear that transferred the power from the turbine.

Mill stones, turbine and parts from the old mill in the Klingerstown Gap, operated by the Deibert Family. Peter Klinger, (1773-1858), son of Philip Klinger, (1723-1811), established the first grist mill and saw mill on this site. This location was a portion of Parcel No. 4. Peter Klinger is identified on page 8 of this book, where he is named as an adjoining land owner of "formerly Manor land". The large grist mill stones in the foreground of this photo were carved on site. Peter used the conglomerate sandstone he found on the nearby Mahantongo Mountain. It is estimated that the bed stone and runner stone each weigh one ton.

Parcel No. 4, Western Portion

The western portion of tract No. 4, is earlier identified as the land of Johannes Klinger. He passed away at the young age of 47, in the year 1800. The western portion was purchased from Johannes Klinger by Johannes Baum Sr. This is presently the farm and lands of Troutman Brothers and the old Williard farm which is now Michael's Foods. According to the "Baum Family History," by L. Gertrude Fryburg, the Johannes Baum family was among the first to settle in the Klingerstown area. Johannes Baum was born December 11, 1754 in Alsace Township, Berks County, PA. He took the oath of allegiance, May 28, 1778, and resided in Cumru Township, Berks County. Johannes served in Capt. Myers Company of Berks County in the Revolutionary War. In 1802 he is recorded as being a miller in Maxatawny Township, Berks County. This is very interesting to note that Johannes Baum, being a miller himself, may have come to this location because of the existence of a mill. In 1803-1804, he moved with his family to the Mahantongo Valley and died there in 1804. Other sources list 1807 as the date of his death. Although no monument exists to mark his grave, he is no doubt buried at the Klinger's Church Cemetery where many members of his family rest. Much of the Baum tradition was preserved through Lena Baum, and aged spinster who died in Klingerstown, at age 94, in 1905. She was a daughter of Henry Baum born 1786.

A Short History of the Baum Family
By Steve E. Troutman
August 20, 2006

The Baum family was one of the earliest to settle the land where Klingerstown is now located. Sally B. Troutman, mother of the boys who founded Troutman Brothers, often told a story about her ancestors. The middle initial in her maiden name of Sally B. Wiest is in memory of the name Baum, as that was her mother's maiden name. Sally told her grandchildren what her grandmother told her.

It was John Baum who first settled west of the Pine Creek. John and his family built a log house in the lowland, not far away from where Elwood Williard's stone house stands today. The cabin was built among the trees, beside a brook. A few foundation stones from this cabin can still be found there when the ground is plowed. Sally remembered glass and broken crockery also marking the location. Most of the foundation stones were reused in building the Williard's stone residence. The Baum's lived off the land. They brought only three things with them when they came up from lower Berk's County. These items were a little salt, a little flour, and three cents. Most everything they needed they made themselves. The brook and the Pine Creek provided fish that was easy to catch. Many animals abounded so that hunting and trapping provided the family with meat.

As time passed, some of the trees were cut and small clearings allowed wheat to be planted. The harvested wheat was put in linen bags and put on horseback and taken back down to Reading where the closest gristmill was located. This may have been Grings Mill, located on the Tulpehocken Creek, close by where it joins the Schuylkill River. A county park is located here today and the old Grings Mill is beautifully restored.

A copy of the Baum family history, by L. Gertrude Fryburg is in the possession of Troutman Brothers. Gertrude Fryburg was an early genealogist of the Baum family. Part of the following is from her research.

The Baum family was among the first families to settle in Berks County. The pioneer ancestor was Theobald Baum who came to Oley in Philadelphia County, now Alsace Township, Berks County, PA. On February 27, 1733 his name appears on the records of Philadelphia County, and it may be assumed that he was already settled there. A survey made April 30, 1734 shows surrounding land vacant with only the name Baum and Spangler as landowners.

Theobald Baum was born March 15, 1693 near Strasbourg, in Alsace Germany. He was naturalized in Philadelphia on April 10 and 11, 1741. Twenty-two years later, April 27, 1762 he died at this home in Alsace Township. Theobald (DeWald) Baum headed a list of signatures presented to Philadelphia County Quarter Session on December 2, 1744 stating that the residents wished to erect a new and separate township named after the place in Germany from whence they came. In 1745 the petition was granted and thenceforth the township was known as Alsace. The first church was built in 1737 on land donated by the Baum and Spangler families who helped build the log church.

Part I: Spread Eagle Manor and the Establishment of Klingerstown and the Klingerstown Grist Mill

The first church in Alsace Township, Berks County, PA, was built in 1737 on land donated by the Spangler and Baum Families. Theobald Baum was one of the first founders of this church and no doubt helped to build the first log building. In the plot of ground, south of the church may still be found the grave of Theobald Baum. The marker of sandstone is the oldest dated stone there. By Gertrude Fryburg.

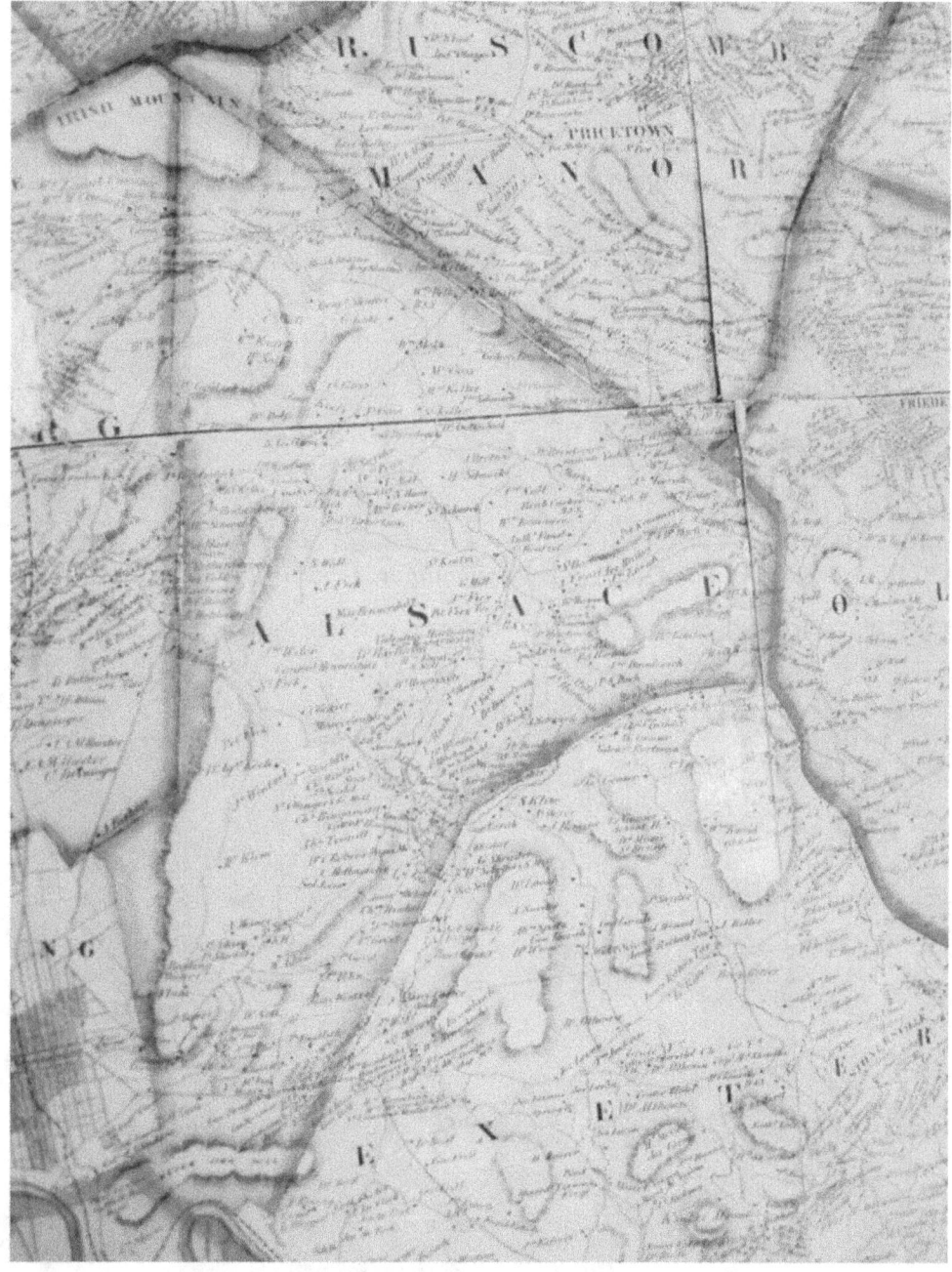

1860 Alsace Township Map courtesy of Allan Wiest
The Alsace Church is located approximately two miles north of the city of Reading on Kutztown Road, between the city and Laureldale Boro. The church is presently in Muhlenberg Township located on the west end of this map. The church, graveyard and D. Baum are identified, two inches west of the letter A in Alsace.

Two farms within the Western Portion of Parcel No. 4

Howard Williard Farm, now Elwood Williard Jr. The site of Michael's Foods.

Troutman Brothers Farm, ca. 1960 earlier Tobias B. Wiest and John Baum.

Family of Tobias B. Wiest Tobias B. Wiest (10 Aug. 1844- 13 Feb. 1912) son of Samuel Merkel Wiest (1819-1866), Johannes Wiest (1794-1881), Johann Jacob Wust III (5 Jan. 1775-4 Aug. 1811), Johann Jacob Jr. Wust (1733-1799), Hans Jacob, the immigrant (1712-1786).Mary Ann Baum (1848-20 Dec. 1931) daughter of David Baum (1816-1893) and Susanna Welker (1819-1893) Mary Ann (20 Dec. 1931-age 83y 6m 10d, married Tobias B. Wiest. David son of Henry Baum (1784-1820) and Catherine Sterner (b. Aug. 14, 1786). Henry Baum married second Salome Gundrum (1795-1852) Henry son of John Baum (1754-1807). He died in Klingerstown. John son of Peter Baum Sr.

Monroe Baum Wiest (5 Mar. 1885-May 1970)

Sally Baum Wiest (31 July 1882-16 Aug. 1972)

John Carlos Wiest (b. 10 Jan. 1892) (Jolie) Logging engineer in Portland, Oregon, WWI veteran, unmarried, raised by Mary Ann Baum for her deceased sister Elizabeth (Mrs. Wm. Wiest) Brothers Tobias B. Wiest and William B. Wiest married sisters, Mary Ann Baum and Elizabeth Baum.

John C. Wiest, son of William Wiest and his wife Liza was raised by Tobias Wiest married to Mary Ann Baum. Liza was a younger sister to Mary Ann Baum. Liza died during childbirth with John C. Wiest. Liza is buried at Klinger's Church, close to Tobias Wiest. Her husband William, then left for Canada and died there and is buried there.

```
Wm. Wiest md. Liza Baum
Children:  Butcher Sam Wiest
           Rich        Wiest
           Mary        Wiest md. Morris Wiest brother of John Wiest and
                             Nathanial Wiest of Nevin and Glippy's Line
           John  C.    Wiest the youngest also known as "Joelie"
```

John C. Wiest was a WWI veteran and John Troutman remembers his leggings as they were wrapped at that time. He went west to Oregon with the lumber camps and died there too, and is buried there. He was never married. He grew up on the farm now being Troutman Bros. and remained there some time as an adult as remembered by Mary Williard, John Troutman, and wife Ada.

Victor Troutman 4-Horse Wagon, ca. 1908, on the Troutman Brother's Farm, Klingerstown, PA.

Victor Troutman (1882-1947) on the wagon seat. Leo (b.1905) standing in the wagon. Ralph Romberger standing at wagon wheel, son of Alice (1880-1920), Victor's sister. Sally (Wiest) Troutman (1882-1972) holding George (b.1907). Tobias Wiest (1844-1912), Mary (Baum) Wiest (d. 1931). John C. Wiest (Jolie), son of William Wiest (b. 1852) and Elizabeth (Baum) Wiest, (1852-1892) deceased sister of Mary (Baum) Wiest. John C. Wiest was a logging engineer in Portland, Oregon and a World War I veteran. He was raised by Mary Ann Wiest for her sister Elizabeth.

Victor Troutman Family on a Carriage. This one-horse carriage photo ca. 1908. Victor Troutman, Sally Troutman, Leo and George. Anecdotal history has it, that they are on a carriage trip to Fountain Springs near Ashland to visit Sally's sister Emma (1869-1914) married to Jacob Dimmler. Jacob worked on the railroad.

A few photos from the Mary Ann (Baum) Wiest Photo Album

Samuel Wiest

Mary Anne Wiest

Jacob Klinger

Ella Wiest

Mary Troutman photo collection- George Troutman's washing machine motor car
Bryant, Bruce, Earl, and Elwood
Williard-1942

George L. Troutman the father of Victor Troutman spent some of his retired years living with his son on the Troutman farm in Klingerstown. Victor's wife, Mary Wert Troutman predeceased George L. Troutman.

Here we see George in front of the Victor Troutman home.

Victor William Troutman, born June 2, 1882, died December 25, 1947. Married September 22, 1904. Sally Baum Wiest, born July 31, 1882, died August 16, 1972. George Troutman holding horse, Ray, Guy and Allen, sons of Victor and Sally.

Children:

- (a) Leo Tobias Troutman, born October 7, 1905.
- (b) George Monroe Troutman, born June 10, 1907.
- (c) Mary Savilla Troutman, born October 4, 1908.
- (d) John David Troutman, born March 27, 1911.
- (e) Ray Clayton Troutman, born December 21, 1912.
- (f) Guy William Troutman, born September 30, 1914.
- (g) Allen Clair Troutman, born August 18, 1916, died February 17, 1920.
- (h) Harry Bryant Troutman, born October 28, 1918.

Henry Baum's log house- with a new addition in the foreground, built by Victor Troumtan for his son John.

David Baum's log house with the summer kitchen built by Tobias Wiest.

*The three houses on the old Baum, Wiest, Troutman farm were painted with three different colors.
Sally Wiest-Troutman's house and shandy was red,
Old Henry Baum house was grey, and
John Troutman's house was white.*

Henry Baum's wagon shed and ladder wagon.

Part I: Spread Eagle Manor and the Establishment of Klingerstown and the Klingerstown Grist Mill

Pine Creek Bottom Land Harvest, by Deanne Wiseman of Wiseman Graphics
The picture is a panoramic view of the old Victor and Sallie farm where many people travel to purchase Troutman Brother's meats. Bruce and Earl Troutman are pictured as well as Ralph Romberger and Howard Williard.

Victor and Sally (Wiest) Troutman
June 2, 1882–December 25, 1947   July 31, 1882–August 16, 1972

Victor Troutman and Sally Wiest Troutman Children

From left to right: Leo Troutman, George Troutman, Mary Williard, John Troutman, Ray Troutman, Guy Troutman and Harry Troutman (in front of the old Baum bake oven).

Parcel No. 5, 201A.

John Schreckengaust. Historian Gary Schreckengast suggests this location including portions of Snowdale Valley may be the original homesite dated 1783-1804. Johann Jost (John) most probably died sometime between 1800 and 1804 and is buried somewhere on Tract 5 or at Himmels or Klinger's Cemetery.

Parcel No. 5, 201 ½ A., granted to William Wightman, Jr., by attorney for John and Richard Penn, 1808. Formerly property of John Schreckengaust. Later owners included Johannes Wiest and his son, Daniel M. Wiest.

Looking east to Herlan Boyer's place. There is a little house along the Snow Creek in front of Herlan Boyer's store. It is barely visible on this picture. (to the left of the two story home).

Jim and Sharon Boyer Residence, previously Herlan Boyer home and store.

Jim Boyer and Sharon (Lenker) share this photo and story. They recall Kenneth Boyer, Jim's father, describing the building of this house and grocery store. The saw mill for cutting the house timbers was located between the house and Klingerstown on the north side of the road. The construction style of the house is a frame of posts and mortised timbers. The carpenter gang slept in the barn for several weeks while building the house.

A red shanty stood west of the big house closer to the Snow Creek. It remained occupied until the 1980's. It may have been only 15 feet from the creek. There was a yard between the shanty and the store-house which was on higher ground. People had to walk up hill to the big house. For a time Louis Smeltz lived in the little red house. Mary Lebo is the daughter of Louis Smeltz. She recalls playing with the Roland Romberger children on the Romberger farm. The Romberger farm was on the west side of the Snow Creek. At that time, the Romberger house was a double house with two Romberger brothers living there.

Mary Lebo attempted to identify the people on the picture. They may be Herlan Boyer, wife Rosie, children, Kenneth, Alberta,(md. Don Lenker), also called Rosie, Hannah, and Arlene (youngest).

Part I: Spread Eagle Manor and the Establishment of Klingerstown and the Klingerstown Grist Mill

Benjamin Markel established a tannery on the north side of Mahantongo Creek nearby the mill which was on the south side of the creek. This originally was a one story building with pits to soak animal skins as part of the tanning process.

The second story was added by Clarence (Toll) Williard. He was a carpenter and stone mason. Tillie, his wife, remembered he repointed these stone walls shortly before he was killed by a lighting strike in Millersburg while working as a carpenter.

Terry and Marla Williard Residence. Tannery in background.

The old Cross Keys Hotel on the Tulpehocken Path one mile west of Klingerstown. N. Daniel Schwalm, Jr. and his wife Noreen are the present owners.

History of Roland R. and Mary K. Romberger Farm
2862 Klingerstown Road, Herndon, PA 17830

by
Roland, Jr., Joyce, Beverly, Gail, and Renee Romberger

Winter View of Farm from Woods Facing North
Circa 1950

If you drive west of Klingerstown for about 1 mile on the Klingerstown to Hebe road, you will pass through a farm with a red bank barn with hex signs on the left, a log house covered with white clapboards, a tractor shed, a pig shed, and a shanty that was an early saddlery. On the right side of the road are a wagon shed and a granary. Earlier buildings also included a corncrib, brooder houses, an outhouse, and a kettle place to heat water for washing clothes, butchering, and making apple butter, and a grape trellis for grapevines.

To the south and east are fields that were formerly used as pastureland and orchards, with a small stream or "run" that goes into the Snow Creek, which joins the Mahantongo Creek in the woods on the southern boundary of the farm. When Roland Romberger farmed the fields close to the Snow Creek, local people would search the newly plowed soil and find arrowheads used by the American Indians.

The first section will present a history of the owners of the land tract based on deeds and surveys in Roland and Mary Romberger's possession. Next will be memories of Klingerstown and the farm told by Roland Romberger which were part of his oral history interviews recorded on film in January of 2004. The land area that includes the village of Klingerstown and the Romberger farm were part of the original Spread Eagle Manor.

History of Owners of the Land Tract

According to John H. Carter's article "Spread Eagle Manor: Ancient Gateway to Northumberland County" (published in the *Northumberland County Historical Society*

Proceedings, Volume XVI, 1948, pp. 21-27), sometime after the Divestment Act of 1779, the Penn's partitioned Spread Eagle Manor (containing 1292 acres) into 8 tracts. These tracts ranged from 3 acres to 262 3/4 acres each. The Roland Romberger farm was part of tract #5 which contained 201.5 acres, granted to William Wightman, Jr. in 1808 by John and Richard Penn. Tract #5 was centrally located in Spread Eagle Manor. Today the Tulpehocken Path borders the western edge of the farm and goes through the southern portion of the property. The Roland Romberger farm is situated west of the Snow Creek, south and east of the Nathan Schwalm farm, and north of the Mahantongo Creek.

From this original Tract#5 of 201.5 acres, Roland Romberger's farm today in 2015 contains approximately 72 acres. Roland R. Romberger's estate had the original deeds from 1827 through the present. Records indicated different acreage at times, but without written explanation, the reasons why the acreage changed could not be clarified through the deeds. For example, in 1827 the farm was roughly 76 acres (similar to today's approximately 72 acres, but included the Clair Troutman property plus a few additional acres.) Yet in 1870, the farm was much larger and included about 120 acres. The farm then included some land behind Clair Troutman's property on a northwest diagonal toward the Barry Erdman house.

The first deed Draught that exists shows Jacob Holben (deceased) to Jacob and Samuel Wiest 76 acres 40 ¼ perches on Nov. 22, 1827. This tract is approximately the Roland Romberger farm today minus the Clair Troutman property and a few acres south of the farm. See Figure 1.

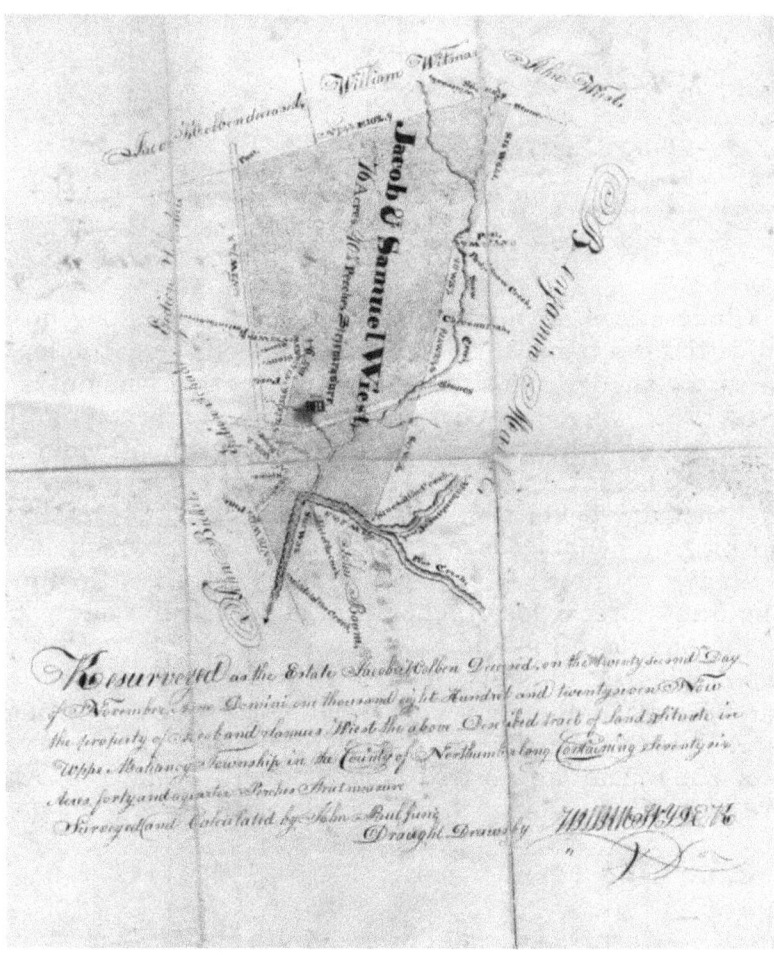

Figure 1: 1827 Jacob Holben to Jacob and Samuel Wiest.

Part I: Spread Eagle Manor and the Establishment of Klingerstown and the Klingerstown Grist Mill

The draft names the owners Jacob and Samuel Wiest. Adjoining land owners named John Bickel, Gidion Schadle, Gidion Hobnits, Jacob Holbein, deceased, William Witman, John Wiest, Benjamin Markle, and John Baum.

Resurveyed as the Estate of Jacob Holben, deceased, on the 22 day of November, A.D. 1827. Now the property of Jacob and Samuel Wiest. The above described tract of land situate in Upper Mahanoy Twp., County of Northumberland containing 76 acres, 40 and ¼ perches. Strict measure. Surveyed and calculated by John Paul Jr.

In 1870 the Sam Wiest tract shows 120 acres, 30 perches which includes land to the north of the current Roland Romberger farm, on a northwest diagonal. Excluded was a small rectangular tract bordering the highway on the west side. All of this land was to the north of the current Clair Troutman property. See Figure 2.

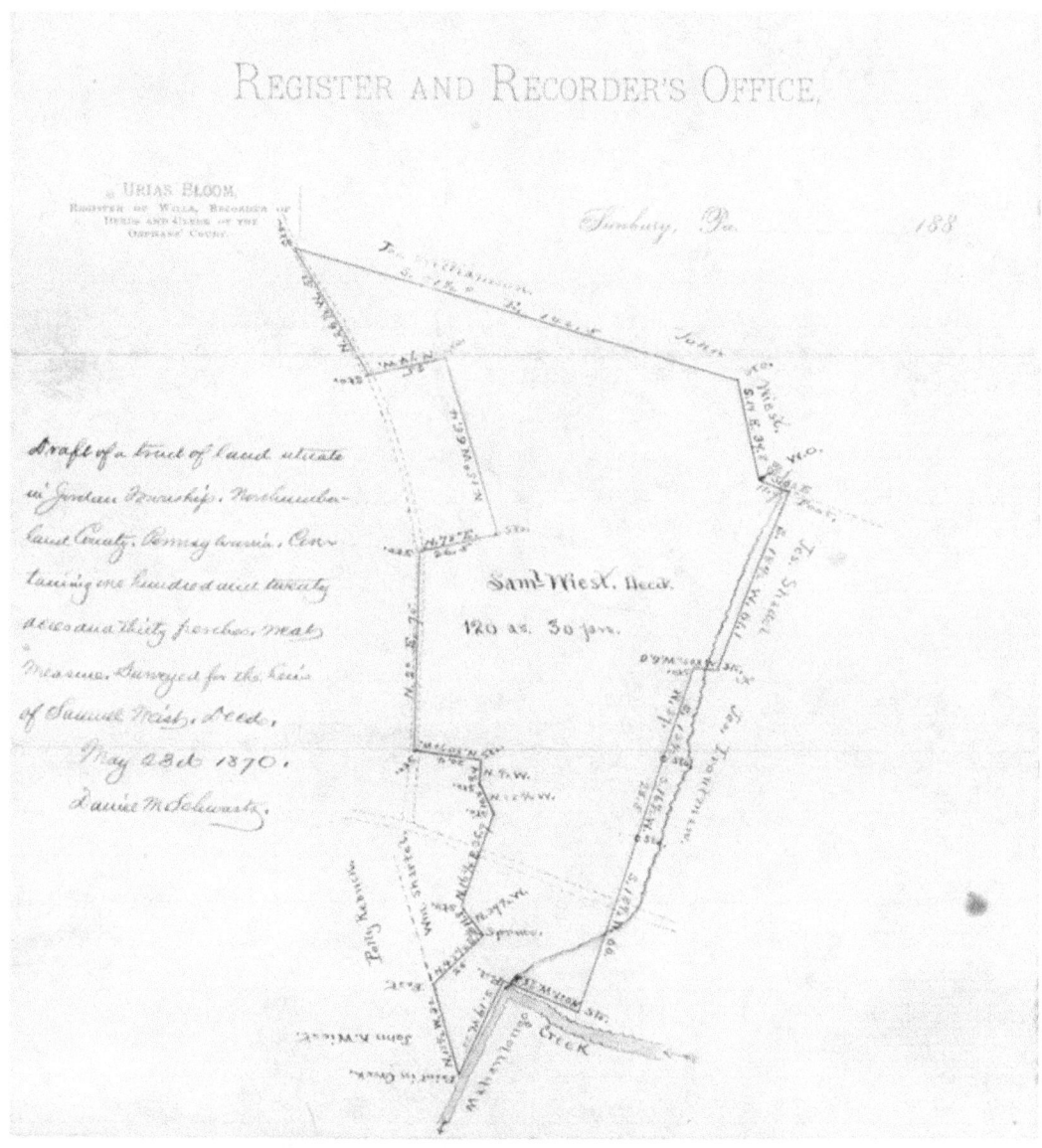

Figure 2: 1870 Samuel Wiest Tract Survey.

In 1874 there was a sheriff's sale managed by Sheriff Samuel H. Rothermel, which sold the lands, goods, chattels and tenements (76 acres, 40¼ perches) of Jacob M. Wiest and Samuel W. Clark. The tract of land sold for $5390 to John Wiest, the highest bidder.

In 1883 the farm was sold to Peter D. Snyder. The indenture was made the third day of April, 1883 by Daniel M. Wiest and A.R. Poffenberger, Trustees, appointed by the Orphans Court of Schuylkill County, to make the sale of the real estate of John Wiest, deceased. The tract showed 86 acres, 47 perches. Peter D. Snyder bought the farm for the sum of $4185.25. See Figure 3.

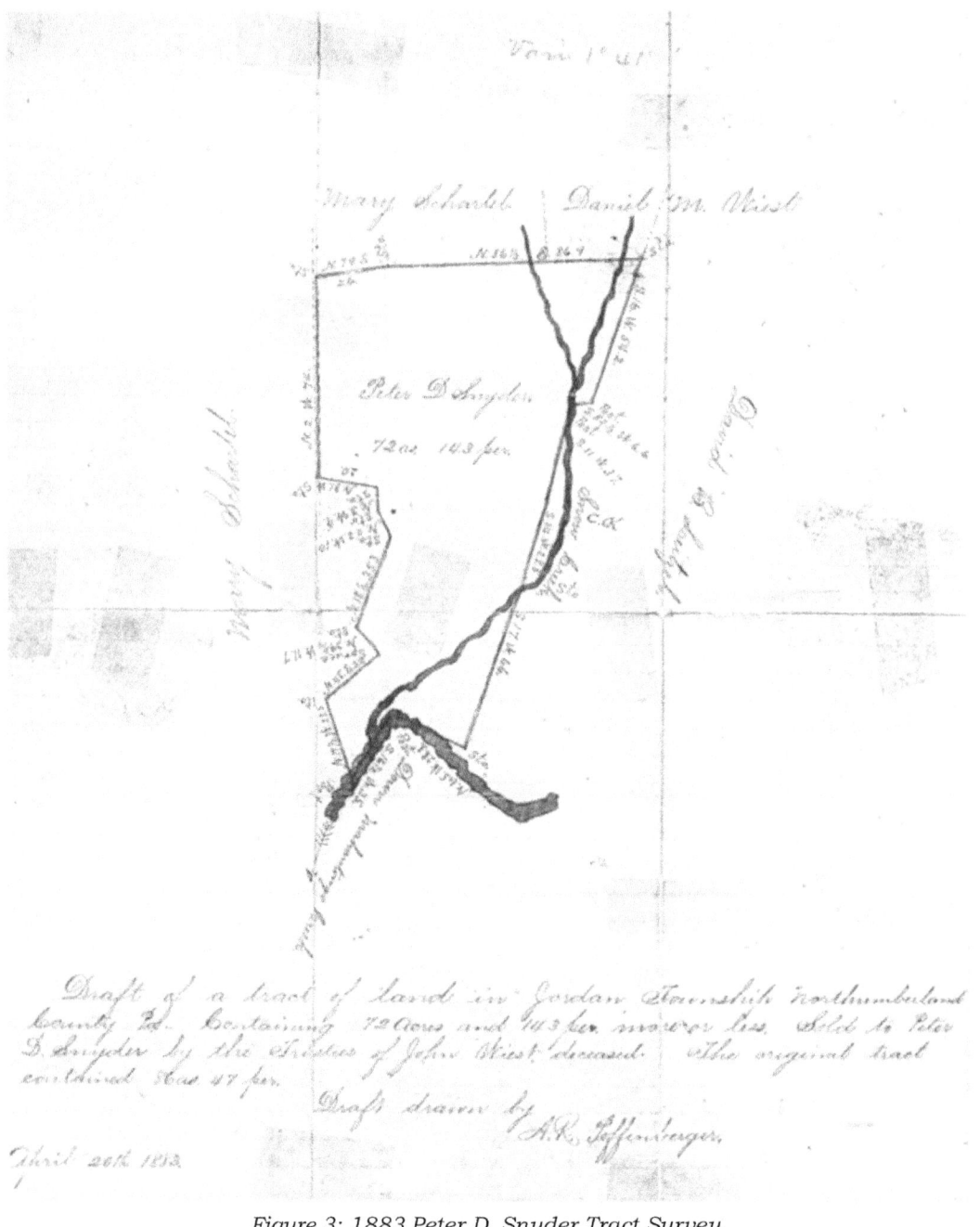

Figure 3: 1883 Peter D. Snyder Tract Survey.

Part I: Spread Eagle Manor and the Establishment of Klingerstown and the Klingerstown Grist Mill

In November, 1906, Peter D. Snyder's heir and wife Fietta Snyder died. On April 2, 1907 John M. Snyder, as Executor of Estate, sold the farm to Monroe Snyder for $3098 and Monroe Snyder conveyed the farm back to John M. Snyder in the amount of $3098 for 86 acres. In September 1907 John M. Snyder also paid his brother Charles I. Snyder $1620. In December 1915, John Snyder had the tract resurveyed and it shows 78 acres, 123 perches. See Figure 4.

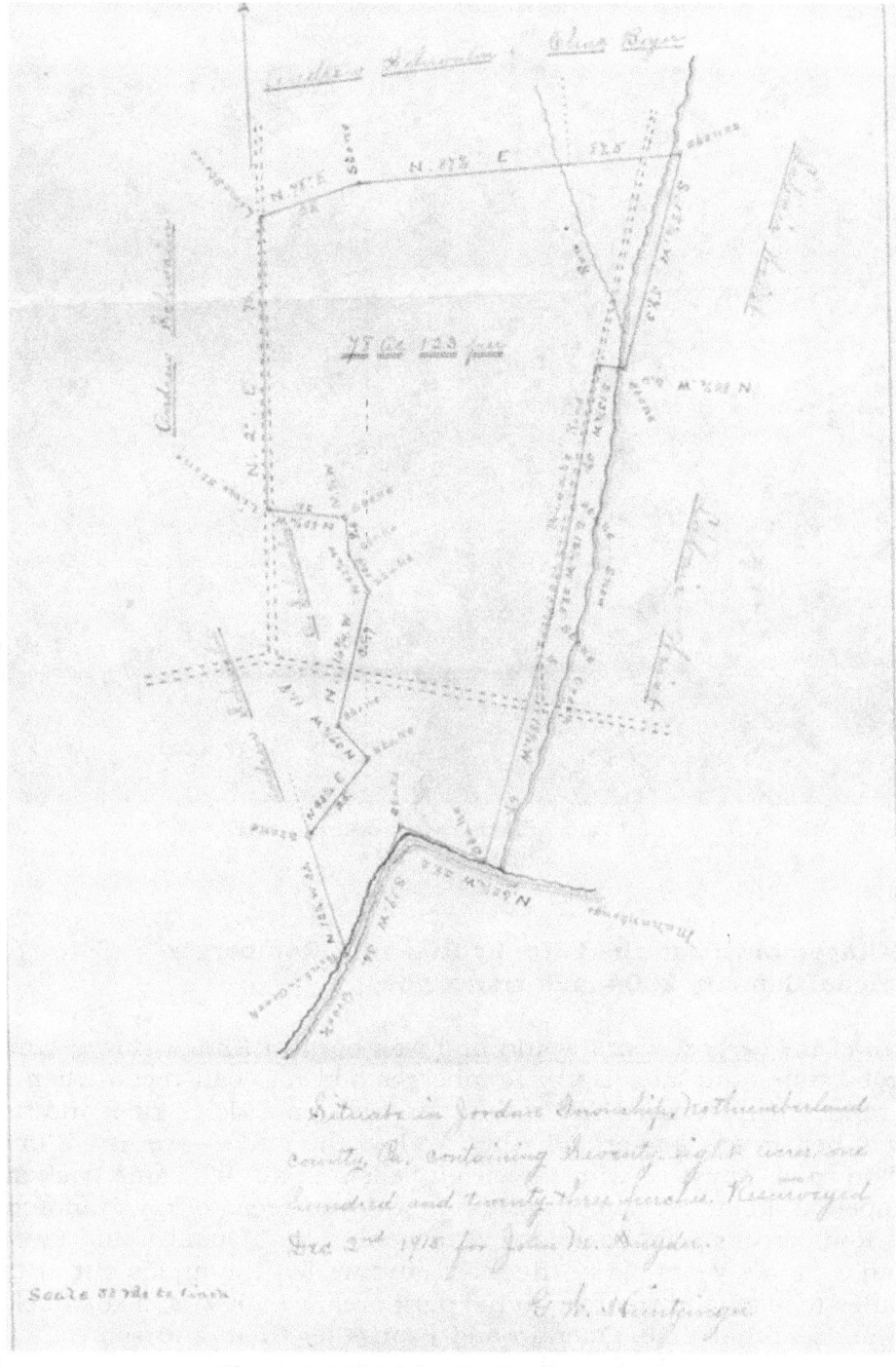

Figure 4: 1915 John Snyder Tract Survey.

On February 4, 1946 Roland R. Romberger and Mary K. Romberger bought the farm from John M. Snyder for $6000. The 1946 deed indicated 86 acres, 47 perches stating, "It is the same farm which Daniel M. Wiest and A. Poffenberger Trustees, etc. by their deed dated April 3, 1883 . . . conveyed to Peter D. Snyder. . . ." The 1883 deed showed the acreage was 86 acres, 47 perches. The John M. Snyder tract survey done in 1915 showed 78 acres, 123 perches.

In 1969 and 1970 Roland Romberger sold 2.942 acres in the northwest section of the farm to Clair Troutman.

*Aerial View of Romberger Farm Buildings
Circa mid-1960's*

**Memories of Klingerstown and the Farm by Roland R Romberger
(Recorded in video, January 2004, and transcribed)**

The first I recall of my earliest years would be I was born in Klingerstown, which was at the Isaiah Romberger store, and later Harry Romberger had it. I can recall when I was about 3 years old my grandmother, Elmira, held me and we went on a sleigh ride, and this is the first I can remember of her. It was a short ride, but we had the mules—we had 2 mules, Rose and Dick, and we had to of course go with the sleigh bells and all. We came back and it was cold and I was wrapped in a blanket. Those are the first days I recall of my grandmother. She was a Clark, Isaiah Romberger's wife. Then later, I remember that Quentin and I were playing and I may have been 3 ½ to 4 years old at the most, and we left the mules out at the back of the barn. These mules took off and went up to the park area, which was located below the church and in the lowlands at that time. Quentin and I ran after them and someone else came and helped us. We finally got them back in the barn. When my father came home from market we got a good whipping. I'll never forget that. I know we never opened the barn doors again.

I began fishing at about the age of 10. It was Good Friday and your Grandpa sent Quentin and me to go fish. We fished in the Mahantongo that goes by John Snyder's farm. We used a long bamboo rod with a line and hook. We used a cork for a bobber. When you saw the cork go up and down you had to yank on the rod to try to catch the fish. Then we caught bass and pike. Whatever we caught, we cleaned and ate—even suckers and catfish. Quentin and I did a lot of fishing. I stopped fishing when I went to high school and didn't start again until 1970 when Lee and Mark talked me into going trout fishing in the Penns Creek.

After I came out of the service [WWII], we bought this farm here. When I came home from the war, I don't believe I was home for more than a couple of days when my Dad said he believed I could buy the farm here from John Snyder, and that other people were after it, but he thought I could buy it. So I talked to John and he said, "yes, if you want to buy it, I'll sell it to you". He said, "You always came down here and helped me and you always liked to hunt here and trap, and you were always good to me, so I'll sell it to you." So we bought it then. That was in the fall of '45, shortly after I got back from the service. We paid $6000 for about 72 acres. Now at the same time, Johnny Rothermel's farm sold for only $1250 on auction. His farm was about 100 acres, but his land was off the main highway. So I felt we paid a fair price.

Roland R. and Mary K. Romberger Wedding Day
September 19, 1942

John had a maid here by the name of Jennie Boyer. They liked to play the card game "Rook." So Quentin and I used to come down here when we were younger and every time we came down here, he made sure we got a little glass of wine. This was big doings for Quentin and me. We would play Rook the whole evening long. John liked to smoke cigars and he always had a cigar. We had fun playing cards in his kitchen.

John lived here all his life. I guess he was about seventy-one, seventy-two when he passed away but he was in Lykens for a year or two. His parents had lived here. He had a brother who was out west. John's father Peter Snyder had what people in Dutch would call a "saudler" shop. He repaired saddles and harnesses and horse lines, collars, leather stuff. This is what they did in the shanty next to the house.

The closest we can tell when this house was built was 1840. According to what I read about homes in this area, I think this house was built even before the hotel up at Schwalm's. This is a log house and the earliest houses were log houses.

There were a number of owners of this farm. I don't remember all the names, but a Poffenberger and a Clark's names were on the deeds. My great-great grandfather owned this place and he had nothing but horses and this whole farm was fenced in. You can still see some of the fence up at the sumac hill grown into the trees. He was a drover. They'd bring the horses to Herndon, I guess by train, and then they'd drive them on the road up here to the fields. Then he'd break them, tame them, and sell them to farmers. This was a Clark and he owned this farm—through Elmira Clark's ancestors. She was my grandmother. At that time the house only had boards upright covering the logs, upright like on the shanty. That's what this house was like. Then later on they put the siding on. Underneath are logs. The west end of the barn is also logs. The original part of the barn was a log barn. We had Fred Peifer extend the barn out on the south side and add the wings. Before that there was a stonewall on the bottom and the above walls extended out. The reason for that is there were stalls underneath and they could walk underneath that extension and be in the dry if it was raining to take feed or go to the different animals. The first stall was horses. You'd put like four horses in there and the next two or three stalls were for cows. And of course, when I came along, we extended it out to have more barn space and put windows in.

John used horses to farm and he had the nicest team around the whole area. They were good. He'd put his plow on the wagon and they would run, run all the way from here up past my Dad's place up the hill [to the fields]. He'd plow all day and then he'd come down through. Yeah, he had good horses, four of them, and they were beautiful. He fed them good and took care of them. A lot of farmers just had mules. I know Al Klinger, he had mules. They would work hard, maybe longer than a horse, but they could be stubborn. The horses were smarter. With mules, if you wanted them to go left, they would go right. Now my Dad, after we kids were born, never had mules or horses. He always had a truck for huckstering. His parents, who owned the store in Klingerstown, did have two mules to go to market. That was back in the nineteen twenties.

Quentin helped my father with the huckstering. My father had started over in Klingerstown when they had the store. At the time they used to go around with store things. They would go from house to house with canned stuff, coffee, whatever store things. From that I think he started. When he'd come around with the truck like that, first it was a wagon, the farmers would ask him, you know, if he had calves for sale or pigs for sale. It wasn't like it is now. He'd start doing it and then of course he took them out to market and he kept it up. That's what he did then.

Before the truck it was all mules and the spring wagon. My Dad would go out to Pottsville, Minersville and that was a long trip for mules. He'd leave early, maybe two o'clock in the morning and then he'd get out there maybe 8 or 9 o'clock. He'd sell everything which he had no problem doing. He always had customers there. At that time pigs were slaughtered and cut into half and then put in white cloth bags cleaned, so they wouldn't get dirty, and that's how they were taken out. One of the reasons he left so early was because of the summertime so it wouldn't be so hot for some of the meat. From the mules he went to a Model T Ford truck with a Swab body on it and then a Model A and he had that Model A all the way until he quit driving.

Stanley Romberger's Model A with Swab Wagon.

In 1928 we had a Chevy car and I remember going up to my grandmother's and he'd go "ba ba" around the turns. I remember Quentin used to laugh when he did it with the horn. Later on, shortly after that, he got this Model T truck. Now when he moved over to his house he brought one along over from Klingerstown. It was also a Model T but it was a very poor one. We got a different one then that he used to drive to market. The windshield wipers you had to do by hand. There was a crank on the inside and (Roland motions left to right)—this is how you made the windshield wiper go. There was no heater in the truck and the gas tank was right under the seat. You had to pull the seat front to fill it with gas. But that Model A Ford went and went and went. He'd leave with the truck to go out to Shenandoah. He might have left at 6 o'clock. I went along sometimes, Quentin went along most of the time. He sold to stores. All except chickens. Chickens at that time—they were all live, that's how you sold them. You'd go down a street in town and yell "chickens, chickens" and the people would come out. You'd put up a scale, weigh the chicken there, and so much a pound, and they would take the live chicken back in their home, maybe out back in whatever they had to put it in, until they wanted to kill it. At that time they killed their own chickens. Everybody. Dad would have to go to the farmers around dark the night before to get the chickens.

I don't remember Isaiah Romberger. I remember my grandmother, I still remember her holding me and I was very young, and that's the only memory I have of her. She was also a very kind lady. She was at the time, but the flu, I forget the early 20's or prior to that, what they called the "faullhaus" in Dutch. But in other words a lot of people died from it. To take care of them they used to wear something over their face to try to keep from getting it but a lot of them got it that way and died also. But at that time it was worldwide. A lot of people died from that. It wasn't like now, you know, that they had antibiotics. My grandmother didn't get it, but my dad had two brothers who died because of it. I forget exactly if they were younger than my dad or older, but they died from it. They were young yet when they died.

I remember Klingerstown was dirt roads. Dust everwhere, and some Sundays they used to bring motorcycles in. Tommy Klinger and a number of people had these motorcycles. They'd come in, drive around, standing on them, stand on their head on them, you name it and it used to be comical I tell you. They always had something going on in Klingerstown. My mother told me they used to have a merry-go-round that would come in and it was on the lawn between the hotel and the store. Every summer this would come in for maybe two weeks and it was run by gas engine –putt, putt, putt, and this was something big at that time.

For fun we used to walk to Klingerstown and we would spend the evening in town, running around with other boys our age, and on the way home, maybe at 10 o'clock, whenever we were told to be home, why we would walk home again. I remember Al Klinger's boys, Marlin Klinger, Ray Klinger, and some of Hauley Snyder's boys, and this was full of people. We'd all come walking home, heading home at the same time, a lot of fun. Dirt roads. No traffic. We'd walk; nobody had a car. Everybody walked and we had just as good a time when we walked.

I remember it seemed like there was a fight every Saturday night in Klingerstown. It was Trevorton against the locals, Rough and Ready against the locals, and if there were no outsiders the locals fought other locals. I remember one winter night there was a group ready to fight on the street, a big V-shaped snowplow came into town from Rough and Ready, plowed right through the group. That stopped the fight!

I was raised just up the hill from John Snyder's farm. John Geiss had just built the home up on the corner when my dad bought it then. He just had finished it. John Geiss was a carpenter and a fisherman, big fisherman. He had just finished it and Dad bought it and we moved over. He was building it for himself and Dad bought it from him. He lived where Mae Rothermel used to live. I know when I broke a window at home, threw a ball through the window; I had to walk down and tell him to come and put another window in. And I walked quite often because I broke quite a few. I didn't have to pay for them but I had to walk down and tell him to come up and put another one in. That was my punishment.

Families also enjoyed music. I really don't know why my brother and I took guitar lessons. Quentin started. Willy Howeiter was our teacher. Music lessons cost 75 cents. He'd come once a week. I played the Hawaiian guitar and Quentin played standard. We played together. I played with Willy Howeiter over in Klingerstown when the Herndon band played there; we had to play a solo with the guitars. Later on, he must have been coming around for about a year, Quentin and I played in church, at the Sunday School picnics, we played all over and we had fun doing it. Later on we used to take the guitar to Marlin Klinger's and we'd be there on a Sunday afternoon and everybody would be singing away. I started lessons when I was going to school. I'd say I was 10 . . . 11 years old. Yeah, I'd say about 12 years old when I played in church and at these places. We practiced, Quentin and I practiced quite a bit, especially when we started and we could play together. Then we liked it and we'd get all the latest music. My dad played the piano in our house and according to the church records my mother also; she played the piano in Sunday School. My dad was very good. He liked the Missouri waltz and boy he could really play nice. Oh yes, I remember my dad playing. He often played. I don't know that any of his brothers or sisters played. I don't believe, not that I know of. I think Anna Wiest taught him. I believe Anna bought the first church organ over here in Klingerstown [at St. Michael's]. She was out in Hollywood later. When dad was young she was at where Boyer's store is now, prior to Spockey's store. He and my mother liked music. We had a self-player piano too. But I know sometimes we'd get over to church early and Rich Leitzel would be there, maybe John Leitzel, not many. Rich would tell Dad to go up and play the Missouri waltz or something like that before church service and Dad would go up and play, yeah beautiful.

Dad was active in the church, very active. He was on the church council for I don't know how many years, but a long time. At that time things were rough. During the depression there were hardly any jobs; people had no work. You couldn't get any money. And then later on even after the depression, it wasn't really good. We didn't have enough money to pay the pastor and my father would go around collecting, with the truck, from house to house trying to get enough money to pay the pastor. He did that many a time. My mother was treasurer of the church. She took care of the money, and well that's how Dad knew there wasn't enough to pay the preacher. So then he went house to house. My mother was treasurer of the church for a long time. Dad was always a trustee or elder or something like that. Of course I was also an elder or trustee too. He was friends with the preachers. I remember Pastor Blank would come over and go hunting with us for pheasants.

A typical day for a woman was about all work. My mother didn't get up with my Dad. Dad would get up very early to go to market. And I won't ever forget this. Every morning he would make two eggs for himself and if you ate with him, you got two eggs. My brothers Lee, Quentin, all of us got the two eggs because that was what Dad made. My mother got up later. Well Dad got up early, often 4 or 4:30 in the morning. Mom would wash and cook and clean and do all the rest of it. At that time washing was a major event, not like today. We had an ice refrigerator, and a man from Pillow would come around once a week with ice and you'd pay 10 cents for a small piece, maybe 1 ft. square and maybe 15 cents for a 2-foot square. He'd bring it in and put it in the refrigerator for you. This refrigerator took care of the water in the bottom, you had to empty the water out still as the ice would melt, but that kept the food cold. The one side had ice and there was little space on the other side where you could keep milk and things like that. At that time all we had was fresh milk. There was no homogenized or pasteurized milk. We used to get it over at Sally Troutman's, five cents a gallon. Over at the butcher shop.

I remember when they build this macadam road through here; it used to be all dirt roads. I was about third or fourth grade in school when they came around with these graters and grated out the ground roads. Then they came with large stones that they got off the Hoofland Mountain. Then they came with people who had stone hammers and they would smash these rocks so that they could fit tight. Then the rollers would roll them and later they came with fine stone and rolled it. This was around 1930 or around there I would say - 1930 or 1932.

During the depression I remember eating a lot of bread and milk. I remember my mother making a bowl with bread and milk and putting a little sugar on it. Milk was a stable food that gave you nourishment. You didn't have everything like you do now. You had milk, potatoes and my mother would bake bread. There wasn't too much. You ate what you had and you didn't get fat.

There weren't deer around here when I was growing up. The first I remember about deer around here, actually hunting deer, was when I came home from the service, after WWII. That was in 1945 when I came home. That fall my dad said, "Do you want to go along deer hunting?" Now I about fell over. I didn't know what he was talking about. I didn't know there was deer hunting around here. During the war years I guess they multiplied because no one hunted them and they increased and then we had quite a few deer. Before that I guess farmers could shoot them on their own farms because they didn't need a license to hunt.

As I said earlier, Quentin went to market with my Dad more so than I did. I went to high school. Now one trip we both went on was when we went with Dad and Rue Erdman. Rue Erdman had a Ford truck and we put a load of chickens in it and took them to Baltimore. He sold them down there near the waterfront or the wharves. Instead of coming back empty we piled up the chicken crates up front. We had about ¾ of the truck full of watermelons. We got them out of a boat down there and we got them for 15 cents a piece, for the big ones. We loaded the truck up with all we could, and then we started peddling over here in Gratz for 50 cents a piece, and they were going like hotcakes. We sold the whole truckload then and we didn't lose any. Quentin and I were carrying watermelons, uh! Dad only did that once or twice. It was a long trip. Quentin and I sat in the back between the chicken boxes. Rue and Dad sat up front. All the way down to Baltimore and back up. It took at least 3 to 4 hours to get to Baltimore. Yeah, we got fresh air back there.

One of the games I really enjoyed playing was croquet. My father loved croquet. I remember in Klingerstown where Paul Shiffer now has his garage there was a croquet sand diamond that was rolled. Rich and John Leitzel and other locals played croquet on the sand diamond. I remember the day Dad brought home a croquet set from market. It seemed every Sunday we played croquet that resulted in serious arguments. You thought you'd lost a car even if the ball was only 2 inches out! It was a serious issue!

I know we had cold winters. I can remember as a child they used to cut ice in Klingerstown on the creeks. When the ice got thick, I'd say 6 or 8 inches, and it usually did every winter. There was a dam, the breast of the dam was at Paul Shiffer's garage, and the water was backed up all the way to the park below the church. The water was quiet in there, not real fast, and so the ice got thick. Then there was a little bit of a get together and the men helped each other. The men had handsaws and they sawed blocks of ice, and then they took the ice tongs and pulled it out and put it away in icehouses. They packed it in sawdust. There was an icehouse where I was born [Romberger's General Store]. I know Quentin and I played in it many a time. It was in back of the store. And the ice would keep like that almost a whole year. There were a number of icehouses in Klingerstown.

I remember Louie Smeltz, who lived in Boyer's shanty next to Herl Boyer's house right below us, would sometimes come up here for a bucket of coal. He and his wife, and two girls lived in that shanty. One day it was so cold I thought I better take a bucket of coal down to him. So I did. When I went inside you could feel the wind inside. There were gaps between the boards. The shanty was like our shanty with boards going straight up and down. And the gaps were about an inch, inch and a half. It was so cold that the water bucket inside next to the stove was frozen solid.

Now when Mom and I first bought this farm, there was an apple orchard on the other side of the shanty below the road. The apples were all Baldwin apples; that was the name of them. They weren't good for eating, but they made good cider and pies. John Snyder had left the grass grow up. It must have been four feet high. Clarence Brown, and my brother Quentin, myself, and my Dad decided we'd cut that grass down because we would see a black snake every now and then around the house. So my Dad got the 12-gauge shotgun, the pump gun, and he stood back. Clarence, Quentin, and I would cut the grass with the scythe. About every 6-, 8-foot or so, bang, another one would be shot. This was full of snakes. Now John, when Quentin and I would be down when we were younger, he wouldn't allow us to shoot any of them. He even put milk out for them, the black snakes. He said they would catch the rats and the mice. I know when Quentin and I were down one time, John had the feed troughs below the barn, and the rats were eating at this. A big black snake came down through the lawn and Quinty said, "Look there!" and lifted his gun to shoot it and John said, "No, no, no, you don't shoot it; it will eat the rats." So John didn't want them killed. But I know when Mom and I had the chickens, there was even one in the chicken nest, when we hunted eggs, a black snake. But after we cut that high grass down, then we got rid of them. Maybe we shouldn't have, but we did.

Here at the farm we had the farm in corn, and we had chickens. Later we raised 10 acres of tomatoes and 12 acres of onions. We had workers from Puerto Rico here to help, eight of them. Eugene Erdman came here with his two-row digger to dig the onions out and then the workers picked them up in baskets and put them on the wagon. Then we brought them down to the wagon shed, cut off the tops, and put them up on top of the wagon shed to dry. We had an awful lot of onions and tomatoes. The tomatoes we hauled down to Hanover. Dad sold the onions at market.

Soon after we lived here, Mary's mother gave us two cows. Then we started getting calves. We had milk and butter. We had a separator and Steins Creamery would stop here every week and take the cream. Mary made butter that my dad took to market. The skim milk, we always had 12 to 15 pigs in the pen, so we'd put mash to the skim milk and they'd eat it up. We used everything.

We had sheep galore for a while. But that was not a paying proposition. They hardly paid anything for the wool or the lambs.

We had chickens. We had brooder houses across the run for pullets, young chickens. We usually got about 500 every spring. They were over there because they would eat the green grass during the day and then at night they went in the brooder houses, so no fox, or possum, or weasel could get at them. They were protected in there. Then in the morning we'd let them out again. When they were big enough to lay eggs they were brought in the barn. My Dad would take all the eggs we could raise to market.

And at one time we went into the pig business. We had over 120 pigs in the barn, fattening them up. That was a noise, what a racket! We raised a lot of Shrove ducks. They'd hustle them off, at hustle matches—playing cards to hustle them off. So we had quite a few different animals.

At first after the war, my brother Quentin and his wife Jean lived with us. They had two rooms downstairs, a bedroom and a kitchen, and then a spare room upstairs. We'd go to G.I. school every week on a Monday evening. They paid you a lot of money for that; I think it was $90 a month to go to school to learn how to farm. My brother Quentin and I both went. We learned how to weld, raise chickens. We had Lloyd Bohner, Gene Dreese, and a fellow up from Sunbury named Richert. They were the teachers and were paid by the federal government. And Bohner would come around to see how we were doing. Quentin helped me with the farming and they lived here about 3 or 4 years, quite a while. I also had Clarence Brown and Louie Smeltz, who lived in the shanty down at Boyer's, help me. Everything was by hand labor at that time. No one had machinery. We husked the corn by hand. I almost had horses. When we bought this place, my Dad wanted me to buy a team that Charlie Lark had. There was a huge barn behind the hotel [Klingerstown Hotel] where Larky sold teams, jockeying in there. He wanted $350 for this team, a nice team of horses, which was a lot of money at that time. But I told my Dad I didn't want any team of horses or mules, I wanted a tractor. And I went over to Troutman's and they said because of the war business, they [agriculture machinery companies] had stopped making farming equipment. They had started again, and they said when they got them in again, I would get the first tractor. But in the meantime, I could loan their equipment—their tractors, and plow, cultivator and disks, and whatnot, until my equipment would come in. They did this, but I had to do it in between their farming, which was quite difficult, but I did. The first year I bought the farm, Rue Erdman farmed it, but then I started after that year. Never having farmed before in my life, I had to learn everything from scratch. We didn't do bad. I started getting the equipment about 2 years after we started. I got the tractor first, and then the plow and the disk. I needed the cultivator to cultivate the onions. A harrow. Then later on a manure spreader and wagon. At that time a new tractor cost me $1450. A harrow might have been $80. A disk $150. A brand new manure spreader, John Deere, about $175. So things were not as expensive as they are today.

Mary K. Romberger Handharvesting Corn
Circa early 1950's

Roland J. Romberger, Jr. on John Deere Tractor
Bank Barn with Overhang in Background
Circa 1948

Part I: Spread Eagle Manor and the Establishment of Klingerstown and the Klingerstown Grist Mill

When I came back from the service, I just wanted to do something on my own. Get away from always being told what to do, like they did in the army. I was in the Third Infantry Division [Company H, 30th Infantry Regiment]. I was a machine gunnist. Our division fought in northern Africa, in Casablanca, Oran, Algiers, on to Bizerte, then Tunis. We fought through Sicily. Then we fought in Salerno, Italy, then through Naples, the Rapido River, and then the invasion of Anzio, which were some of the worst days I've ever experienced. In three hours our company of men went from 150 down to 75 men. Then we took Rome. We then invaded southern France and went up through the Rhone Valley, all the way up to the Alsace-Lorraine area where we linked up with Patton, through the Vosges Mountains into Germany, all the way down to Salzburg, Austria, where the war ended on the 8th of May, 1945. I was gone from spring of 1942 to the fall of 1945 and was wounded twice. So when I got back I just wanted to stay put. I think the farm was good for me. I really do.

Roland R. Romberger Farm, 2003. View looking southwest.

Roland R. Romberger Farm, 2009. View looking south-southeast.

Parcel No. 6, 83 ¾ A. within the Manor, approximately ½ more acreage north of the Manor boundary. The Tulpehocken Path crosses this Tract which is presently the farmland of Nathan Daniel Schwalm and the residence of Barry Erdman. Early land owners of this real estate include Peter Troutman and Philip Spohn who jointly owned several more tracts outside the Manor. They purchased their lands together from the sons of William Penn. See "Trautman-Troutman Family History," by Steve E. Troutman.

John (Han) Williams Farm on the Tulpehocken Path north of Klingerstown.

Looking South from Parcel No. 6 toward the Klingerstown Gap, on the Tulpehocken Path.

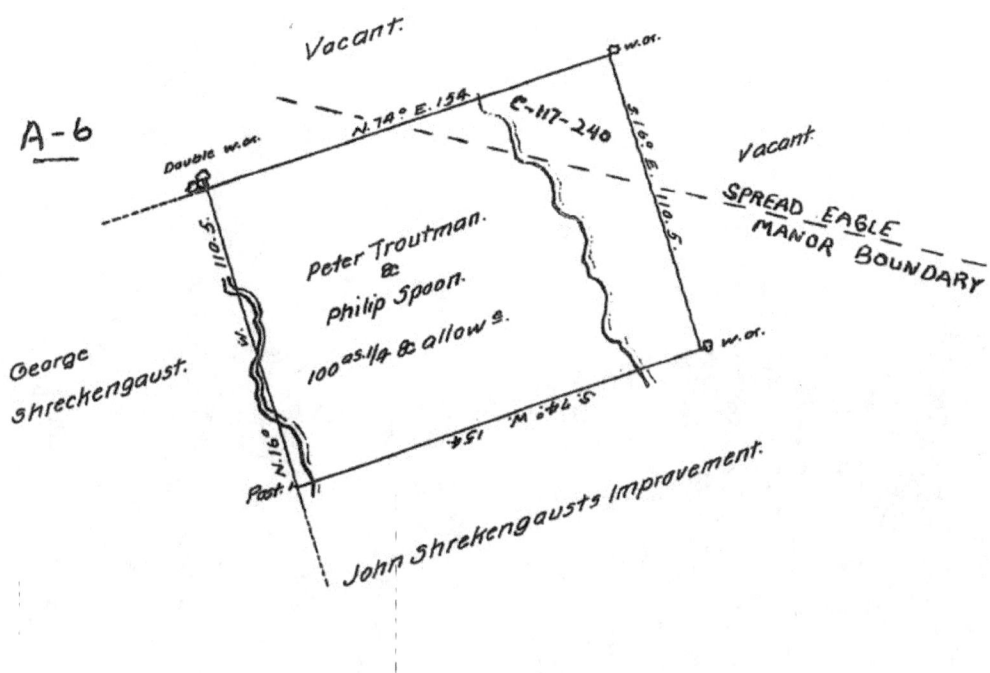

A Draught of a tract of land called ———— Situate on the waters of Mahantango Creek in Mahanoy Township Northumd County Containing one Hundred acres 1/4 & allows of six ⅌ Cent. for roads &c. Surveyd for Peter Troutman & Phillip Spoon the 6th Day of Decr, 1788 in pursuance of a Warrant Dated the 30th Day of April, 1788.

To John Lukens, Esqr, Survr Genl.   by   *Wm. Gray, D.S.*

A-6 Location Information. Barry Erdman residence on this land. Spread Eagle Manor's Northern boundary cuts across this land. North west of Klingerstown 1½ miles. Jordan Township, Northumberland County, Pennsylvania.

Steve E. Troutman
1985

Philip Spohn, the son of Philip Spohn, (named above) migrated to Ohio with the Peter Zartman family also intermarried with the Peter Troutman family. In fact, Philip Spohn, Jr., Justice of the Peace, married Peter Zartman Jr., and Elizabeth A. Reed in 1872 in Lancaster, Ohio.

Looking North toward the John Williams Farm location.

Warrant No. 137 dated 30 Apr 1788 to Peter Trautman et al (et al- and others) for 100 acres in Mahanoy Township, Northumberland County, surveyed for 100 ¼ acres in Mahanoy Township but never patented. This land adjoined, and extended into the Spread Eagle Manor. At the time of the survey, neighbors adjoining were George and Jon Schreckenguast and vacant land. The "et al" was Philp Spoon. This was the same Philip Spoon who showed up with the family Peter Zarman St. and wife Catharine (Trautman) Zartman in Lancaster, Ohio was a Justice of the Peace, and in fact married Peter Zartman Jr. and Elizabeth A. Reed in 1872.

At this location on the right hand side of the road an old pioneer dwelling existed. Dale Erdman has found an old coin from the very early 1800's at this location. The house no doubt stood close by the road which was earlier the Tulpehocken Trail. As the land in this vicinity on both sides of the road was earlier warranted by the Schreckengast Family, this dwelling may have been a Schreckengast house.

The John William's place was on the east side of the Tulpehocken path beyond the trees.

Parcel No. 7, 92 3/8 A.

Original owners include John Reed. He purchased it from land speculator Abel James and Company. On April 20, 1804, it was sold to Jacob Wust III by John Reed, 93 Acres in Spread Eagle Manor, located in Mahanoy Township, Northumberland County. Parcel No. 7 shares a common boundary with Parcel No. 4 and Parcel No. 8.

Parcel No. 7

This parcel contained a farm in years past, known as the Willard Schadel property. The pond and barn seen here mark the location known as "Dosa Platz," which takes its names from the Tobias family that lived here generations ago. The letters "T" and "D" are often interchangeable in the PA Dutch pronunciation of words. See 1875 Map of Upper Mahanoy Twp., Northumberland County naming J.W. Tobias. The Schadel name is very much associated with this farm, also. Heinrich Schadel is recorded as living here or nearby on parcel No. 8. See Schadel History recorded by Mr. Floyd in 1911. It is recorded here, naming Moses Schadel. In the 1960's, this farm was owned by Willard Schadel, who asked Earl Troutman to build the pond seen here. An old house foundation existed when the pond was built. A spring was here as well, which was the water source for the old dwelling place. Perhaps this is the Heinrich Schadel foundation ruins named in Mr. Floyd's History.

Earl Troutman built a farm pond where an earlier house and spring was established. Local residents recall this location as the "Dosa Platz" which originates with the name Tobias Place. The Tobias' lived here as well as the Shadles.

Parcel No. 8, 34 A.

Originally Christian Stutzman to his heirs. It is of interest to note that the Stutzman pioneers intermarried with their Schreckengaust neighbors. The Stutzmans occupied the farm where Ricky and Amy Masser live today. An old stone farm house east of the present residence was removed 50 years ago.

The name Stutzman is identified with this land, which is only a small part of a large farm, most of which is outside the Manor boundary. There is a definite relationship between the Stutzman and Schreckengast family who lived on Manor Parcel 5 and 6 in the Snowdale Creek Valley. Gary Schreckengast, family historian writes: " In 1775, Jost Schreckengast's eldest son, Heinrich, age 24, married Maria Catharine Stutzman, the daughter of Christian Stutzman, who lived to the east, on the other side of Snowdale Valley, on Parcel No. 8 of the Manor, (NE corner). The Schreckengaast men, Henry, Conrad, and John, decided not to convert their land warrants into land patents, and moved west to Armstrong County, soon after 1803."

Conversation with Rick Masser on April 27, 2015, who lives on the farm lands of Parcel No. 8, recounts the Schadel history which ties in to "The Genealogical Biographical Annals of Northumberland County," by Floyd, in 1911. Moses Schadel owned 3 farms, all adjoining. 1. The "Doza Platz," in past generations known as the Willard Schadel farm. 2. Rick Masser's homestead farm. 3. The old Willard Schadel farm on the intersection of Water Shed Road and Smith Road. Steve Haas is the current land owner and John and Natalie Ryan own the resort home near the pond, on the 3rd farm. Moses Schadel was a wealthy farmer, owning approximately 600 acres on his 3 farms. Moses accumulated gold coins and stored the coins in a bucket. The story is told that he moved or carried the bucket of gold from place to place. Some of the descendants of Moses are Silas (md. Lottie), and Penrose (md. Mable). Silas and Lottie had sons Afton Schadel and Willard Schadel. Penrose and Mable did not have children. Penrose Schadel inherited the western farm, ("Doza Platz") and the eastern farm (now Haas and Ryan). Silas inherited the center farm, now owned by Rick Masser.

Rick and Amy Masser live on the center farm which had a 2 story stone farm house with a spiral staircase. The house was dilapidated and removed in the early 1960's. Silas and Lottie lived here in the stone house in the winter months and moved into the summer/spring house in the warmer seasons. Rick and Amy's house is the remodeled summer house. Penrose owned the eastern most farm. Afton Shadel built a log cabin home on a lake, now owned by the Ryan family. Steve Haas owns this farm land. Penrose also owned the western most farm, within the manor, where Earl built a pond on the "Doza Platz".

Henry Shadle Transferred Land to George Shadle

The 34 acres of Parcel No. 8 are identified on a land survey draft for George Shadle as follows:

Resurveyed the first day of Sept. A.D. 1852 at the request of George Shadle. Letter A is part of what is called Manor of Spread Eagle Land containing 35 acres and fifty perches, the same which was surveyed unto Henry Shadle in pursuance of a warrant dated the 11th day of April, 1817, surveyed the 20th day of May, 1817, by Jacob Rockefeller. The draught Letter B represents the original courses and distances situate partly in Schuylkill County and partly in Northumberland County, containing 138 acres, 144 perches. Parcel A plus Parcel B total 174 acres, 34 perches, as identified in Archives Book, A-47-193. Information from page 570 of the Trautman/Troutman Family History, Vol. I, by Steve E. Troutman. This survey draft is included in the appendix of this book.

Part I: Spread Eagle Manor and the Establishment of Klingerstown and the Klingerstown Grist Mill

Eva Scheddel	Heinrich Scheddel
b. Jan. 5, 1769	b. May 24, 1761
d. Sept. 5, 1856	d. Nov. 22, 1828
age 87y 7m 28d	age 67y 5m 29d

Heinrich and Eva Scheddel are buried at Zions or Klingers church just across the county line in Dauphin County. He does appear on the tax lists for Upper Mahantongo Township and also on the 1800 census list for Mahantongo Township in Schuylkill County. Henry Schadel Sr. and Henry Schadel Jr. are both listed with service in the Berks County Militia under Capt. Jacob Ladich in 1781. Ref. Pa. Archives, Series V, Vol. V, page 281. *Schuylkill County Vital Records, Rice and Dellock, p. 523, Vol. 2.*

This family is said to be descended from Urban Schadel, who was a German by birth, coming to Berks County, Pa., about the middle of the eighteenth century. He had a son Heinrich who was a man of small stature. His wife, Eve Leisenring, was a native of Berks County. Heinrich Schadel came from Berks County to Northumberland County, settling on the farm now owned by his grandson Moses. Some of the buildings Heinrich erected are now crumbling, the wall of a house standing in a meadow being almost in ruins. He was an excellent woodworker and mechanic making spinning wheels, reels, flax brakes, and various other devices fashioned of wood. His wife bore him 14 children as follows: Jonas; Solomon (1790-1857); Gideon (1794-1848); Jacob; David (1796-1876); Johannes (1799-1862); George; Samuel; Daniel (1801-1833); Abraham L.; Hannah, married to John Ossman; Catharine, married to Jacob Buffington; Mrs. Abraham Maurer; and one whose name is forgotten. All those of dates of birth and death are buried at Klingers Church. The family all are Lutherans. *Genealogical and Biographical Annals of North. Co., Pa., Floyd, p. 667, 668.*

Heinrich Scheddel stone carved by Rev. Isaac Stiely.

The Population of Klingerstown in the mid 1800's

The 1850 and 1860 Census and the 1875 Map of Schuylkill and Northumberland County provide an accurate cross section of the population in the Klingerstown area.

The 1850 Census for Upper Mahantongo Township, Schuylkill County, PA names the residents of Klingerstown. They are recorded by the order in which he made his visits. Jacob S. Klinger is named as occupation of grist miller. Sometimes the middle initial "P" is interchanged with the "S". He is the son of Johann Peter Klinger and Catherina Steinbruch. Jacob's age is listed 38 and Daniel M. Wiest, also listed as miller, is age 28. Daniel must have been apprenticed to Jacob Klinger.

Max E. Klinger, author of "The Descendants of Johann Peter Klinger and Catharina Steinbruch," published in 2005 by Sunbury Press states on pages 13 and 17 the genealogy. Jacob S. Klinger is the son of Peter Klinger and the grandson of Johann Phillip the immigrant. Peter Klinger operated a mill on the Pine Creek near Erdman, PA, a lovely stone arch bridge marks the mill location on Luxemburg Road. Peter Klinger's mill existed prior to the construction of the stone arch bridge. A fording place existed here to pass through the waters of the Pine Creek when this Klinger mill was first established.

"Bridge Over Pine Creek" by Deanne Wiseman, Wiseman Graphics
Peter Klinger's Mill predated this bridge as evidenced by the small stone arch over the mill race at the eastern approach to the bridge.

Part I: Spread Eagle Manor and the Establishment of Klingerstown and the Klingerstown Grist Mill

1850 Census, Upper Mahantongo Township, Schuylkill Co., PA, Village of Klingerstown

Household No. 251 - Moses Wiest, laborer, age 25, son of John Wiest
    252 - Daniel M. Wiest, miller, age 28, son of John Wiest
    253 - John Wiest, farmer, age 56, son of Jacob Wiest III
    254 - Maria Tobias, widow, age 47
        Anna Maria, d/o Jacob Wiest III
    255 - Wm. Deibert, innkeeper, age 35, md. Hannah B. Wiest, d/o John Wiest
    256 - Michael Sallede, laborer, age 74 (md. Barbara Wust, widow of Jacob III)
    257 - Henry Baum, farmer, age 65
    258 - Jacob (P.or S.) Klinger, miller, age 38
    259 - Wm. Bickel, wheelwright, age 35
    260 - Frederick Heitzman, watchmaker, age 45

Jacob Klinger is in the mill house next door, who operated the grist mill in 1850. It would seem that Johannes Klinger's mill was in the hands of the Wiests within a few years after it was built. Johannes Klinger died in 1800. We can assume the log grist mill was completed at the time of his death. The 1850 Census of Upper MahantongoTownship names Jacob S. Klinger's occupation as grist miller.

1860 Census, Upper Mahantongo Township, Schuylkill Co., PA, Village of Klingerstown

Household No. 977- Joseph Tobias, 22, cattle dealer (son of Joseph and Maria Wiest Tobias)
    978- George Stokes, 36, blacksmith
    979- James M. Hart, 32, grist miller
    980- Jacob P. Klinger, 48, farmer (previous grist miller)
    981- Jacob Tobias, 27, cattle dealer (son of Joseph and Maria Wiest Tobias)
    982- Mrs. Polly Tobias (Maria), 58, lived with Benjamin Leitzel, 57, land lord. Maria is the daughter of Jacob Wiest III, md. Joseph Tobias
    983- Henry Baum,73, Jacob Baum, 48, David Baum,43, farmers
    984- Daniel M. Wiest, 38, grist miller, Sarah Rickert, 24, (son of John Wiest)
    985- Jacob M. Wiest, 25, merchant (1835-1915) (son of John Wiest)
    985- John Wiest, 66, merchant, store and post office (son of Jacob M. Wiest III)
    986- David Klinger, 33, merchant, md. Barbara, (d/o John Wiest)
    987- Moses M. Wiest, 33, farmer, grist miller (son of John Wiest)

Editors Note: It seems as indicated by the 1850 and 1860 Census Records that the Wiest Family certainly dominated the Village of Klingerstown for those 2 decades. The 1860 Census lists Daniel M. Wiest now 38, as grist miller, no doubt living in the brick mill house. James M. Hart, age 32 lived next door to Jacob P. Klinger, who was the previous grist miller named in 1850. Moses M. Wiest, age 33, remembered also as a miller, lived where the Amish Stolzfus family lives today in the brick farm house on the property known as the "Billy Wiest place" of a generation passed. Moses could have walked along the mill race from his home to the mill. The mill dam on Mahantongo Creek, was built not far from his house.

The Penns' Manor of Spread Eagle and the Grist Mills of the Upper Mahantongo Valley

1875 Map of Schuylkill County, Beers Atlas

Jacob Klinger residence is opposite the mill. S. Klinger is identified as occupying the mill house. This is Samuel Klinger who purchased the mill property from Daniel Wiest in 1864. The black smith's shop is located near the center of town. A. Rothermel lived in the gap near the grist and saw mill located where Deibert's saw mill is built today. A. Rothermel was no doubt, the operator of this mill on Pine Creek in the gap. Arlene Deibert reports her husband's family included millers by the name of George E. W. Deibert, William Allen (Al) Deibert, and George N. Deibert.

The 1875 map of Upper Mahantongo Twp., Schuylkill Co., identifies a dwelling across the roadway from the Klingerstown Mill, as the residence of J. Klinger. This must be Jacob S. Klinger, the son of Peter Klinger. Jacob and Louisa (Alspach) Klinger had four children in 1850. In 1880, Jacob Klinger is also named in Schuylkill County census records, working as a miller in Klingerstown. See the book, "There is Something About Rough and Ready," page 187, published by Sunbury Press.

Bruce Teeple for the Daily Item Newspaper wrote a column about Union County mill operators. On February 8, 2015, he writes: "Stone milling is more than an 'art trade and mystery'. Millers not only had to adjust the milling process to temperature and humidity conditions; they needed excellent political and social skills, for the mill was the center of community life. Farmers went to mills to have their grains ground into flour or distilled into more profitable whiskey. Waiting in line gave them the chance to get the news, discuss and vote on the issues, or buy lumber if the miller also operated a saw mill. Success required a trustworthy, engaging personality, able to handle competition effectively."

The study of lands within the Manor concludes with the maps below.

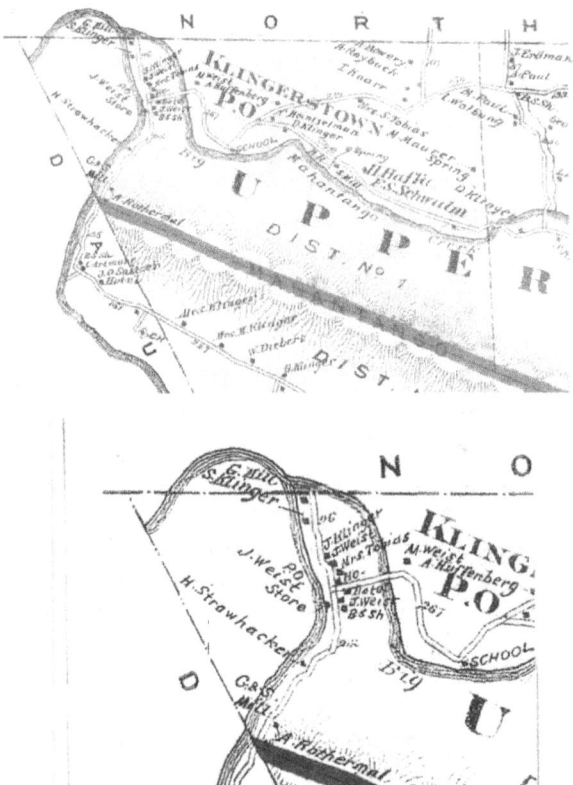

1875 Map of Schuylkill County showing Klingerstown and vicinity.

Part I: Spread Eagle Manor and the Establishment of Klingerstown and the Klingerstown Grist Mill

Lands Adjoining "The Manor of Spread Eagle" to the West and the People

The Little Red House - Caption Below by John A. Romberger

Carrie (Bahner) Romberger, 1897-1983, in her kitchen in the little red house. This photo is reproduced as a print commissioned by Dr. John A. Romberger as a memorial to the life of his mother. The print is available from Wiseman Graphics, Herndon, PA.

The "Little Red House" (Tenant House) on the George L. Troutman Farm in 1920 (looking southeast)

This posed picture was made at 12.45 PM on June 4, 1920, by Ralph T. Romberger. As the sky was overcast, he used an 8 second time-exposure at f-32, with the camera on a tripod. The people sitting on the porch were (left to right): Eva Shutt (a hired house-maid), Carrie E. Bahner Romberger; and John Klinger Romberger (my grandfather).

The road in the foreground is the Klingerstown to Pillow Road, which was not paved until 1936. Though traffic was rather light in 1920, road dust was even then an unpleasant consequence of this location in summer and fall.

My father, Ralph T. Romberger, lived in this small house with his parents from April, 1903 until 1910, when he moved across the road to the "Big House" to live with his grandparents, George L. and Mary Wert Troutman. His parents continued to live in this "Little Red House" until 1920 when his mother, Alice A. Troutman Romberger, died on February 15 during the "flu" epidemic. My parents also lived here for a short time after they were first married in 1918, and then again briefly in 1920.

This enlarged and enhanced print was made from an original 1920 contact print by scanning and computer processing of the digital file using Adobe Photoshop CS and an HP Photosmart 7960 inkjet printer. The original 1920 contact print is only 2.25 by 4.25 inches in size and is quite faded. This old image, nonetheless, is a valuable record of this small house which few living people now remember.

John A. Romberger
January, 2006

George L. Troutman farm house and the "Little Red House."

Part I: Spread Eagle Manor and the Establishment of Klingerstown and the Klingerstown Grist Mill

The George and Mary Troutman farm, Jordan Twp., Northumberland Co.

The log farm house seen here was built by John Eister in 1836. The barn was built in 1840.

The Wiests lived here. Samuel Wiest bought the property from Mr. Eister for his son, Jacob Klinger Wiest (1826-1878). He married Elizabeth Trautman (1825-1881), daughter of Peter and Elizabeth Batteiger. They occupied the property for 35 years. Elizabeth was killed by lightning in the kitchen. (Source: page 736, "Genealogical and Biographical Annals of Northumberland County, PA," by Floyd.)

George L. Troutman purchased the farm and rebuilt the barn in 1898. George married Mary Wert. George M. Troutman, grandson of George L., married Mary S. Rabuck and raised their family here as well.

"Winter Shadows along Fisher's Ridge" by Deanna Wiseman of Wiseman Graphics.

The George Lesher Troutman Family in the Fall of 1906
(This is the family of my paternal grandfather)

The probable occasion of this family photograph was the marriage of George and Mary Troutman's youngest child, Dora Agnes, to William Baum Wiest, Jr., in June 1906. This newly married couple was planning to move to Lebanon, Pennsylvania, in the fall. This picture was probably taken in September or October, as the leaves are still on the trees, but the geraniums have already been taken indoors (visible in the window).

The people left to right are: Back row, John Klinger Romberger (b. 17 June, 1876; d. 16 January, 1954), Alice Amelia Troutman Romberger (b. 15 August, 1880; d. 15 February, 1920), Victor William Troutman (b. 2 June, 1882; d. 25 October, 1947), Dora Agnes Troutman Wiest (b. 21 July, 1888; d. 21 October, 1927), William Baum Wiest, Jr. (b. 19 February, 1883; d. 19 April, 1962). Front row, Mary Louise Wert Troutman (b. 17 December, 1856; d. 26 December, 1925), George Lesher Troutman (b. 21 June, 1858; d. 7 October, 1934), Sallie Baum Wiest Troutman (b. 31 July, 1882; d. 16 August, 1972). Standing in from of George is his grandson, Ralph Troutman Romberger (b. 29 December, 1900; d. 20 June, 1974. Sitting on Sallie's lap is her son Leo Tobias Troutman (b. 7 October, 1905; d. 13 April, 1980).

The site of this family portrait was the lawn near the southeast corner of the George Troutman farmhouse, which is still relatively unchanged today. The size of the original print is 8 by 10 inches. It is pasted onto a heavy grey cardboard mount about 12 by 14 inches. There are no identifying marks. The original photograph was somewhat underexposed and lacking in contrast. I was not able completely to overcome these deficiencies while copying it.

This picture has been in my family, packed away in a box, for as long as I can remember. I had it framed in 1998, and now have it hanging in my study.

This ink-jet print was made on 15 December, 2000, after scanning, and computer enhancing the original print. John A. Romberger, December 17, 2000.

Wiest History as found in "The Troutman Family"

by Ralph T. Romberger

The following Wiest history is appropriate, for two reasons, to be included in this book. The farms described are at or near the western boundary of the Manor of Spread Eagle. The account also illustrates the pervasive manner in which the Wiest family dominated this local throughout the early to mid 1800's. The account also illustrates the wanderlust of many Wiests as they migrated north to Canada to homestead unsettled areas. Many other Wiests migrated to the west coast to Washington and Oregon to establish sawmills and work in the bourgeoning lumber industry at the turn of the century. Many of the Wiest family were very ambitious and fearless in their endeavors. Quite a few died out West, working in the lumber industry. They were courageous in their accomplishments. The following account was written by Ralph Troutman Romberger (Dec. 29, 1900-June 20, 1974) and represents one small chapter in his book, "The Troutman Family". He worked to complete his book at least five years, spanning the years of 1965 through 1970.

William Baum Wiest, born 1852 and died 1918, Shelby, Montana. Married Elizabeth, daughter of David Baum and Susanna (Welker) Baum. After Elizabeth's death he moved to Travers, Alberta, Canada. William and Elizabeth had 10 children. Richard, Samuel, William, Worth, Ira, John Carlos, Clara, Mary Jane, Ella, and Elizabeth. William Baum Wiest, Jr., born 19 February, 1883, died 19 April, 1962. Married Dora Agnes Troutman, 21 July, 1888, died 21 October, 1927. Worth Baum Wiest, wheat rancher at Rosemede, Alberta, Canada. John Carlos Wiest, born 10 January, 1882. He traveled to Washington and Oregon to work in the logging industry near Portland, and served in WWI.

This large farm, presently the Buurton Residence, was lately known as the George R. Wolfgang Farm. The original 48 acres occupied by William B. Wiest, Jr and Dora (Troutman) Wiest, are included. William Wiest Jr's father, William had owned this farm at an earlier date. Prior it was the John K. Clark place and the Samuel B. Clark residence.

The following five pages by Ralph T. Romberger as prepared on his typewriter.

(1)

Dora Agnes Troutman, the third child and second daughter of George L. and Mary L. (Wert) Troutman, was born July 21, 1888 and died October 21, 1927, at the age of 39 years and 3 months.

Dora was born at the Troutman homestead, located in Jordan Township, Northumberland County, Pennsylvania, about one and one-half miles (by road) west-northwest of Klingerstown (which town is situated in Schuylkill County). She attended the Noble (Rothermel's) school, No. 4, located about one-half mile east of the homestead, and about one mile northwest of Klingerstown. This was a one room little red school house, typical of that era. Dora quit school before she was fourteen years of age; however, by continued effort in home study she attained a fair education. Dora was brought up to farm life and became a very efficient housekeeper in every way.

Dora was married on June 4, 1906 to William Baum Wiest, Jr. born February 19, 1883, and died April 19, 1962. William B. Wiest, Jr. was a son of William Baum Wiest, Sr. and Elizabeth Baum Wiest, his wife. The parents of William B. Wiest, Jr. started housekeeping on a farm in the Powell's Valley, Dauphin County, and lived there for some time. Their next move was to a farm located about two miles (by road) west-northwest of Klingerstown on the Hebe road, in the Mahantango Valley, Jordan Township, Northumberland County. There William B. Wiest, Jr. was born. This farm is now (1967) owned and occupied by George R. Wolfgang. After farming there for a number of years, William B. Wiest, Sr. and family moved onto a small farm located in Lykens Township, Dauphin County, near Erdman, where they lived for about one year. Following this, they moved to the Klingerstown Hotel located in Upper Mahantango Township, Schuylkill County, and conducted the hotel business in that town for some time. While they lived there Elizabeth died. Later, William B. Wiest, Sr. moved onto a farm located on the right bank of the Mahantango Creek about one-fourth of a mile north-northwest of the square in Klingerstown. This farm is partly in Jordan Township, Northumberland County, and partly in Upper Mahantango Township, Schuylkill County. It is now (1967) owned

(2)

and occupied by Clarence (Tol) Ray Williard. Later, William B. Wiest, Sr. went to Alberta, Canada where some members of his family had lived at one time or another. Following this, years later, it is said William B. Wiest, Sr. was murdered at a hotel in Shelby, Montana.

William Baum Wiest, Sr. and Tobias Baum Wiest were brothers, whereas their wives, Elizabeth Baum Wiest and Mary Ann Baum Wiest were sisters. William B. Wiest, Jr. and Sallie B. (Wiest) Troutman were first cousins on both the paternal and maternal sides of the family. William B. Wiest, Sr. was born and raised on a farm (owned by Samuel B. Wiest during the 1920's) located about one and three-fourths miles (by road) northwest of Klingerstown, in Jordan Township, Northumberland County. Samuel and Hettie (Baum) Wiest were the parents of William B. Wiest, Sr. Samuel was reared in Klingerstown where now (1967) William R. Romberger lives. Samuel the father of William B. Wiest, Sr. was accidently killed while felling a tree in the wood lot on the Wiest homestead, located about one and three-fourths miles (by road) northwest of Klingerstown. This Samuel Wiest's parents were John and Catharine (Merkel) Wiest.

In the fall of 1906, Dora and William started housekeeping on North Fourth Street in Lebanon, Pennsylvania because William had secured employment with the Bethlehem Steel Company there. After a period of time, due to the excessive heat in the steel plant, William decided to start farming.

And so it was that, in the spring of 1907, William and Dora started farming for shares for Mrs. Mary (Straub) Baum on her farm located about one-third mile west of Klingerstown. After farming for some time William and Dora decided to go homesteading in the province of Alberta, Canada. In the late winter of 1907-08, they disposed of their livestock, farm equipment and household goods at public sale.

Following the sale, in the early spring of that same year, William started (by train) for Lethbridge, Alberta, Canada. Dora stayed with her parents, while William

(3)

traveled ahead to take up a quarter section of land (160 acres) and built a small house. Arriving in Lethbridge, William then took up a quarter section some forty miles to the north of that place, in the vicinity where now (1967) the town of Travers is located. Some members of the Wiest family had emigrated to Alberta before William and no doubt they gave him some assistance in his settlement. William purchased and hauled enough lumber from Lethbridge to his quarter section some forty miles distant, to build a small house. Although he had plowed a fire break around his lumber and building site, a prairie fire on a stormy day, crossed the fire break and burned nearly all his lumber for the house. Undaunted, William bought some more lumber to build a small house.

While William was trying his best to start farming and build a house, Dora, at the home of her parents back in Pennsylvania, on May 11, 1908 gave birth to a daughter which she named Mabel Louise Wiest, who in later years became the wife of Irvin D. Williard. When the daughter was about four months of age, in early September 1908, Dora started (by train) from Herndon, Pennsylvania for Lethbridge, Alberta, Canada to join her husband. The trip was a hard one with the small child; however, both mother and daughter got to Lethbridge safely. When Dora and her daughter arrived in Lethbridge, Worth Wiest (brother of William B. Wiest, Jr.) was in town (with a team of horses) to get some lumber. Nevertheless, he took Dora and her daughter along on the lumber wagon to William's homestead.

In the area where William and Dora settled, the main crops raised were spring wheat, oats and a little hay. Field corn was not raised as the growing season was too short. While William and Dora were living there, it was very dry in some years and the yields of grain were poor, therefore, they finally decided to return to Pennsylvania.

In the late fall of 1912, the William B. Wiest family returned to Pennsylvania. Mabel was about four years and seven months old at that time. For the next several

(4)

months the Wiests stayed with Dora's parents. During the winter of 1912-13, William and Dora purchased from William A. Zerbe, the farm consisting of about 48 acres where William Jr. was born in Jordan Township, Northumberland County. This farm is on the Klingerstown-Hebe road about two miles west-northwest of Klingerstown and adjoined Dora's parents farm on the west. At an earlier date, William's father had owned the above farm. It is now (1967) owned and occupied by George R. Wolfgang. In about 1913, William and Dora also purchased from William A. Zerbe a tract of timberland containing about 10 acres located near Erdman.

In about 1916, William and Dora bought from Paul A. Updegrave a farm consisting of about 77 acres. This farm, then locally known as the "Schadel Farm" is located slightly less than one mile (airline) northeast of Hebe in Jordan Township, Northumberland County. While living on this farm, in October 1927 Dora died. The farm was later sold to Albert T. Strohecker and is now (1967) owned by him.

Around 1920, William and Dora purchased a farm consisting of about 140 acres from Frank and Charles Balsam (brothers). This farm is located about three-fourths of a mile southeast of Hebe in Jordan Township, Northumberland County. In about 1930, this farm was sold to Jacob W. Strohecker and is now (1967) owned by Earl G., Bruce A., and Bryant A. Troutman, all brothers. They named the farm "Green Acres." It is occupied by Bruce A. Troutman and family. William at one time also owned the large double house in Hebe locally known as the "Big House."

Dora was fairly tall and medium in build. She was a good mother and provided well for her family at all times. Dora was a hardworking woman and a conservative, efficient housekeeper in every way. She was outspoken when she had something to say, however, after all, that might be the better way. Dora was rather stern, but good natured at heart. Dora and William were both well known in their home community and were numbered among its substantial citizens.

William was a Democrat in politics, however, it is not known that Dora ever

(5)

voted in the USA. William was a member of the David's Reformed Church (now 1967 called the United Church of Christ) at Hebe. Dora died at the "Schadel Farm", on October 21, 1927. She had been affected by double pneumonia. Pneumonia it seems was rather prevalent in the family. Dora and William along with their daughter Alice E. who died in infancy, are buried in the Union Cemetery near Pillow, Pennsylvania. This cemetery is located in Jordan Township, in lower Northumberland County, about three-fourths of a mile northeast of Pillow which town is situated in Dauphin County.

Quite some time after Dora had died, Williwm entered into a common-law marriage agreement with Polly Sophia (Wolfgang) Land. They lived together at several different places including a farm between Herndon and Red Cross in Jackson Township, Northumberland County. A son, Stanley James Wiest was born to them on February 27, 1931. Among his other farms, William had purchased (about 1930) a small farm consisting of about 9 acres from Charles A. Bohner. This small farm is located about two-thirds of a mile (airline) north-northeast of Hebe. There in his old age, William resided with his son Stanley and wife for a number of years. William was admitted to the Northumberland County Hospital near Shamokin, Pennsylvania a very short time (about twenty-four hours) before his death which occurred there. William is buried in the Union Cemetery near Pillow, Pennsylvania.

Dora and William were the parents of four children, three daughters and one son, in order as follows: Mable Louise, Helen Marie, Mark Woodrow and Alice Elizabeth (died in infancy) Wiest.

Lori Scott lives on the old Harter homestead lately recalled as the Bruce Troutman Farm. Her neighbor William S. Wiest (Toby) lives on the Hebe Bypass. Toby told Lori that the Johannes Harter log house was dismantled where the barn is now built on Lori's farm. Logs from this house were reused to construct the present residence of Toby Wiest.

William Wiest Jr. and Dora purchased this farm in 1912-1913 from William A. Zerbe. Parcels 1 and 2 were purchased.

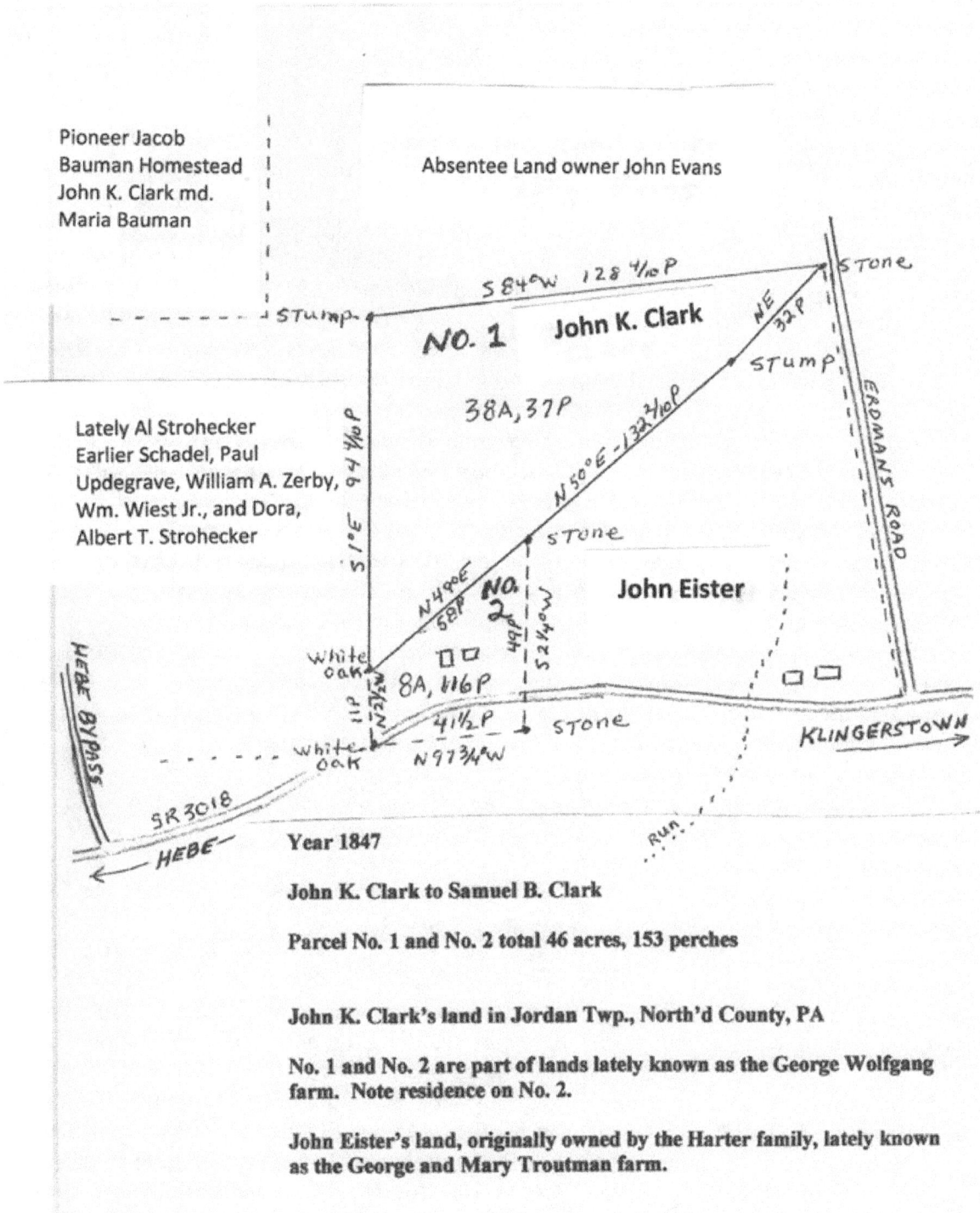

Year 1847

John K. Clark to Samuel B. Clark

Parcel No. 1 and No. 2 total 46 acres, 153 perches

John K. Clark's land in Jordan Twp., North'd County, PA

No. 1 and No. 2 are part of lands lately known as the George Wolfgang farm. Note residence on No. 2.

John Eister's land, originally owned by the Harter family, lately known as the George and Mary Troutman farm.

The Penns' Manor of Spread Eagle and the Grist Mills of the Upper Mahantongo Valley

John K. Clark's land between Klingerstown and Hebe, Jordan Twp., Northumberland Co. PA at or near the farm lately owned by George Wolfgang, now the Burton residence.

Northumberland County Courthouse, Sunbury, Pa.
Deed Book FF, Page 250
Deed, John K. Clark to Samuel B. Clark, May 29, 1847
This indenture made the 15th day of May, in the year of our Lord, 1847, between **John K. Clark** of Jackson Twp., North'd. Co. and Commonwealth of PA of the first part and **Samuel B. Clark** of the Twp. County and Commonwealth aforesaid of the other part. Witness that the said John K. Clark for and in consideration of the sum of $1100.00 lawful money of the United States of America unto them well and truly paid by the said Samuel B. Clark at and before the sealing and delivery of these presents. The receipt – whereof is hereby acknowledged, have granted, bargained, sold, aliened, enfeoffed, released, conveyed, and confirmed, and by these presents do grant, bargain, sell, alien, enfeoff, release, convey, and confirm unto the said Samuel B. Clark, his heirs and assigns. All that certain messuage, tenement-and **two tracts of land adjoining to each other** situate in the township of Upper Mahanoy, now Jackson, North'd Co. and Commonwealth aforesaid. Bounded and described as follows: To wit. **The first**. Beginning at a white oak thence by land of **John Eister**, North 50 degrees East 132 and 2 tenth perches to a stump, thence Northeast 32 perches to a stone. Thence South 84 degrees West – 128 and 4 tenth perches to a stone, thence South 1 degree East, 94 and 4 tenth perches to the place of beginning, **containing 38 acres and 37 perches of land** neat measure. This being part of a larger tract of land which the Commonwealth of PA by letter Patent dated the 16th day of December A.D., 1793, granted unto **John Evans**, surviving executor of Dr. Cadualeder Evans, dec., intrust for the heirs of deceased, and whereas **William Witman Jr. and Mary** his wife, by their indenture bearing date the 15th day of April, A.D., 1820, did grant and confer the same onto **John Holben**.
The second piece is part of a larger tract of land called Union. Bounded and described as follows: To wit. Beginning at a white oak in a line **Jacob Bowman** now **Peter Rettinger**, thence by the same North 2 and one half degree West, 11 perches to a post. Thence by the above described land North 49 degrees East 58 perches to a stone. Thence by land of **John Eister**, South 2 and one fourth degree West 49 perches to a stone. Thence North 97 and three quarter degrees West 41 and one half perches to the place of beginning, containing **8 acres and 116 perches** of land neat measure. This being part of a larger tract of land which was surveyed for **Andrew Harter** in pursuance of a warrant dated the 14th day of May, A.D., 1805, and the Commonwealth of PA by patent bearing date the 5th day of June, last past (1805) did grant and confirm the same unto the said Andrew Harter and to his heirs and assigns forever which is enrolled in the rolls office for the Commonwealth aforesaid in patent book #61, page 55. And whereas the said Andrew Harter and Magdalena, his wife, by their indenture bearing date the 23rd day of June, last past (1805) for the consideration therein mentioned did grant and confirm the same with other land unto **Mathias Harter** and to his heirs and assigns forever. And whereas the said Mathias Harter and Elizabeth, his wife, by their indenture bearing date the 24th day of November, A.D., 1807, did grant and confirm this last described piece of land unto John Hobben and to his heirs and assigns forever relations being had unto the in part – recited indenture more fully appear. **Containing together 46 acres and 153 perches**

neat measure. And whereas John Holben and Susannah, his wife, by their indenture dated the 6th day of March, A.D., 1831, granted and confirmed the same unto **Joseph Tobias** and unto his heirs and assigns forever. And whereas Joseph Tobias and Maria, his wife by their assignment dated the 13th day of March, A.D., 1837, granted assigned and confirmed the same unto **John K. Clark** party hereto and to his heirs and assigns forever, which is recorded in the office for recording of deed at Sunbury in the County Northumberland, in deed book AA, pages 121, 122, and 123 recourse being thereto and more full at page appears together with all and singular the buildings, improvements, ways, waters, water courses, rights, liberties, privileges, hereditaments, and appurtenances whatsoever thereunto belonging or in anywise appertaining and the reversions and remainders, rents, issues, and profits thereof, and all the estate right, title, interest, property, claim, and demand whatsoever of him the said **John K. Clark**, in law, equity, or otherwise howsoever, of, in, and to the same and every part and parcel thereof. To have and to hold the said **46 acres and 153 perches** neat measure of land. Hereditaments and premises hereby granted or mentioned and intended so to be with the appurtenances, unto the said **Samuel B. Clark**, his heirs and assigns to and for the only proper use and behoof of the said Samuel B. Clark, his heirs and assigns forever. **Except about one fourth of an acre of land which John Holben sold unto George Heil Sr.** and which the widow and heirs of said Heil now have in their possession. And the said John K. Clark, his heirs, executors, and administrators doth by these presents, covenant, grant, and agree to with the said Samuel B. Clark, his heirs and assigns. That the said **John K. Clark**, his heirs, all and singular the hereditaments and premises herein above described and granted or mentioned and intended so to be with the appurtenances unto the said **Samuel B. Clark**, his heirs and assigns, him the said John K. Clark, his heirs and assigns and all and every other person or persons whomsoever lawfully claiming or to claim the same or any part thereof by from or under him, them or any of or either of them shall and will warrant and forever defend. In witness whereof the said parties to these presents have hereunto interchangeably set their hands and seals. Dated the day and year first above written except as above excepted. **John K. Clark (seal)**
Sealed and delivered in the presence of us Isaac H. Knorr
Received the day of the date of the above indenture of the above named Samuel B. Clark and the sum of $1100 lawful money of the United States, it being the consideration money above mentioned in full.   John K. Clark
Witness at signing Isaac H. Knorr

Schuylkill County
On the 15th day of May, A.D., 1847, before me Isaac H. Knorr, one of the Jutices of the Peace, in and said County personally appeared the above named John K. Clark and in due form of law acknowledged the above indenture to be his act and deed and desired the same might be recorded as such. Witness my hand and seal the day and year aforesaid.
Isaac H. Knorr (seal)
Recorded May 29th, 1847

(John Harter originally warranted the John Eister land, later owned by George and Mary Troutman. Andrew Harter recorded the survey. Mathias Harter md. Elizabeth Bowman, d/o Jacob and Susannah Bauman.) (S.E.T.)

Johannes and Anna Maria Hartter - Mahantongo Valley Pioneers

The Hartter Family always interested me because I grew up on the land where this early pioneer family settled. John Hartter warranted two tracts of land in 1774 and dwelled there until 1800 when John and Anna Maria died within four weeks of each other, having been married 47 years.

Most of this land is now owned by Earl, Bruce and Bryant Troutman. (See Troutman\Trautman Family History pg. 588 - 596). The southern boundary of this land is generally followed by the Mahantongo Creek.

As a young boy I often walked the vanishing trace of an old "wagon road". The road began in Klingerstown, crossed the creek to Bobby Hoffman's farm and continued past Bryant and Earl Troutmans. From Earl Troutmans the road continued west along the creekhead to Bruce Troutman's farm. This road followed on the north side of the Mahantongo Creek, crossing many hollows with small streams which descended rapidly down the steep cliff to the Mahantongo Creek below.

I believe this old road to have been an earlier path for the native Indians, traveling from the well-known campsite at Spread Eagle to a smaller campsite in the lowland below where the Hartter log cabin once stood. We know of this ancient Indian dwelling place because of the large number of flint points and pottery fragments found by my grandmother, Mary Troutman. These artifacts were found near the creek, south of Bruce Troutman's home (1995).

As the pioneers followed this Indian path it became one of the valley's earliest roads and connected several pioner dwellings now long gone, evidenced only by springs, hand dug wells, foundation ruins and Easter lilly flowers which bloom in early spring. This old road was south of the present day field road which passes from Bryant Troutmans' to Earl Troutmans' to Bruce Troutmans'.

Johannes and Anna Maria lived in a small log house, located north west of the farmhouse Bruce Troutman lives in now. Communication with Mark W. Wiest (16, Feb. 1995) show a photograph from 1926, taken at the south west corner of the old log house which had several windows and a small porch on the south west side. In the photograph William Wiest Jr., the father of Helen and Mark, is seated on the chair. He built a new house about fifty feet south of the old house, completed in 1926. As soon as the new home was finished the old log house was torn down. This farm land borders Mahantongo Creek and Tumbling Run. This would have been a good spot for a grist mill. No doubt this is why Johannes Hartter chose to patent this land since he was a miller by trade.

The Balsam family was a later generation of residents of this original pioneer home. At this time the location became known as" Balsams' Loch". Mrs. John Williams (Dorthy Strohecker) of Hebe, recalls visiting the Balsem children to play with the neighborhood girls. Dorthy remembers a beautiful spring, partly enclosed, some distance south of the log home. Of the Balsam family, she recalls the father as originating from an East European country, perhaps Romania. During World War I, when there were many unemployed men, Hobos were common in this area. The Balsam Family often gave refuge to these traveling men, by leaving a mark on a post at the main road marking their lane as a path to food and shelter. Dorthy recalls the Balsam Family was not Pennsylvania German and came from the Shamokin area.

Florence (Rothermal) Hoffman shared her early memories of living in this same area where the pioneer Hartter family lived. She was born on the farm where she now lives with her son Robert Hoffman, just east of the Hartter homesteads. Florence is the daughter of Manassas Rothermal.

In 1914 Philip Lupold, a cobbler, lived south of the Earl Troutman residence on a tract of land known as the "Cassy Patch", so named for the owner Catharine Schadle, a neighboring store owner. Philip was the last resident of this small homestead, but he was certainly not the first.

Earl Troutman bulldozed the barn remains when he built his new house. The handdug well is still there in addition to the house foundation and white lilac bushes. Florence said she often walked by the Lupold house on her way to visit her Aunt Lull (her father's sister) who was married to Paul Kratzer. Paul and Lull Kratzer lived on the Hartter homestead farm in the new house, built by William Wiest Jr. Paul Kratzer was small in stature. Mr. Lupold later moved to Hoofland area in the Fisher's Ridge Gap, where the Land family later lived in a green shingle home, close to the main road at the telephone exchange building.

Florence said there was also another house, now long gone, east of Bryant Troutman's residence, near the edge of the woods, several hundred feet south of the road leading to Florences home. Only the location remains marked by a flat spot in Bobby's field where he finds glass and crockery when tilling the soil. The water source remains as a spring in the hollow to the west. The names of any residents are forgotten but the apple trees are remembered.

On the earliest maps of the area, "Hartters Improvement" is noted as being near the residence of Mary Troutman. (see pg.596 Troutman\Trautman History) There are several springs on this farm. Two are located in the hollow north east of Mary Troutman's house. This hollow was a pioneer home location. Very nearby, just south of Mrs. Eugene Erdman's home is a known homesite. Foundation stones and crockery are evident when plowing. Earl Troutman owned this location for many years and cleared the land of thorns and brush which had overgrown the abandoned site. This was one of his first bulldozing jobs as a young man. He also closed up an old handdug well at that time. Earl's mother, Mary Troutman, recalls this location as "The Peelers Patch". There is an old story that "Zwei kinner sind dat vergraben". Translated : Two children are buried there.

It is very possible that Johannes Hartter's sons lived at some or all of these early homesites.

Johannes and Maria Hartter Homestead. Recently the Bruce Troutman Farm.

Lands adjoining "The Manor of Spread Eagle" to the East and the People of the Past

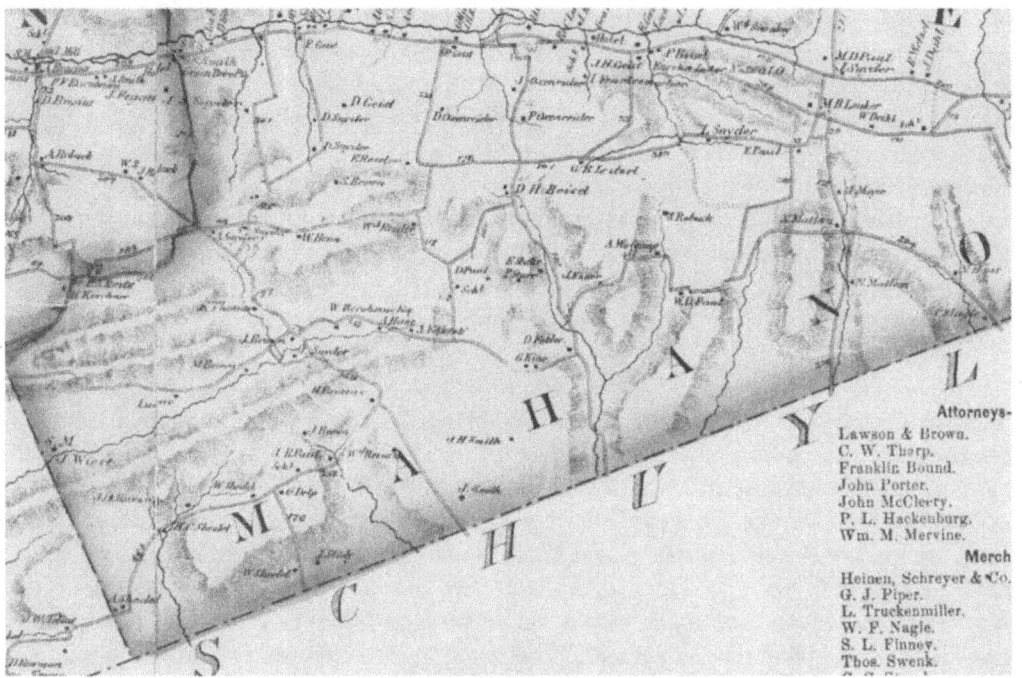

1875 Map of Mahanoy Township, Northumberland County, PA.

John F. Braun Farm. Photo courtesy of Thomas Umholtz of Valley View, PA.
According to Tommy these Brauns were descendants of Michael Braun. These early settlers were some of the Mahantongo Valley cabinet makers. The door and window moldings of this home were made with the same planers and joiners used by John Braun to build furniture and blanket chests. These farm buildings are now gone and the land has reverted to a game preserve owned by the sons of Ernest and June Masser. Ernest recalls potatoes being grown here along Snow Dale Road.

Part I: Spread Eagle Manor and the Establishment of Klingerstown and the Klingerstown Grist Mill

Jim and Melinda Romberger Family
Jim was John F. Braun's hired farm worker for many years as young man. According the Mae Romberger Kahler, Jim continued his education and became a superintendent of Blue Mountain School District. Jim was a relative of her first husband, William Romberger of Pitman.

Michael Braun pioneer home along the Line Mountain. Rusty Blyler has a new home built on this location. The old stone house was built in 1829 and the old stone barn was built in 1826 with date stones and M. Braun. This photo courtesy of Rev. Raymond L. Brown 1999 Sassafrass St., Selinsgrove, PA.

John Rabuck   *Emanuel Erdman, cousin of S.W. Brown*

These photos were sold at public sale at the Charles Brown residence which was previously the Delp School House. These photos courtesy of the Guy R. Brown photo collection, as purchased by Thomas Umholtz, Valley View.

Robert Clark's Pioneer Land East of the Spread Eagle Manor Boundary

Robert and Susanna (Kauffman) Clark removed from Oley Twp., Berks County, PA to Upper Mahantongo Twp., Schuylkill County, PA, about spring of 1807 and purchased 125 acres from William Whitman, Jr. and his wife, Mary, of Reading. A weaver by occupation, Robert Clark and his family, nevertheless, developed this land until Robert's death in September of 1813. He was survived by his widow, Susanna, and 7 children. Susanna gave over the administration that same year to sons Jacob K. Clark and John K. Clark. The land was sold to John Peter Clark, a "tin peddler" because it was un-dividable without prejudice to the heirs. The deed was dated March, 1815. By this time Susanna had also died.

Jacob K. Clark and his brother, Daniel K. Clark, moved to Stark Co., Ohio, by April 15, 1816. Peter was a merchant in the city of Philadelphia; John K. Clark had removed to Northumberland County, PA. Abraham K. Clark died in Berks County, PA, circa 1836/37; Samuel and Hannah became the wards of George Klinger in Schuylkill County, PA. The above information compiled by Charlene Dixon of Walnut Creek, California, in 1990.

Robert Clark's homestead adjoined the land of Gideon Williamson, as seen on the draft on page 125. The name William Witman is written on the land that Mr. Witman sold to Robert and Susanna Clark. Note that Robert Clark's land survey is included in the appendix of this book.

More Land Along Ridge Road, East of "Spread Eagle Manor"

To Samuel Cochran Esq., Surveyor General of Pennsylvania

Situate in Upper Mahantongo Township, Schuylkill County containing 85 acres 81 ¾ perches and allowances of 6% for roads and part of 323 acres 153 perches all surveyed to Phillip Galman by an Application No. 3476 dated 19 July 1768, now surveyed for Gidion Williamson, August 28, 1823.   By Jn. Dreher, D.S.

Author's notes: The land described is located east of Spread Eagle Manor. It includes property on both sides of Mahantongo Creek. This would be near Benigna's Creek Winery and the present residence of Darwin and Carol Mauser. No doubt Gidion built the log house on the Mauser farm.

A record of the transfer of ownership includes the following: Phillip Galman, 19 July, 1768 – Henry Bingamon, 9th August, 1804- Gidion Williamson, 28th August, 1823- John Wiest, 17 September, 1852.

This survey from 1768 names Phillip Klinger, brother of Alexander Klinger, as an adjoining land owner on the south side of Mahantongo Mountain. By this early date, 1768, the Klingers are documented here as being in this area. The map previous shows a survey of the same land in 1792. Alexander Klinger is named on this survey transferring land to Gidion Williams.

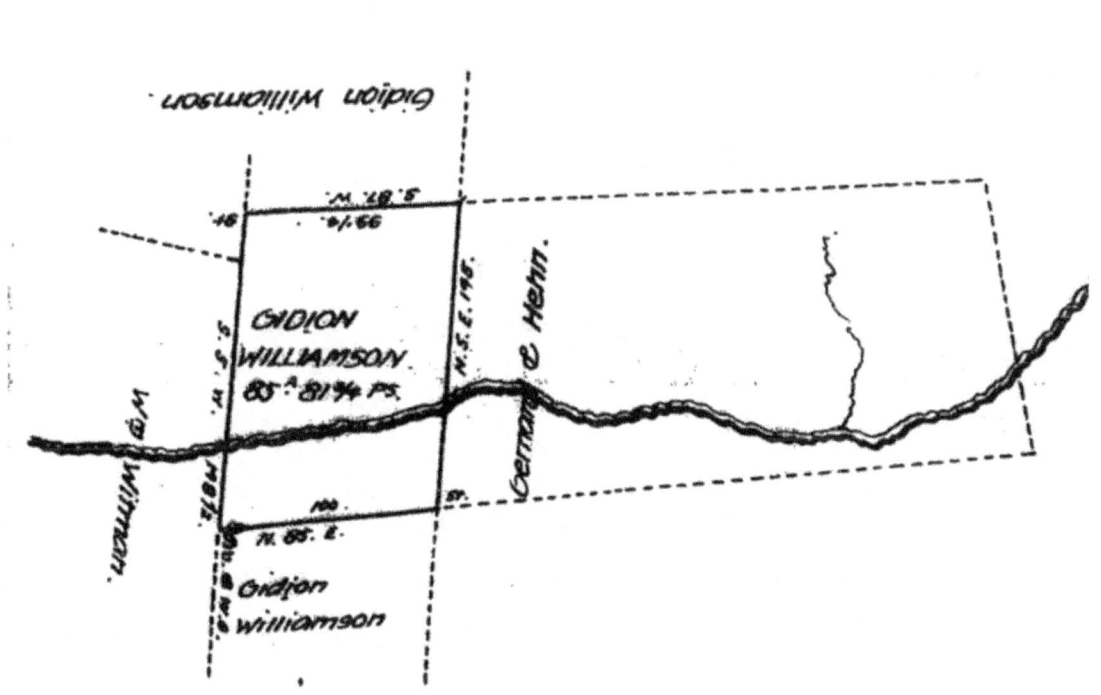

The Gidion Williamson draft is now the residence of Darwin and Carol Masser.

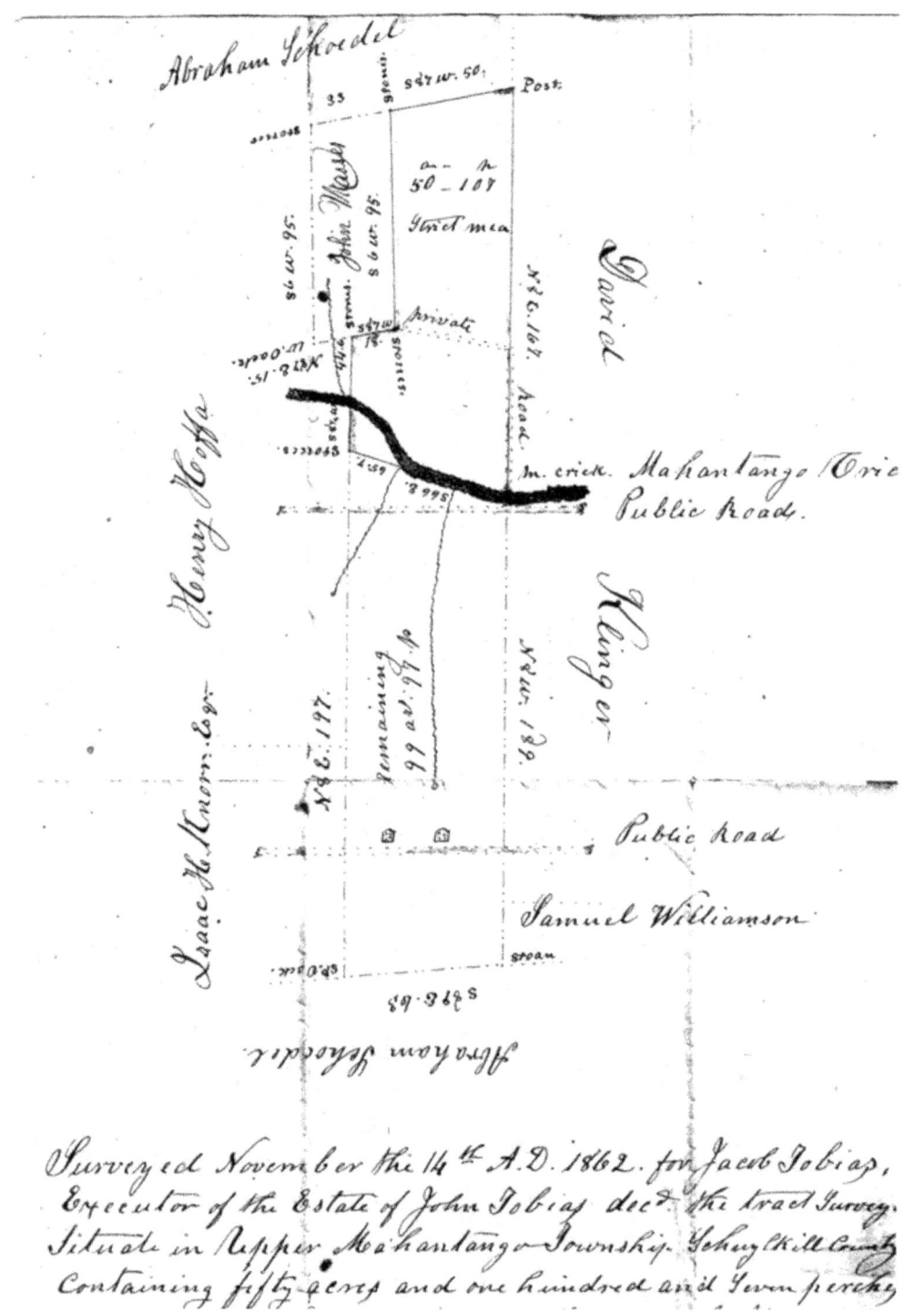

Darwin Masser Farm. Prior owner John Tobias to Jacob Tobias, survey, November 14, 1862.

Isaac H. Knorr, Esquire, adjoining land owner, daughter Ida Knorr married Elsworth Klinger. Elsworth's daughter Verna married Stanly Romberger. Stanly's daughter, Marion A. Romberger married Earl G. Troutman

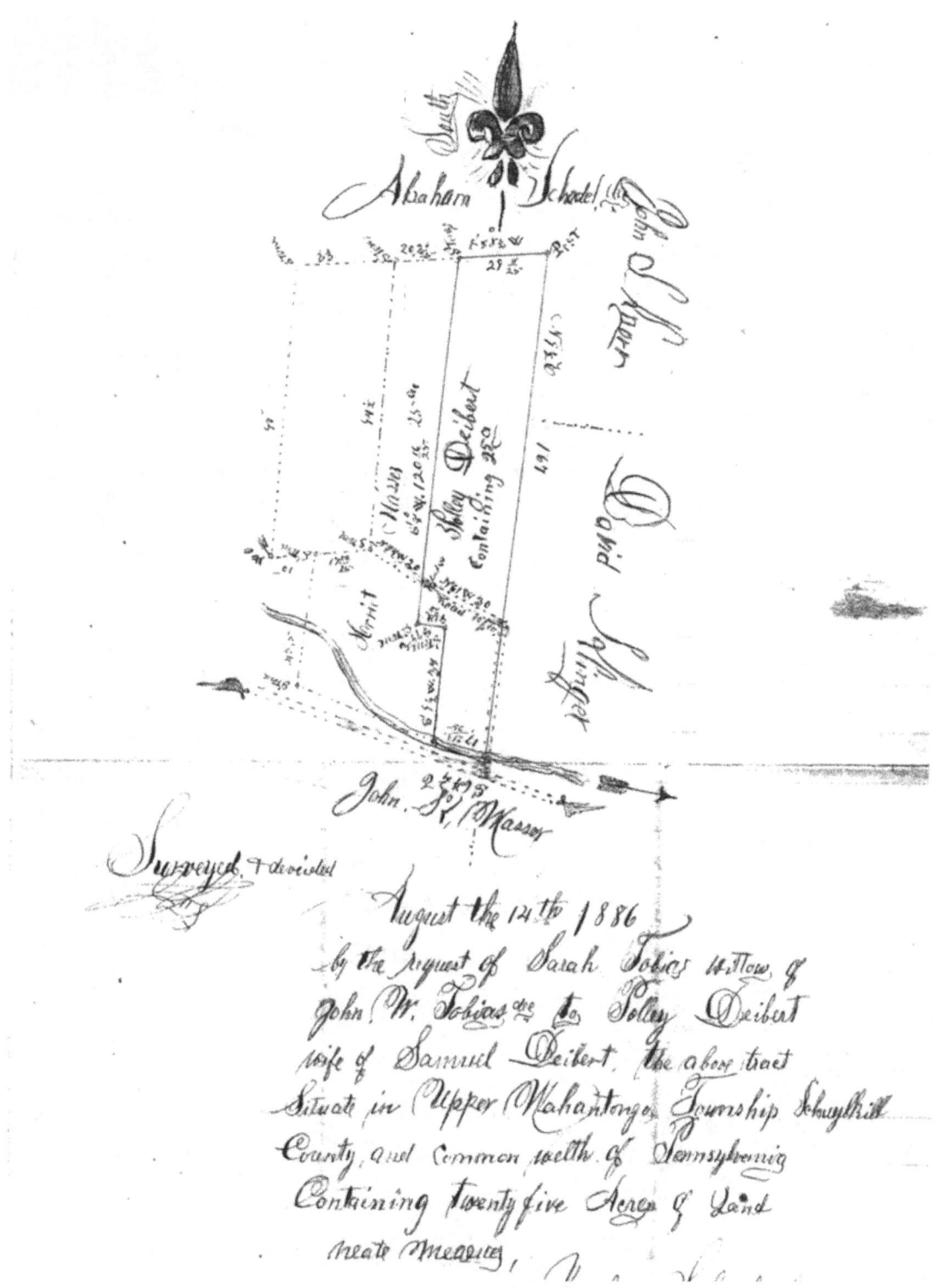

Sarah Tobias, widow of John W. Tobias, survey August 14, 1886.

Note adjoining land owner David S. Klinger, son of Alexander and Elizabeth Schwalm Klinger. David learned the trade of millwrite. He married Barbara Wiest, daughter of John and Katherine Merkel Wiest

Another Tract North East of "The Manor of Spread Eagle"

To Samuel Cochran Esq., Surveyor General of Pennsylvania

By virtue of a Warrant dated 25th of May 1805 Surveyed 7th of June 1805 unto Jacob Wiest and David Myers the above described Tract of two hundred and fifty acres of land and allowance including an improvement adjoining lands Frederick Weaver and the Manor land in Mahanoy township, Northumberland County.   By Wm. Montgomery D.S. I suspect this land has been before appropriated on a warrant to Wm. Simpson. W.M.

Description by author: This tract of land located north of the Spread Eagle Manor boundary line would be in the area called Snow Dale. It would seem to include lands between the Manor and Fisher's Ridge. Jacob Wiest would be Jacob Wiest III who was the Wiest pioneer from Oley and David Meyers is the brother of Eve Elizabeth Meyers who was married to Peter Trautman. David and Eve Elizabeth Meyers' parents are George and Barbara Meyers of Tulpehocken, Berks County. Peter Trautman owned adjoining land within the Manor. See Connection Draft of the Manor by E. Terry elsewhere in this book.

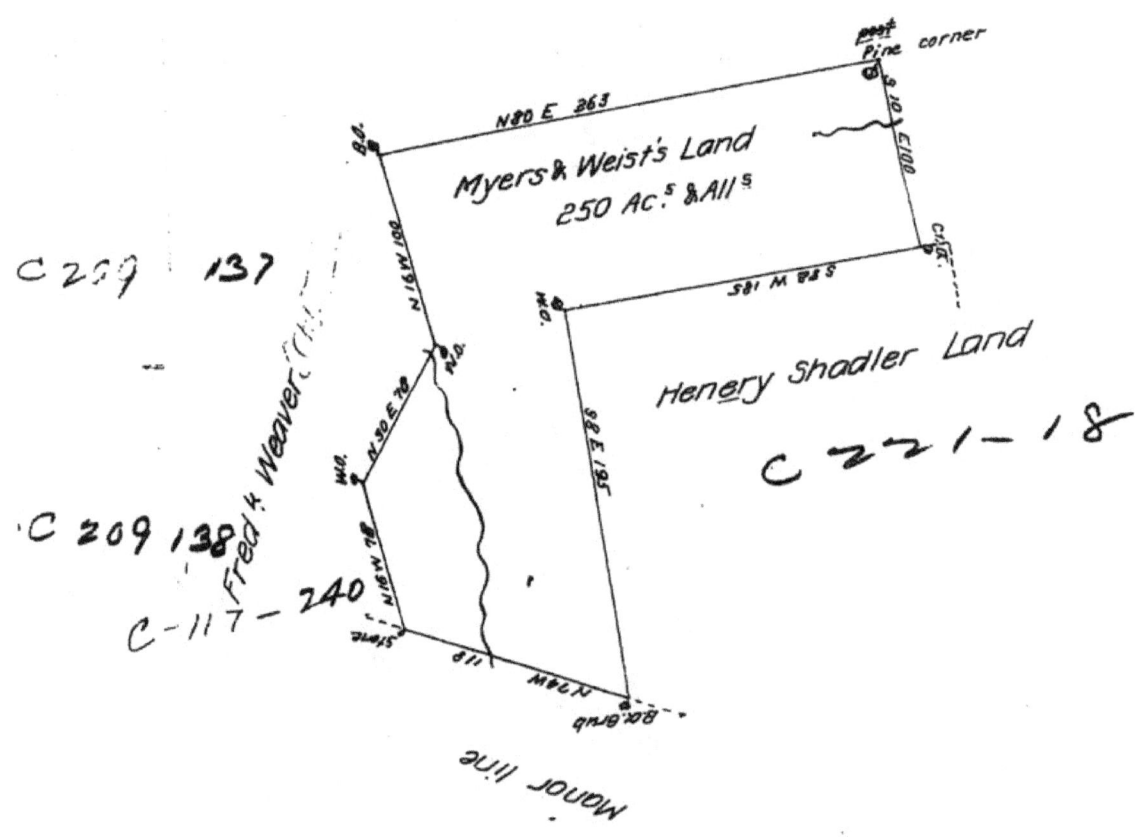

TSCHOPP FAMILY

(Tschopp is pronounced "Chubb" or "Job". It is spelled Tschopp, Job, Shupp or Shop.)

The Tschopp family settled early in the Mahantonga Valley. John Tschopp, Jr. was born in Switzerland. He married Magdalena Stohler in Switzerland and emigrated to the United States with his wife and three children in 1767. The family emigrated on the ship Sally from Rotterdam, last from Cowes, England, Patrick Brown, Master, 62 passengers. Arrived in Philadelphia on Nov 10, 1767.

The emigrants were listed as:

Hans Tschopp, no age, Magdalena, wife, Johannes, Felix, and Magdalena

According to Faust "Swiss Immigrants to the American Colonies" Hans Tschopp, son of Hans, is listed as an emigrant who left secretly with his wife and three children under age. It is presumed he went to the United States. Fridlin Stohler, his father-in-law, declared he was willing to meet his debts.

His three children were baptized at Protestentisch, Bubendorf, Basel, Switzerland. These dates are found at the LDS site on the internet in film number 128156.

The baptismal dates of the children were:
Johannes 12 Jul 1761
Felix 04 Dec 1763
Magdalena, 30 Jun 1765

Magdalena Stohler was born 31 Aug. 1740 and was baptized at the same place as the children on Sep 4, 1740. Her parents were Felix Stohler and Ursula Glintz. Other ancestors can be found at Rootsweb.com

John Tschopp, Jr was born on 29 July 1740 and baptized at the same place as his children on 31 July 1740. He was the son of John Tschopp and Barbara Thommen. John and Barbara were married at the same place 10 June 1739. This couple also had another son, Christian, born 12 Feb. 1747.

It seems likely—but has not been proved—that John Tschopp Sr. was the son of Peter Tschopp and his wife, Barbara Rudin who married 6 March 1708 at Bubendorf.

Peter and his wife had four children baptized at Protestantisch, Bubendorf. These were:
Barbara (born19 Oct 1708)
Anna (born 13 August 1711)
Johannes (born 31 Jul 1714)
Martin (born 30 June 1716

John Sr. apparently settled in the area of Schaefferstown, Lebanon County.and John Jr. met him there; John Jr. and Magdalene had a son John Jacob Tschopp, born: 05 Dec 1767 and bap: 28 Mar 1768 at the Heidelberg Reformed Church.. Sp. Jacob Tomme and wife, Ursula Graef

Johannes, Felix, Magdalena and Jacob are four of the children later listed in John Job's estate settlement.

John Tschopp, Sr. who had immigrated earlier than his son is probably the person listed in the council minutes of Amt Waldenburg on 27 May 1750 where it is noted that Hans Tschopp, Hollsteiner's sons, left, destination unknown. His name has not been found on an immigration list but many Swiss came to America on the ship "Crown" in 1749. There was a Martin Tschopp aad a Jacob Tschopp on that ship/ John Tschopp probably immigrated about that time . John Tschopp left his wife and children behind. when he left Switzerland.

By 1778 the Tschopps were on the tax list for Mahanoy Township, Northumberland County.

They paid a state tax of 5.7 in 1785 for 80 acres, 1 horse, 1 cattle. Then in 1787 a state tax of 9.0 for 100 acres, 2 horses, 2 cattle was paid.

John Tschopp Sr. died 26 Novenber 1784. In his will , probated in 1784, there is no mention of a wife or children other than John Job, Jr. and Madelin Job who were appointed executors of his estate.

.John Tschopp Jr died in 1813 in Northumberland Co. His estate settlement named ten children. On 10 Jan 1814 his oldest son, John, was named executor of the estate. The children were:

1. John who married Barbara
2. Magdalena married George Kemble .
3. Philip (Felix) died between 1792 and 1813 when his father's estate was settled.
4. Jacob
5. Christian
6. Henry
7. Rachel (Regina) married Henry Trautman. She was deceased in 1813. Rachel's children received her share of the inheritance when John Tschopp died .(Durs Thommen was a sponsor at the baptism of Regina Tschopp.)
8. Catherine married William Fisher
9. Elizabeth married Abraham Trautman
10. Maria married John Weikerly

Remembering that a hypothesis is a tentative assumption which needs to be proved or disproved, I present the following hypotheses concerning John Tschopp.

John Tschopp, born in Switzerland in 1714, is the son of Peter Tschopp and Barbara Rudin.

Barbara Tschopp, born in Switzerland in 1708 is the daughter of Peter Tschopp and Barbara Rudin

Barbara Tschopp is the wife of Hans George Meyer of Cumru Township, Berks County.

Barbara Tschopp Meyer is the sister of John Tschopp.

At the Millbach Church there were baptisms as follows:

Peter Ecker and wife, Barbara had a daughter Anna Barbara baptized Dec 1749
Sp. John Meyer and Barbara

Peter Ecker and Barbara had a son, Peter baptized 20 Apr 1751 Sp: John Schupp and his sister, Mrs. Meyer

Schupp is probably one of the spellings for Tschopp.

John Tschopp's two granddaughters married two grandsons of Barbara Meyers and her husband George, so there is a connection between the families.

"Mrs Meyer," wife of Hans George, is probably the sister of John Tschopp.

Courtesy of Beatrice Leemhuis, for genealogy see the website:
http://www.mahantongo.org/genealogy.html

Part I: Spread Eagle Manor and the Establishment of Klingerstown and the Klingerstown Grist Mill

Troutman, Spohn, Ruth and Meyer relationships

In Dec. 1, 1786 Peter Troutman, Philip Spohn, and Jacob Ruth applied for 200 acres of land in Northumberland county. Peter Troutman lived on this land, but the others lived in Berks county.

On August 27, 1785 Peter Troutman applied or 100 acres of land adjoining land of Philip Spohn, Jacob Ruth, and George Mayer in Mahanoy township, Northumberland county.

Philip Spohn lived in Heidelberg township, Berks county, adjoining lands of Michael Ruth. He was born in that township Sep. 24, 1737, a son of Adam Spohn. On April 26,1766 he married Maria Krick, a daughter of Frantz Krick. On Sep 13,1807 Philip died in Heidelberg township. He had a brother, John. He had 2 sons and 9 daugters.

In his will, probated in Berks county, Philip mentions tracts of land in Mahanoy township, Northumberland county. One was "held in partnership with Peter Troutman".

Jacob Ruth lived in Cumru township, Berks county. He was a son of Peter Ruth. Peter had four sons when his first wife died. He then married Catherine Meyer and had ten more children.

Jacob Ruth was married to Catherine Krick, a daughter of Frantz Krick. Philip Spohn and Jacob Ruth were brothers-in-law.

An Ancestry.com family tree of "Hurst, Pittman and allied families" says that Catherine Meyer was born August 1715 and died 28 Nov 1783 in Bernsville, Berks county. They say she married Peter

Ruth August 10, 1740 in Berks. No other source is given.

On July 11, 1740 Peter Ruth and his wife, Catherine Meyer were sponsors at the baptism of Anna Catherine Meyer, a daughter of Hans George Meyer and Barbara (Records of Rev. John Casper Stoever). The Meyers were Peter Troutman's in-laws.

The Troutmans, Spohns, Ruths and Meyers were interconnected.

My hypothesis is that Catherine Meyer was a sister of Hans George Meyer.

Catherine was a baptismal sponsor of one of the Meyer children.

Catherin's step-son, Jacob Ruth had a daughter, Susanna, who married David Meyer, a son of the Meyers.

Catherine Meyer Ruth and George Meyer lived in the same general area and their ages were compatible to be brother and sister.

This may seem like flimsy evidence, but it may be a basis for further exploration.

Tschopp, Troutman, Spohn, Ruth and Myer family history courtesy of Beatrice Leemhuis
2631 W. Sixth Street, Erie, PA 16505

Present residence of Roy and Marlene Paul at the intersection of Ridge Road and Water Shed Road. In 1875, Isaac H. Knorr lived at this location in an earlier dwelling removed before this photo was taken. Isaac H. Knorr was a Justice of the Peace and his name sometimes appears on legal documents as Isaac H. Knorr, Esq.

Part I: Spread Eagle Manor and the Establishment of Klingerstown and the Klingerstown Grist Mill

Property on Old State Road North East of The Manor

John H. Knorr Land

The following document was purchased on public sale at the residence of George Klinger who had recently deceased. George's residence was on Old State Road between the Charles Masser house and the Delp farm house (now removed), in Upper Mahanoy Township, Northumberland County, Pa. Willard Reiner has built a new house on the property. Prior to the sale of the Klinger farm to Charles Masser, a plot of land was kept separate for the George and Charles Klinger dwelling. This following deed seems to be for their residence, as well as the earlier location of the John H. Knorr residence.

This indenture made the 24th day of April in the year of our Lord, 1854. Between Magdelena Williamson, the wife of Joseph Williamson, of the township of Upper Mahanoy, Northumberland County, and state of PA the first part and John H. Knorr of the township, county, and state aforesaid of the second part. Witness that the said Magdelena Williamson in and for consideration of the sum of $10 lawful money of the United States of America unto them will and truly paid by the said John Knorr at or before the sealing and delivery of these presents the receipt whereof is hereby acknowledged ....all that certain tract of land situate lying in the township, county, state aforesaid bounded and described as follows: Beginning at a stone by land of George Schedel, North 86 degrees East, 19 Perches to a stone. South 8 degrees East, 17 Perches to a stone. South 86 degrees West, 18 Perches to a stone. North 1 degree West, 15 Perches to the place of beginning. Containing 1 acre, 128 and ½ perches.

It being part of a larger tract of land confirmed by deed dated 10th January, 1826, unto George Schedel. And whereas George Schedel by his indenture bearing data 17th of March, 1848 confirmed the same unto Magdelena Williamson.
Magdelena Williamson hereby granted unto the said John H. Knorr his heirs and assigns forever.....the said parties to these presents have here unto set their hands and seals dated the day and year first above written.

Sealed and delivered in the presence of us, Isaac H. Knorr, (Justice of the Peace), Magdelena Williamson and husband Joseph Williamson (signed in script letters). Magdelena Williamson (mark).

Received the day of the date above indenture of the above named John H. Knorr, the sum of $10 lawful money of the United States, it being the consideration money above mentioned in full. Witness present at signing, Isaac H. Knorr, Magdelena Williamson, (her mark).

Note about the Williamsons and Schedels

Gideon Williamson married Eve Elizabeth Klinger, the daughter of Alexander Klinger. The Williamson homestead was on the land now known as Darwin Mausser's farm on Ridge Road. Benigna's Winery is also established on the land Alexander Klinger once owned. The Schuylkill Co., Northumberland Co. line is nearby.
The well known Schedel farm neighbors the Darwin Mausser farm to the north.

John Knorr Place on Corners Road, North East of The Manor of Spread Eagle

Conversation with Ray Davis, April 2012.

John Knorr's place was where Milton Paul lived. Milton was a school teacher. John Brown told the story that John Knorr, the undertaker, was without a wife. So John Knorr asked the Brown ladies to do the hair of the deceased women, when a lady died. The Brown homestead was north of Ernest Masser's farm, along the township road to Snowdale. Ray stated John make coffins and furniture.

Editor's note: I believe Isaac K. Knorr married to Elizabeth Fetterolf was known by the name John to the neighbors. He is identified on page 65 of **The Descendants of Hans Peter Knorr** by Lawrence Knorr, Sunbury Press. My mother also referred to her great-grandfather, Isaac K. Knorr, as "Old John Knorr", in reference to his line of forefathers.

Ray recalled another undertaker in the Klingerstown was named Musick. He lived in the Hoofland Valley near the old wooden corn houses which still stand at the east end of this valley. The Musick home was near the intersection where the road to Greenbriar meets the Hoofland road. This house burned down.

Family of Wilson Elsworth Knorr and Selarah Amanda Deppen about 1914. Wilson and Selarah were married in Northumberland County in 1891. Selarah died soon after this photo.

Wilson Knorr, 49, Selarah Deppen, 47, Guerney E. Knorr, 22, Estella, 16, Rosie, 10, Boyd, 6, Mabel, 5, Allen, 4, Kermit, 2. This is Ida Knorrs brother's family who lived where the Smith farm is today. Note the exceptionally well dressed men. They appear to be some of the Knorr line of morticians.

Water Shed Road, North East of The Manor of Spread Eagle

The William Strohecker log house on Watershed Road was removed and rebuilt by the Hermitage of Pitman, PA. They dismantled the log house in 1991 and rebuilt it in 1995as a residence. William Strohecker bought the farm from Al Klinger who lived on Old State Road, where Charlie Masser lives today. The 1875 Map of Northumberland County shows J. Stiely as living here. Notes of interest: About 1945, Parvin Wm. Troutman was killed by a farm tractor upsetting on him. He was traveling on the road near the "Salt Hill" west of the Smith farm and unexpectedly met the US mail carrier. Parvin was working for William Strohecker at the time of the accident. Mike Deibert, neighbor to the east, recalls the story of William Strohecker's barn on fire. The embers were carried by the westerly wind to the Gideon Erdman barn adjoining to the east. The floating embers, carried by the wind, burned Gideon Erdman's barn also.

William Strohecker Log House.

Al Klinger sold this farm to William Strohecker.
Al is the father of William Oscar Klinger named below.

The old log house from the William Stohecker Farm, nearby the residence of Leonard Strohecker, is seen here being rebuilt on The Hermatige, by Johannes and Christian Zinzendorf, Pitman, PA.

Going to Market with the Klingers from Rough and Ready

William Oscar Klinger was a farmer and produce market man from Rough and Ready. He lived on the farm owned now by Eric Klinger along Old State Road. One of the market towns he visited was Heckstersville. This was a coal mining community. Eston Klinger (his wife's brother) often went along to market. On the way home while crossing the Red Shale Mountain, three robbers tried to stop them in a hold up. Robbers on the mountain were always a concern for the produce farmers. W.O. Klinger gave the reins to Eston and told him to keep going. William went to the back of the wagon where he picked up a hatchet. He used it to chop their fingers as the robbers tried to climb on board the back of the wagon. Eston kept the horses running and the robbers gave up the chase. W.O. Klinger later said, "I should have marked them with the hatchet." What he meant was that he should have hit them on the head as well. W.O. Klinger was the father of Paul Klinger, Eric's grandfather.

Part I: Spread Eagle Manor and the Establishment of Klingerstown and the Klingerstown Grist Mill

Knorr Family Heritage
by Steve and Joan Troutman, January 23, 2012

Fifty years ago, when I was about 10 years old, the Earl and Marion Troutman family would drive about the Mahantongo Valley. Sometimes when in the area of Rough and Ready, Mom would point out the house where her grandmother Klinger lived. This was the second farm house north of the USDA Water Study headquarters, on the west side of the road. Here Ellsworth and Ida (Knorr) Klinger lived. Mom said she often visited here and even stayed over night. I knew she had some old fashioned kitchen chairs which were some how connected to the Knorrs, and Dad had a Knorr/Fetterolf marriage certificate and birth certificate framed, hanging together in the living room.

Ellsworth had a small farm overlooking the Klingerstown Gap, on the sun sided hill. The farm was located between the present residences of Leonard Strohecker and Calvin Knorr. Mother said that while she was a little girl, a community fair was held on the hilltop above Ellsworth Klinger's home, in a picnic bush. Evidently it was a well established grove, as I have talked with other people of my mother's generation, and they also remember it being there. Mom said she had a ride on a merry go round which was a special treat for the children of the area. The wood lot is now gone and a field has taken its place.

On one of the family drives through Rough and Ready, I remember Mother saying the Knorrs made coffins in the meadow below Ellsworth Klinger's farm house. At the time I thought what a gruesome work that must have been. I pictured rough plank boxes of unplaned wood. Only lately, after conversation with Larry Knorr, did I begin to appreciate the Knorr's cabinetry work. Larry Knorr wrote a family history book, The Descendants of Hans Peter Knorr. After I purchased his book, and talked with him personally, many unanswered questions became answered. Larry asked me if I knew any Knorrs in the funeral business in Rough and Ready. I had heard of the old Art Rothermel mortuary on the Ray Dietz farm north of Karterman's School. In the horse and buggy days, this was where the black horse drawn hearse was kept, and the mortician did his work in a small building on the east side of the road, opposite the Ray Dietz farmhouse. Larry told me that the Knorr family also had a mortuary tradition as well. Larry's ancestor Caton Knorr left Rough and Ready and traveled to the Reading area. He was trained as a coffin and cabinet maker. Perhaps this move was prompted in order to avoid the Civil War recruiters, who were actively enlisting young men to fight in the Civil War. Caton established a funeral business in the Reading area and became well known and very successful. He was also an established cabinet maker and several family members of Caton's descent have pieces of furniture he made.

The Knorrs of Rough and Ready made furniture. Quite a number of their works can be found today in the area. All the Knorr made furniture that I have seen is made of lighter colored oak with pronounced grain of wood, finely planed with dove tailed joints. This furniture has spoon carved vines and leaves for decoration. There was a decorated bed recently sold at Bryant Boyer's estate sale, with spoon carved leaves on a vine. Beverly

Romberger, who attended a preview of Bryant Boyer's sale items, identified the spoon carving. Beverly had seen other local pieces of furniture decorated with the same motif.

Ernest Klinger of Rough and Ready, remembers his father Ralph Klinger speak of attending funerals at a Knorr house lately known as the Milton Paul residence. This was the place that my mother said the Knorr's made the coffins. Beatrice Paul lived her entire life at this Knorr homestead, even as an elderly unmarried spinster. Beatty told the Smith's who presently own this farm, that the Knorrs had a mortuary on the hill above her house. Nothing remains of the building except the foundation stones and a medium sized tree which grows there. Beatty said "Nothing else seems to grow there, except the tree." This single tree can easily be seen from the main road where the Smith's barn is located. The tree marks the mortuary location about half way up the hill when facing south. In earlier times, a township road passed by the Knorr homestead, (Beattie's place) and climbed the hill in a south westerly direction, past the mortuary to the top of the hill. This township road then joined the main road near Benigna's Winery parking lot. Because Beatty Paul did not drive a car, this driveway was abandoned. Beatty walked wherever she needed to go, and the township road reverted to a foot path and animal pasture trail still visible today.

A conversation with Roland Romberger within the year before his death, resulted in an interesting story. Roland said he and his older brother Quentin, would sometimes stay over night at Grandfather Ellsworth Klinger's farm. Ellsworth had a saw mill in Snow Dale. This is logical, because Ellsworth's father, Marcus Klinger also had a saw mill in Snow Dale. Surely his sons helped him in the business of logging and sawing of wood. In those days the belt driven saw mill was powered by a steam engine. Ellsworth would have the young grandsons walk from his residence over to the Marcus Klinger homestead where Charlie Masser's new house is today. The boys continued on walking down the steep south rim of Snow Dale, sometimes covered in snow, to the valley below. Here the saw mill was set up. Logging was done in the winter when frozen ground and snow allowed the logs to be pulled easier. Quentin and Roland had the job of building fire in the fire box of the steam engine. They used wood to build the fire, which heated the water jacket boiler to make the steam. This would seem to me to be a man's work that these youngsters were doing. Evidently, Ellsworth knew his engine and he had confidence in his grandsons.

Quentin and Roland stayed with the steam engine and kept the fire burning until the workmen arrived. The steam pressure was already building by then, so the men could soon begin to run the mill.

These pages from the book "There's something about Rough and Ready" published by Sunbury Press

Ellsworth Klinger Family Photo

Ellsworth Klinger and Ida C. Knorr Klinger family. This family picture taken at their home near Rough and Ready. Ida is descendant from the Knorrs that did the coffin making and funeral service and mortuary work. On this picture Ida wears a robe style dress decorated with embroidery work. Perhaps she assisted with the funeral work. Photo center: Elizabeth Delp, Ellsworth Klinger, Ida Knorr Klinger. Allen Timothy Klinger and wife Alpha (Starr) are behind his mother, Ida. Stanley Romberger stands behind Ellsworth. Verna holding Roland Romberger stands behind Elizabeth Delp. Carrie Vesta Klinger sits next to mother Ida with husband Charles H. Boyer behind Carrie. Mabel Gertrude Klinger married to Henry Lesher stand on the right. Quentin Romberger sits on the ground center front row.

The Last Days of the Ellsworth Klinger Family Homestead
Photos courtesy of Roger Strohecker, son of Leonard Strohecker who lived next door

In 1956, three families lived in his very large farmhouse built by Elsworths Klinger
Lawrence Maurer md. Violet Clark, son Ronald, age 6 (Upper Floor)
Russell Mace md Pauline Clark (Upper Floor)
Robert Wendt md. Marilyn Bowman (1st Floor)

Other Neighboring Residences and Locations on Old State Road and Watershed Road, Rough and Ready, PA

The Delp School – Now a residence east of the Delp Farm.

*Joel Zimmerman, school teacher, at Delp's School.
Photo by J.H.L. Gallery, Philadelphia, PA.*

Old dwellings along Old State Road north of Rough and Ready. Markus Klinger's log home and barn now removed. Presently the residence location of Charles and Nancy Masser.

The Delp Farm on the intersection of Old State Road and Water Shed Road, house and barn now removed.

July 30, 2012 Steve Troutman spent time with Darwin Erdman to verify the John H. Knorr 1 acre land location. He farms the 100 acre Delp farm at the intersection of Old State Road and Watershed Road, about 1 mile west of my home. During the 1960's, the Delp house which stood on the intersection was burned down by vandalism. The smaller Rabuck house to the west, along Old State Road was burned at the same time. Straw from the Rabuck barn was used to start both fires. The straw was seen scattered along the roadway from the barn to the Delp house. Darwin told me Gideon Erdman and Gideon's father owned this farm before the Delps. Today Delp's one room school connected to a residence, is on this farm, as well as the Shawn Erdman residence, Darwin's son. This land adjoins the John H. Knorr property. Darwin purchased the farm from Clair Hoffman, who was a blacksmith in Rough and Ready, south of Salem Church, first on Vista Road, and 2nd at his home on Hoffman Road, next to Zerfing School.

Mike Deibert, who owns the Gideon Erdman homestead location, recall Gideon's barn burned the same time William Strohecker's burned down. Westerly winds carried the sparks to the Erdman neighbors. The Gideon Erdman homestead location is referred to as "Judy's Patch" named after Gideon's wife.

Milton Paul, school teacher, lived on the Smith Farm on Corners Road, where John Knorr's cabinet wood working shop was previously described.

Milton S. Paul, teacher (above), at Delp's School. The bottom photo shows teacher Milton S. Paul with students thought to be at Delp's School. Another area school was Paul's Academy, located 2 miles further east from Delp's, both on Old State Road. Mr. Paul's handwriting was beautiful.

Interview with Darwin Erdman, July 29, 2012

Darwin Erdman is a farmer from Rough and Ready. He presently resides south of Zion (Klinger's) Lutheran Church, in the Village of Erdman. Darwin and his family farm land on both sides of Water Shed Road. The property occupied by the USDA Water Study facility was earlier part of a Shadle farm. Darwin's fore fathers farmed the Delp farm, located at the intersection of Old State Road and Water Shed Road. The Delp farm is approximately 100 acres. The Delp school house is located on his farm. The Delp farm house stood on the intersection on the east side. It was a log house. The barn was on the north side of Old State Road. Neighboring to the west was a house and barn on Old State Road, associated with a Rabuck family. Both homes were abandoned by the 1960's, and were set on fire by vandals, during the night, destroying both houses. Straw from the Rabuck barn was used to ignite the Delp farm house. The straw was scattered along the road. The Rabuck farm location was across the road from the present residence of Willard Reiner. George Klinger lived on this land prior to Willard Reiner. (See John H. Knorr document.)

Darwin recalls Clair Hoffman farming the Delp farm. Clair told Darwin that before the Delps lived on the farm, the property belonged to Gideon Erdman's father. Darwin's family line includes: Farus (1888-1968) md. Mazie, Gideon (1854-1941) md. Elizabeth, John (1824-1896) md. Judith, and Andreas (1779-1863) md. Rachel Williamson (1780-1852). All are buried at Salem except Andreas and Rachel are buried at Zion (Klinger's) Lutheran Church.

The Tennant House on Ernest Masser's Farm
East of Delp's School

Two Pictures from Snow Dale

Klinger's saw mill in Snow Dale. Ellsworth Klinger had the mill deep in the Snow Dale Valley. Marcus Klinger had the mill before his son Ellsworth.

Thmas Family Homestead in Snowdale
Jacob Thomas (1767-1843) married Maria Schmelzer (1774-1842)
They are buried at Salem. Peter and Elias Thomas, later generations lived here also.
Dennis and Christine Masser residence in 2012.

"The Erdman boys, Killian, Frank, Wilson and Nathan."
I assume these are the sons of Nathan and Rachel Montelius Erdman. The second is perhaps the Wilson Erdman who owned the mill in Steve's pictures. A younger sister of the boys, Jane Priscilla Erdman, was my great grandmother, the mother of my grandmother Edna Rachel Knorr Ramberger, who was married to Charles Edgar Ramberger.
Photo and Caption Courtesy of Lorraine Andary - 6/26/12

Part I: Spread Eagle Manor and the Establishment of Klingerstown and the Klingerstown Grist Mill

Local History from Rough and Ready, North East of The Spread Eagle Manor

A Winter Market Day

By late afternoon, on a Wednesday in February, of 2010, the Lewisburg Farmer's Market was almost over. Most of the customers had gone and many of the vendors had packed up to head for home. Har-Del Klothes Korner's was packing up also. Harvey and Delphine Brown sold clothes. Steve and Joan Troutman sold meat for Troutman Brothers. We saw each other every Wednesday, as our stands were on opposite sides of the market aisle. Harvey was keen on historical matters so I asked them about an old house foundation near by my home in Rough and Ready.

Delphine called it the "Kima-Haus" and she told me she lived there for a few years as a young girl. Delphine's parents were Willard Mattern who was married to Verna Geist. As a young man, Willard lived on the next farm to the west where Samuel Mattern, his father, owned the farm. Today Dennis Mattern lives on this farm. The "Kima-Haus" stood near the top of Mattern Hill Road on the north side of the intersection with Heim Hill Road. Willard and Verna Mattern's family was the last to live in this house. Only the stone foundation walls remain. This small home had a front room and a back room. Inside there was a set of two steps in front of the door of the enclosed stairway which led upstairs. Delphine played on these two steps, pretending to be in a one room school or in Sunday School at church. If the door was opened, then they went up to bed. Harvey knew Charles and "Poll"(Polly?) Keim lived there before Willard and Verna. Verna Mattern remembered "El" (Ellen) Keim lived there before Charles. The old Keim folks picked potatoes with Samuel Mattern.

The 1858 map of Northumberland County, Pa., shows C. Keim living here. Widow Kline lived next door adjacent to the west. Two foundations remain here today. C. Fetrulf (Fetterolf) lived ½ mile to the west where Ray Davis lives today.

Delphine remembers that it was a cold house in the winter. The location is scenic with a near by woods and a meadow in a hollow. The hollow leads water to Beisel's Run. Heim's Hill Road intersects Salem Road which parallels Beisel's Run. Willard Kahler removed the house for building materials. The Keim house was framed like a barn with chestnut beams and timbers pegged together. Willard built a new home where Paul's Academy previously stood. This was a near by one room schoolhouse. Broad hemlock boards were on the floor of the house. Inside the walls were covered with plaster. There was no insulation. Willard Kahler used the floor boards from the Keim house as wall covering in the construction of his new house in 1963. He also used some of the chestnut timbers. The barn to this farm stood on the south side of Heim's Hill Road across from the house.

When Delphine was 4 years old in 1943, she moved with her parents, Willard and Verna Mattern, to their new farm previously owned by William and Verna Mattern on Pumpkin Center Road. Harvey said he heard the old folks tell that "only the middle initial changed when the farm was sold". Verna (Geist) Mattern lives here today as I write this on 19th of April, 2012. Verna is 91 years old today, this being her birthday.

Mattern Hill Road, Rough and Ready, PA

For more information about Willard and Verna Mattern's farm on Pumpkin Center Road, see the book The German and Welsh Origins of the Charles and Lottie Fetterolf Family, by Steve and Joan Troutman. It is published by Sunbury Press. Page 21 pertains to the Northumberland County Fetterolf pioneers.

The Kime House stood at the intersection of Mattern Hill Road and Heim's Hill Road.

Another old house on the Elvin Knorr family farm east of Willard Kahler. Residents in recent time include John Wiest, Dallas Miller, Dale Reynolds, Fetter, and Henry Klinger, son of Calvin Klinger from Snowdale. Henry was the last to live there. A fire spoiled the house inside, and "Henny" moved out.

Valley Road, Rough and Ready, PA

July 11, 2010
Conversation with Kyle Brown in the Leck Bush at Lee Peiffer's homestead. This farm is owned by Andy Rothermel and rented by Kyle who has cattle in the barn. Kyle recalls of the legend of graves along the Leck Bush road. The Peiffer's were related to the Howerters who own the adjoining farm to the north of Pumpkin Center Road. A drilled well, only shallow, perhaps only 30 feet deep, provides water, even in drought conditions, for the cattle. The farm house, long gone, had a nice hilltop location.

Hepler Hotel and Exchange Stable Carriage House

The Carriage House Restaurant and Bar, now known as the Ridge Road Inn, occupies the old horse stable. Photo courtesy of Leroy "Pitty" Hepler who resided next door to the Carriage House.

Hepler Hotel, Hepler PA. Built 1900 Burned 1973

Part I: Spread Eagle Manor and the Establishment of Klingerstown and the Klingerstown Grist Mill

Hepler Hotel, Hepler, PA

Bird's Eye View, Hepler, PA

The village of Hepler was important to the early settlers as a place to purchase merchandise.

Part II:

The Klingerstown Mill

In the year 2007 the bicentennial celebration for Klingerstown was held. Early maps prove the existence of the mill by this date. The mill itself is identified on the 1807 document. Two houses and a barn are also identified. The mill construction date must precede the 1807 map date. Erroneous conclusions by the bicentennial committee attributed the mill builder to be Daniel Herb for Johannes Klinger. Bell's history of Northumberland County was incorrectly interpreted by the committee. The mill built by Daniel Herb is now recognized to be the old Samuel Knorr mill lately known as Stehr Brother's Mill built in 1808.

The Klingerstown Mill is now recognized as being built by Johannes Klinger in the last years of the 1700's, just after the Revolutionary War period. There has been no definitive paperwork found to date enabling the determination of an exact building date. As part of the 2007 bicentennial study, access to the old building became common. Quite a few early and later generation items were removed by many interested persons. It is satisfying to know that portions of the old mill still exist although now the building is completely gone.

The Klingerstown Mill existed for most of my lifetime. I was born in 1952 when the mill was still in operation, although its usefulness was already declining at that time. It closed in 1958 and at that time the building was secured and remained tightly shuttered for forty years. The unoccupied building was passed by motorists many times a day and the local folks simply viewed the old landmark as being immortal. The 200 year old original log building supported the framework addition completed over 100 years after the original mill building was established. Decades of neglect and the work of mother nature took its toll. Slowly the metal roof addition began to leak rain water. The tin valley on the roof above the millstones dripped water unto the stones where only grain was allowed to touch the millstones for many generations. The broad pine floor boards, cut from virgin hemlock and pine, many 20 inches and greater in diameter, eventually soaked and softened allowing the stones on the second floor to fall through to the first floor below. The stair steps next to the gaping hole in the floor remained untouched. The stairs remained until the very end of the building's existence. Shafts and pulleys which turned the stones remained attached to the timbers above the location of the millstones. Equipment within the mill itself remained just as the day it was last used. Many line shafts with flat belt pulleys, large and small, and iron and wooden gears still turned freely to the touch. Canvas and leather belts hung limply over the pulleys.

The first floor of the building was constructed of four stone walls. The purple foundation stones may have been quarried at the nearby intersection of Klingerstown Road and Old State Road. The bedrock silt stone with thick layers are still exposed here. Another quarry could have been on Spain Road south of the mill. The purple bedrock is easily seen below the residence of Elwood Williard Jr. The mill office was located on the first floor enclosed by a wall of stonework 8 feet high. It had windows on the south side, toward town. Some of the original wooden posts greeted anyone who entered the building. These posts polished with age had beveled corners creating a wooden 8 sided column. Wooden bins, constructed as a later addition, lined the east wall as funnel shaped pockets. They must have held whole or ground

The Pennsylvania Historical and Museum Commission studied the Klingerstown Mill and concluded that the mill was built in the late 1700's to early 1800's.

Some Mill History

In September of 1991, the Bureau of Historic Preservation did a study in anticipation of a new bridge construction over Pine Creek. This report is titled: <u>Phase I Archaelogical Survey of the Replacement and Relocation of Schuylkill County Bridge #59, Klingerstown, Pa.</u>, by Fred Kinsey III. The following description is included:

The Klingerstown Mill is probably the oldest standing mill in the Mahantongo Valley and perhaps one of the oldest in Schuylkill County. This feed and flour mill appears to date from the late 18th to the early 19th century. Originally the mill was powered with water diverted from Pine Creek but in the 20th century a gasoline motor replaced water power. Lawrence C. Stiely recalls working in the mill when he was 12 years old and later he managed the mill. His daughter Nancy Shaffer and son-in-law Leonard Shaffer now live in the 154-year old brick house adjacent to the mill which probably replaces an earlier miller's house. Mr. Shaffer filled in the millrace in the 1950's. The present owner of the mill is Charles Masser.

Marion (Romberger) Troutman recalls that the Klingerstown Mill sold supplies, building supplies, and farm equipment. A dealership for Lehigh Trucks was also established. Local people involved in milling were: Moses Wiest, Charles Bingaman, Landis Witmer, Ira (Pit) Hoffman, Austin Davis, Lawrence Stiely, Fred Leitzel, Harry (Henner) Brown, Bill Zerby, Ralph Romberger, Ivan Boyer, and probably more.

grain. The deep pit of the mill race, located under the north side, originally held the water wheel. I believe it to have had the shape of a wooden spool, similar to that shape of a spool used to hold thread. The original wooden wheel was replaced over time by an iron turbine and perhaps over 100 years ago, the iron turbine was replaced by an iron flat belt pulley. This largest pulley was 7 feet in diameter and 12 inches broad. This large wheel was powered by a stationary gasoline engine which stood outside the mill on the north side on a massive cement foundation. This same engine was later used to generate the first electricity produced and used in the town. These changes to the original mill works replaced many wooden gears and wooden shafts. A belt system of elevator cups carried grain throughout the building. It carried grain from the first floor to the third floor high above under the roof rafters. The old mill was now renamed the Klingerstown Manufacturing Company. Flour and animal feed were the products originally made. In the last decades of the company's operation, other businesses were established at the mill including farm implement sales, general farm hardware, sporting goods, and other items as well.

The second floor of the mill was constructed of a ring of 6 logs on top of each other. The mill stones were located here as well as the belt driven line shafts and pulleys, which rotated the stones. Other machines were located on this floor as well. A machine to bag flour or animal feed stood along the north wall. It was fastened to the floor joists above, attached to a funnel shaped bin above. This machine was powered by an auger within it to push the ground grain into burlap bags. The bags were placed on a movable platform on the machine. The platform could be raised or lowered by turning a crank. A work man's wooden work table was fastened to the east wall below a window which faced the macadam road. The windows provided ample light here to perform necessary repairs. Two sets of mill stones occupied a large portion of the second floor space along the west wall. The mill stone's operator's station was a room located nearby the mill stones in the southeast corner of the building. Here the miller spent his time in a room heated by a stove. The walls were neatly plastered and painted, providing a comfortable setting. The miller could not be far from the stones while they were working, in case the grain stopped flowing. If the stones would run dry they would be ruined and require re-cutting.

On the third floor of the mill many machines were kept in motion by belts which derived their power from the master pulley in the raceway. The original belt driven rope spool was used to the end to lift the grain bags from the outside area below to the top of the mill. This rope spool was located above the mill stair well and was controlled by a lever 8 feet long. It had an attached clutch mechanism consisting of a pulley 12 inches wide, being movable on a pivot point to engage and disengage the power of the drive pulley. The lever operating the clutch controlled the rope spool speed as it wound up the rope and lifted the grain bags. This method of lifting the grain bags remained in use for over 200 years. The remodeling of the mill equipment perhaps 100 years ago, included the installation of a windmill machine to remove chaff from the grain. This windmill was located on the west side and remained visible for many weeks while the old building was being dismantled. Several flour sifting machines were located on this third floor. One sifter with the name Monarch was in the shape of a lengthwise cylinder. Dimensions were almost 8 feet long and 3 feet wide. It utilized cloth on a revolving framework to sift the flour. Another flour sifter much larger, was square in shape. It was a large as a double bed, being at least 2 feet in height. This flour sifter rotated on an off set shaft which created a shaking movement to the sifter. This sifter remained movable to the end of the mill's operation and was so well balanced that it could be made to revolve by pushing it with your hands. The sifter revolved on a shaft fastened to the floor below and hung on iron rods from above. Canvas tubes surrounding the sifter carried the flour to the cup elevator nearby. This was undoubtedly a very expensive handmade machine of the finest workmanship. The name Sprout was emblazoned on the name plate of the machine.

Dust is an inevitable problem in a mill and belt driven fans, designed like airplane propellers with two blades, were installed in the highest reaches of the mill at a window. It was interesting to see the planks used by the mill operators high above the flour sifter on the building cross beams. The planks were laid there to allow a man access to oil the fan bearings.

The open spaciousness of the newer addition adjoined the old third floor of the log mill. The newer addition contained wooden storage rooms for grain and milled feed. Deteriorated paper feed bags littered this floor level to the last days of its existence. A large round iron bin operated by some metal gears was also located here on this third floor. The grain pockets which were earlier described located on the first floor, had open access here on the third floor along the east wall. The whole grain entered the millworks in bags on the third floor. The burlap bags were emptied into what I describe as an open well which emptied itself above the millstones on the second floor below as controlled by the miller. The ground up grains were then moved by gravity or endless belts of cups enclosed by square wooden tubes to other places in the mill, for example, the bagging machine which was on the same floor as the grist stones.

In the era of the operation of Grist Mills in the valley, the farmer who delivered the grain to grind did not pay in monetary compensation for the service. The miller accepted a portion of the grain as his payment. There is a Pennsylvania German word often used by the farmers and the miller for this bartering. Muldere means to take miller's toll. The millers toll is termed multere, few people recall this word today.

For additional information on the mill, see the book, "Klingerstown Bicentennial Album, 1807-2007," available from the Klingerstown Fire Police. Contact Steve E. Troutman.

Wheat shocks on the Victor Troutman Farm across the Pine Creek from the mill ca. 1940.

Part II: The Klingerstown Mill

The model is a lovely replica and includes the pulley at the peak of the roof.

Jim Boyer of Klingerstown built this model of the Klingerstown Mill, benefit Klingerstown Fire Police for the Bicentennial Celebration.

Steve E. Troutman poses at the front door of the Klingerstown Mill. The office window is to the left and the door is split with a separate top and bottom

Joan E. (Masser) Troutman stands in the doorway of the first floor of the mill. The first floor was all stone construction.

These pictures from 2007 were taken during the preparation for the Klingerstown Bicentennial. The mill race bridge is in the foreground. The mill house was built in 1833 and is marked by a brass plaque at the roof line.

The old mill is quite weathered but pretty much in tact. Note the vertical boards next to the second floor doorway which shielded the building from the lifting of the grain bags. The original windows flanking the ground floor entrance are 5 feet from each corner. The west window was 6 inches higher than the east window.

The north side shows evidence of the original red painted weather boards which were placed over top of the original log construction. The foundation was for an outdoor power unit which operated the mill most recently.

The east side mill race entrance is seen where the arch of white sandstone is now partially buried. The little door at ground level in the middle of the stone wall was access to the wooden water powered gears, which originally powered the mill.

Some speculators propose that the white block near ground level at the south east corner may have been a date stone removed by an artifact collector.

The old mill had a large addition built on the west side and on the north end. The original log mil measured outside dimensions 30 1/2 ft. by 47 ft. The new addition had a separate front door flanked by two windows.

The main belt driven power pulley was located above the mill race. An outdoor engine provided the power after the wooden water wheel and the iron turbine was no longer in use. The pulley was the third power source.

Light snow covers the mill. The old mill and the new addition had a door facing the mill house on each level.

High Water, 2011, surrounds the mill house and the mill.

Collapsed line shaft and pulleys which fell down into the water race way.

The mill office on the first floor inside the split wooden mill entrance door. Zeppelin the mastiff was along for the visit.

The view of town from inside the mill office on the first floor.

Grain or ground feed bins were built against the east wall. The bin openings were on the first floor.

The stairway from ground floor to second floor was located in line with the front door. The chamfered post on the right side of the stairs was salvaged. It was over 200 years old.

Behind the stairs in the mill race water way a belt hangs loosely on the line shaft. Note the rope hanging on the clutch mechanism.

On the second floor the wooden wheels above the grind stones remain in tact although the floor supporting the stones has broken down. These line shafts could be hand turned.

This west side door was originally a window before the addition to the mill. The old log mill, second floor, was constructed of six logs on top of each other. Stones and horsehair mud filled the space between the logs.

This mill machine was located on the second floor in 2007.

Second floor line shaft with grain elevator tubes behind.

This south east corner room on the second floor was the mill stone tender's office. The walls were plastered and the room was heated for a comfortable retreat not far away from the rotating mill stones.

The mill had been closed for almost 50 years and remained undisturbed inside.

This east side window provided light for a work bench seen here with the top removed. The mill's second floor windows left a lot of light into the mill.

Rev. Mark Rothermel and Clair Troutman on the third floor.

This iron bin was located on the second floor toward the west side.

This is the grist mill stone location. There were two sets of stones. The floor rotted and collapsed. The stones fell to the ground floor from the second floor.

Second floor stairs to the attic level. The mill stones were to the left of these stairs.

The second floor was constructed of four log walls built of six big logs. This view of the north wall shows a door replacing an original window.

This view of the west wall shows a door replacing an original window. This door led to the new mill addition.

The rope winch was in the attic. The long lever moved up and down to start and stop the winch seen here with a small rope on it. A pulley below the winch moved with the clutch lever.

Fan above the flour sifter seen below.

As labeled, this is a self-balancing Sprout Waldron flour sifter. It rotated on the off set bearing below and was suspended on metal rods from above.

Attic machinery, unidentified person.

The mill had an elevator system of cups on belts which moved inside square tubes. The pulley in the peak of the mill powered this line of elevators.

Attic level, third floor flour sifter, round reel.

Elevator system in the attic of the mill showing the maintenance plank for walking.

There was a fan attached to the elevator drive pulley in the highest reaches of the mill.

Another view of the rope winch showing the clutch pulley below the rope spool. The round reel flour sifter was turned by a belt.

This ladder like object is part to the internal workings of the square flour sifter located in the attic on the north side.

Wooden pulleys above the millstones must have powered the stones.

Water accumulated where the mill stones broke through the floor.

A spare wooden flow control valve.

Bianka Klinger, descendant of a long line of German grist mill builders and operators poses here in 2011. There were four windows on the east and west sides.

The third floor wind mill separated chaff from the grain These bins may have held cleaned seeds.

The original rope spool remained until 2015. It is seen in this 2011 photo. Note the wooden power pulley on the right edge of the photo.

An extra wooden pulley on the third floor.

In 2011, photos of the flour sifter show the canvas bags below which led to the collection boxes. A wooden auger in the boxes moved the flour to an elevator.

A fan constructed by the mill operators above the flour sifter moved the dusty air. Elevator tubes seen in the background led the flour into the top of the sifter.

The rope winch mechanism in 2011 in the attic on the third floor.

Second floor machinery- Note the heavy framework of the mill center beam.

A window in the top of the mill provided some ventilation from a fan nearby.

Note the metal plaque on the rope spool control lever. The plaque displayed a measure of rope speed according to the position of the long lever.

The bagging machine augered feed and flour into burlap bags on the second floor.

Bianka Klinger demonstrates how the bags were filled. A movable platform at the base of the bag moved up and down.

Pioneer Life in Upper Canada
Grist Mill
La vie de pionnier dans le Haut-Canada

[Pioneer Home] [School] [Saw Mill] [Grist Mill] [Blacksmith Shop] [General Store] [Doctor's Office] [Church]
Back to the Village

Bread was a very important food that pioneers ate every day. To make bread they needed flour.

Flour is made by grinding grains of wheat, corn, rye or oats. The pioneers could grind the grains by hand but it was a very difficult job and took a long time.

In most pioneer villages, a grist mill was built as soon as possible because it used machinery to grind the grain.

How a Grist Mill Worked

Water flowed into the buckets on the waterwheel and made it turn.

Gears and rods connected the waterwheel to the grindstones which turned and ground the grain into flour.

The *miller* ran the grist mill and had to know how to grind the grain properly and fix all the machinery.

Back to the Village
[Pioneer Home] [School] [Saw Mill] [Grist Mill] [Blacksmith Shop] [General Store] [Doctor's Office] [Church]

http://www.projects.yrdsb.edu.on.ca/pioneer/grist_mill.htm   9/30/2007

This illustration of how a grist mill worked is from the website listed above. The machinery required to turn the mill stone is clearly visible here.

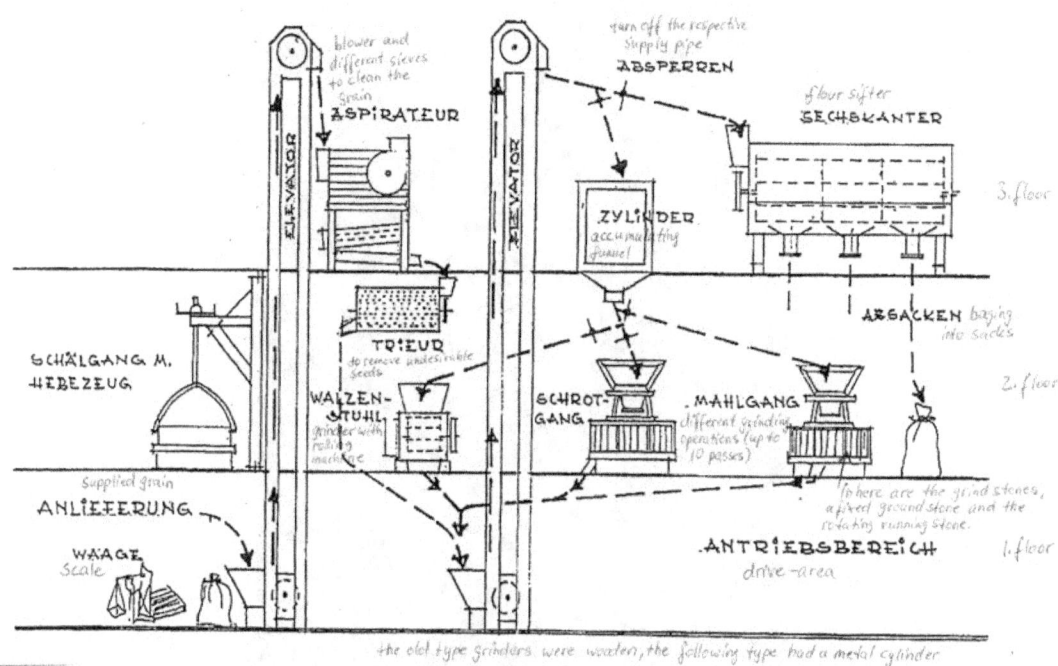

This illustration above of the machinery located on three floor levels of a grist mill shows the various equipment typical of each floor. Photo courtesy of Bianka Klinger.

The Klingerstown Mill Flat Belt Pulleys are on display at Troutman Brother's in Klingerstown.

The south east corner shows the notched logs. The stone wall was 8 feet high.

Stones provided chinking between the logs. The small stones filled the small spaces and the larger stones filled the large spaces.

Large flour chest was removed as part of the mill's demolition. Note these windows have the same level lintel as the door lintel. The middle window was probably added later.

The first floor foundation stones appear to have been quarried from the silt stone bedrock layers within the valley nearby. An outcrop of this rock type is visible on Spain Road below the Willard farm house. This location is across the creek.

The heisting pulley at the mill peak, attic window and door. The three front doors were split doors, with the bottom part separate from the top.

The mill demolition in progress, late summer 2014. The high addition with green shingles was needed for the elevator system of belts and flour sifters. Nathan Stoltzfuss, son of Sylvan Stoltzfuss of Fearnot, began the salvage work.

Joan Troutman, back right, posing with her daughter Valerie Specht and granddaughters Emma and Leah Specht.

South east corner of the mill showing the log construction on top of the stone foundation first floor. The general measurements of the original mill as paced by Steve E. Troutman were 12 paces wide and 19 paces long.

A view of the stair well on the second floor after light snow. Photo taken on the day some local men salvaged the bagging machine located on this floor and the mill rope windless located in the attic.

The mill stone tenders quarters with the plastered painted walls, second floor.

Part II: The Klingerstown Mill

The mill race way beneath the ground floor level. The water wheel was located here first, replaced by an iron turbine which was removed when the stationary engine was located outside the building. Three different sources of power existed for this mill.

The main stair case inside the front door leading to the second floor. The center beam supporting the mill upper stories is to the right of the steps.

North side showing original windows. The stationary power unit was located here on the concrete foundation. It was at the opening in the wall.

West side exposed during demolition. View of the windmill machinery. Nathan Stoltzfuss worked on the demolition of the new addition in July of 2014.

The interior of the old and new part are now visible during demolition. Note the opening in the stone wall of the first floor. This may have been a window converted to a doorway. The mill race exited the northwest wall through an archway which was 3 ft. lower in elevation than the entrance archway.

Second floor line shaft. Note the large beam supporting the third floor of the mill. This photo taken February, 2015, shortly before Frank Krammes demolished the old log portion of the mill.

The mill machinery was installed in a compact fashion. The wooden pulley was above the mill stones. Some timbers were salvaged which were white in color and very hard. They may have been ash. The floor boards were very broad hemlock and pine. Some were 20-24 inches wide or greater.

Second floor. The collapsed floor seen on the left is where the mill stones were located. Ten cup type elevators may be seen on the right hand side, behind the stairs to the third floor. The elevators have been cut open and examined by workmen from Sprout Waldron who came to view the old machinery made by their company in Muncy, PA. They took samples of the elevator belt of cups.

Part II: The Klingerstown Mill

The stone wall was 8 feet high. Note the maintenance opening at ground level and the mill race archway water entrance. The race was where the green grass is pictured. The bins pictured below were built against this wall.

Storage bins lined the east wall seen here on the first floor.

This opening door allowed maintenance of the original wooden shaft and gearing on the ground floor, west side. The east side had an opening also. It was adjacent to the stone arch mill race entrance.

The third floor newer addition was built on top of the old log mill. The flour sifters and the elevator belt system were constructed within this high portion of the building.

The removal of the new addition allowed the red painted weather boards to be visible.

Used building materials were salvaged, including heavy sawed timbers which are seen here stacked where the newer addition once stood.

Frank Krammes Ecavation of Sacramento, PA, completed the removal of the log mill structure. Many of the flat belt pulleys which powered the mill in its latter years were salvaged by the Krammes workmen and are on display at Troutman Brother's.

Third floor. This is a reel type flour sifter. The flour collection chamber is open at the bottom. A worm gear was located inside the collection chamber.

The company insignia on the reel type flour sifter. It names the Monarch brand of Muncy, PA. In September of 2010, Steve Troutman spoke with John Hefty of the Hefty Milling Company in Watsontown, PA. Mr. Hefty did business with the Klingerstown Milling Company. He traded wheat for flour to be used in the manufacturing of glue for wood products.

Leah and Emma Specht stand on a large platform scale on the third floor of the mill.

Three generations descended from Jacob Klinger, who was one of the earliest grist mill operators. Pictured are: Valerie Specht, ground floor, Emma Specht, second floor, Steve Troutman and Leah Specht, third floor.

Emma Specht, January 7, 2009; Leah Specht, February 22, 2011

Valerie Troutman Specht September 23, 1980

Steve E. Troutman, May 4, 1952

Marion Romberger Troutman, December 26, 1929-May 13, 2005

Verna Klinger Romberger, March 30, 1901-July 11, 1979

Elsworth Klinger, October 28, 1862-1933

Marcus Klinger, May 24, 1839-February 6, 1901

Jacob S. Klinger, early Klingerstown miller, January 29, 1813-January 23, 1883

Johann Peter Klinger, November 3, 1773-August 10, 1858

Johann Phillip Klinger, Immigrant, July 11, 1723-September 30, 1811

Part III:

The Mills of the Upper Mahantongo Valley

Carrie Schade with her flock of chickens in front of the Herb-Erdman's Mill. Carrie was Oscar Erdman's niece. Looking east from the mill house.

The Salem Church, Rev. Isaac Stiely, and the Gristmills of Rough and Ready

I want to write about the area where I live near the Village of Rough and Ready in the Mahantongo Valley. In the past, the waters of the Mahantongo Creek provided power for four grist mills and many generations of millers near Rough and Ready. There were water powered saw mills as well. The families that built and operated these mills were all associated with the Salem Church. They include Isaac Stiely, Samuel Knorr, Monroe and Harvey Stiely, Herbs, and Erdmans. First let us consider the origins of the Salem Church.

I can see the Salem Church from my house. The building we see today is the third church at this location. The cornerstone of the present building was laid Sunday, June 9th, 1895. The church is located on a hill in the middle of the valley, able to be seen at great distance. One record states that the Salem Church was organized in 1820, and its meetings were first held in an old school house near where the present church was built. No doubt this church and schoolhouse were one and the same log building, similar to the first church - school building built in 1807 at Jacob's cemetery located at Line Mountain, Pa., where the St. Jacob's (Howerter's) Church was established in 1803.

Other accounts give much earlier dates for the establishment of an organized church for Salem's location. The Northumberland Co. Historical Society Proceedings, Vol. XXX, 1990, page 47 records an interview with Myron Sausser of the Sausser Memorial business. He indicated that another earlier log church stood to the west of the present building. As a child he recalled coming to Salem with his father and grandfather to reset fallen stones of the cemetery. He remembered many stones being stacked in the basement of the church building that now stands and others stored in a caretaker's shed that stood near the site of the first log church. Sausser remembered playing on the foundation of the log church and he recalls it having a separate cemetery. He recalls his grandfather stating that the early cemetery at the site of the log church—now a plowed field- had more than 50 graves dating from the 1790's. In the present graveyard there are a few stones from the 1830's, fewer from the 1820's and none before 1810.

Mrs. Naomi Starr was interviewed by Rev. Eldon Ehrhart for the 150th Anniversary of Salem Church, (1830-1980). Naomi tells us she remembers her grandfather speaking about another log church located east of the present structure, containing a balcony and a wine glass pulpit. This would be the second structure with a corner stone dated, 1831.

The establishment of this church has an interesting story. Naturally the first necessity to build a church is to have some land. Jacob Whery and Peter Schlegel were appointed to secure some property. These trustees were successful and found some land available to purchase from Mr. George Simmy, a free black man of Upper Mahantongo Twp., Schuylkill Co., Pa. This deed dated, Sept. 12, 1823, was for 2 acres of land. We will discuss more of George Simmy later in this presentation. George and Kathryn Henninger and Jacob Bechtel graciously purchased the land for the sum of $8 and donated it for the building of the new church. A building committee was appointed in 1829 and soon after that, (near the end of 1830) work began on the church building.

According to the oldest records of the Reformed Church, the Reformed congregation was organized in 1824 by Isaac Stiely, who was still a student. He was not ordained until 1827 and the building itself was erected in 1830. Pastor Stiely was paid $25 a year. By 1880 there were about 200 members.

According to the oldest records of the Reformed Church, the Reformed congregation was organized in 1824 by Isaac Stiely, who was still a student. He was not ordained until 1827 and the building itself was erected in 1830. Pastor Stiely was paid $25 a year. By 1880 there were about 200 members.

The Salem Church before remodeling

George Simmy's burial was performed by Rev. Isaac Stiely. He carved the following dates on the headstone himself in English. All his other tombstone carvings for his deceased parishioners are carved in German. The date carved on the headstone records: George Simmy, born 4 July 1796, died 8 Jan. 1860, 63 years, 6 mo., 4 days. Text Galations 7:58. Before George Simmy died in 1860, he sold a portion of his land to Abraham and Mary Erdman. George Simmy's grave lies between the headstones of Abraham and Mary (Troutman) Erdman.

George Simmy stone carved in English by Rev. Isaac Stiely.

George Simmy must have been a close family friend of Abraham and Mary Erdman as he is buried between them. Just east of Simmy's grave rests Hannah Snyder, the second wife of Abraham Erdman. Their dates are recorded:
Abraham Erdman (Oct. 20, 1818)-(Nov. 19, 1881), age 63yr., 29 da.
Mary, wife of Abraham Erdman (May 20, 1822)-(Oct. 25, 1869), age 47 yr.,5 mo., 5 da.
Hannah Snyder, wife of Abraham Erdman (Feb. 26, 1826)-(May 26, 1886) age 60 yr., 3 mo., 8 da.

George Simmy is buried at Salem Cemetery in Rough and Ready. The stone was carved by Rev. Isaac Stiely in the English language. All the other stones that Rev. Stiely carved were in German. George Simmy rests surrounded by the graves of the Abraham Erdman family. As recorded on the stone:
In memory of George Simmy, (4 July 1796)-(8 January 1860), age 63 yr., 6 mo., 4 da.

Some records state that George Simmey was the son of William Simmey. At present we know of one William Simmy who was only 10 years old when George Simmy was born. Pastor Isaac Stiely performed the burial service for William Simmey in 1862, this being 2 years after the death of George Simmey. Pastor Stiely's records state William Simmey, born 20 November 1786, died 6 May, 1862, 75 years, 5 mo., 16 days. Text Hebrews 9:27. No place of burial recorded. Northumberland County Historical Society Director, Cindy

Pastor Isaac Stiely performed the burial service for William Simmy Jr., in 1862. He is likely buried on the Ernest Klinger Farm in the Simmy Family plot.

Clervin and Edward Wehry are seen working on the steeple of the Salem Church.

Jacob Wehry monument is located at the northeast corner of the church social hall.
1775-1847, 71y 6m 21 tag
Jacob Wehry and Peter Schlegel were instrumental in purchasing the land which the Salem Church is built upon.

The Rough and Ready Store

Shadle's General Store was last operated by Francis Shadle was the focal point of the Village of Rough and Ready. The post office was located here, named for President Zachary Taylor.

Pastor Mark I. Rothermel serves Salem Church in Rough and Ready. The following is his history as recorded in the <u>Lifeline of the Line Mountain Charge</u>, August 10, 2008, entitled "Brief History Lesson on the Origin of the Name Rough and Ready."
One of Salem's nicknames is the 'Rough and Ready Church'. It sounds intimidating at first, but it should not be so. The village and hence the church of Rough and Ready is named after our 12th President, Zachary Taylor. He was both a gentleman farmer and a general officer in the US army. He earned the nickname, Rough and Ready, from his soldiers while serving in the Seminole War in Florida. He got the name because he shared the hardships of the common soldier. General Taylor became a household name during the Mexican War by leading the US army to several victories in northern Mexico. In 1848, he was elected President of the US as head of the Whig Party. He died in office in 1850. He served a mere sixteen months.
Zachary Taylor was a bit a contradiction. He was a southern slaveholder who opposed the extension of slavery. Even though a Southerner, he was a staunch union man and rejected any talk of secession. His early death was a severe blow to the nation, which lost a real leader who may have lead it away from Civil War. The village and the church can be proud to be called 'Rough and Ready'.

Photo, July 2001. The Rough and Ready store was earlier known as Adam Herb's store. This establishment sold everything the local people needed, including gasoline. The pumps were in front of the porch.

A Tobacco Chewing Story

Pennsylvania German Folk are typically described as being thrifty people. Often times little money was available and the barter system existed for payment of goods or services provided. For example, the grist miller took a portion of the farmer's wheat for his payment when grinding flour or feed for the farmer. Some items required currency. Tobacco was usually something purchased by the men. Some of the more thrifty farmers from Rough and Ready attempted to grow their own, rather than to spent money to buy it.

    Ray Davis told this story concerning the Schlegels of Rough and Ready. As you may recall, they lived north of the Salem Church. Peter Schlegel helped purchase the land for the establishment of this church. According to the story passed down from Belton Davis, the father of Ray, the Schlegels were very thrifty farmers. In fact they did not want to pay money to buy tobacco, so they grew their own. There were several farms in the valley that did this. The Schlegels did have a hired man. In Pa Dutch the word "hired man" would be translated "knecht". Joan and I often heard that word used in conversation with farmers. Die "knecht" was allowed only one chew of tobacco each day. At the end of the day he needed to return his chew to the Schlegel household where it was put on the back of the stove to dry. In order to not waste this chew, it was crumbled and reused as smoke pipe tobacco. Ray thought the old gramma smoked the pipe. Now after gramma was finished smoking the pipe, she saved the ashes. These tobacco ashes could then be used again as snuff. Some folks, including the Schlegels, put this snuff in their nose. Anyone who has ever done this knows that this requires a handkerchief to blow your nose. By this time, you are wondering if this is the end of the story, but it continues. The contents of the handkerchief was then put on the work boots to water proof them! I really should spend more time with my neighbor Ray!

The old Schlegel Homestead with the large fire place and chimney on the Steve Haas Farm north of the Salem Church.

Introduction to Rough and Ready Mills

The Mahantongo Valley is known for its agriculture. The Village of Rough and Ready is centrally located. The Salem Church is built on a hill overlooking the village and much of the surrounding valley. The Little Mahantongo Creek and the Mahantongo Creek join nearby within scenic hills and dales visible from the church. The farmland cleared mostly by PA German speaking folks was quite productive. Grist mills were needed to grind wheat into flour and grain into animal feed. Sawmills and linseed oil mills were established also. All these early mills were powered by the waters flowing in the creeks. The mill dams created ponds of deep slack water which was channeled by mill races which led the flowing water to the mill. Here a millwheel turned under the weight of the water. Rotating shafts, wheels with gears, and pulleys, turned the millstones to grind the grain.

There were 4 gristmills established near the Village of Rough and Ready. These mill locations are within several miles of the Salem Church. The Rev. Isaac Stiely Mill and the Monroe and Harvey Stiely Mill were located on Mahantongo Creek. Samuel Knorr's mill lately known as Stehr Brother's Mill, is located on Little Mahantongo Creek. The Herb/Erdman Mill is located closest to the church where the two creeks join.

The families that operated these mills, Stiely, Knorr, Herb, and Erdman are all associated with the establishment of the Salem Church and many rest there today. Should the reader be interested in these family histories, the following books are recommended:

"The Relations of Isaac F. Stiely, Minister of the Mahantongo Valley", by Lawrence Knorr

"The Descendants of Hans Peter Knorr", by Lawrence Knorr

"There is Something about Rough and Ready", edited by Lawrence Knorr

All three are available from Sunbury Press of 50 –A, West Main Street, Mechanicsburg, PA 17055.

The old mill house which stood next to Rev. Isaac Stiely's mill. Rev. Isaac Stiely and Anna, his wife, resided on the opposite side of the creek from his mill, in a different house. Donald Stiely's home is built upon this foundation which was probably built by Anna's ancestors named Knorr.

For additional history on Rev. Isaac Stiely and his wife Anna Knorr see ....
The Descendants of Hans Peter Knorr, by Lawrence Berger Knorr, Sunbury Press, P.O. Box 178, New Kingstown, Pa. 17072-0178. E-mail lbk@sunburypress.com and Klingerstown Bi-Centennial Album 1807-2007 available from Steve E. Troutman, 1442 Ridge Road, Klingerstown, Pa. 17941. E-mail troutman425@hotmail.com, for $25.

Part III: The Mills of the Upper Mahantongo Valley

First Stiely Mill
Rev. Isaac Stiely
Rough and Ready, PA
South of Salem Church
Donald Stiely Residence, 2004

The first Stiely Mill, operated by Rev. Isaac Stiely, in Rough and Ready. The mill was located south of the Salem Church on the Mahantongo Creek.

Anna Knorr Stiely   **Isaac Faust Stiely**

For more information about Rev. Isaac Stiely, his family, descendants and ministry in the Mahantongo Valley see the books below:

Klingerstown Bicentennial Album (1807-2007)
Published By: The Anniversary Committee, Klingerstown Fire Police,
Books available from Steve E. Troutman

The Relations of Isaac F. Stiely, Minister of the Mahantongo Valley (and)
There is Something About Rough and Ready
By Lawrence Knorr
Sunbury Press, Inc.
50-A West Main Street
Mechanicsburg, PA 17055

Isaac had a pet, a parrot, who was kept in the corner of the parlor. When a couple would be standing in Isaac's parlor to be married, the parrot often piped up, speaking in German of course, "Pretty Polly, Ugly Pauli". I can't help but wonder what effect this would have on the nervous bride. One day the parrot escaped and flew away - to be brought home again when someone saw him sitting on a fence post reciting "Parra Schtiely, Parra Schtiely," and knew where the bird belonged.

The Isaac F Stiely house before it was demolished circa 1920

Photo courtesy of Thomas Umholtz, Valley View, Pa. 2008

Covered bridge over Mahantongo Creek at Isaac Stiely's mill, Rough and Ready, Pa.

Conversation with Donald Stiely of Vista Road, who lives at this location gives identification. Donald's grandfather, Perry Stiely, is the man with the big hat. Perry had many daughters. Perry's father, Jared Stiely, was the son of Rev. Isaac Stiely. Perry had some fingers one half cut off in a shingle mill. He was over 6 feet tall. Jared and Perry operated steam powered traction engines to run sawmills and threshing machines.

Donald's father was Harry Stiely. Harry's first wife, Evelyn, was a born Klinger from near the Delp's School. There were only 3 Klinger girls in the Allen Klinger family. Harry and his first wife had 18 children. She married Harry at age 20, gave birth to a child every year until she was 38 years old, when she died.

The family generations include: Isaac, Jared, Perry, Harry, and Donald.

Stiely Girls fishing the Mahantongo Creek with their Father Perry Stiely.

Part III: The Mills of the Upper Mahantongo Valley

Making Shingles

Perry Stiely and his shingle mill. Perry is the son of Jared Stiely. The wood fired steam engine seen here is powering the circular saw cutting wooden shingles. Note the log cut to proper shingle length standing upright on the mill. A belt driven by the steam engine powered the saw blade. Many cut logs are pictured ready for the mill. A belt driven planer is also on the picture as well as the wooden shavings from the saw. Donald Stiely, (descendant), recalls Perry had some fingers half cut off in the shingle mill. Perry seen here standing with 3 other workmen sitting nearby.

Perry also used the steam engine to pull and operate a threshing machine. He went from farm to farm at harvest time to thresh the grain crop. One story recalls how the heavy steam engine had to cross a wooden plank bridge over Mahantongo Creek. The steam engine wheels broke through the bridge deck near Rough and Ready, Pa.

Second Stiely Mill
Monroe and son Harvey Stiely
Along the Mahantongo, South of Rothermel's
Funeral Home, Schuylkill County, PA.
Walter Burns Residence, 2004

Monroe and Harvey Stiely mill on Kopp Road, Upper Mahantongo Township, Schuylkill County, Pa. Note the rope hanging in front of the open doors which pulled the grain up to the top floor. Here the bags were pulled inside to begin the milling process. Monroe Stiely stands in the open mill door with flour in bags. Harvey Stiely stands in front of the first floor window next to the farmer's wagon. Perhaps the farmer who had his grain milled is standing with the flour bag at the corner of the mill. Monroe Stiely's wife, Emma, stands at the left mill corner wearing a dark apron. Her daughter, Katie, (married an Erdman) stands in the white dress behind the wagon. A maid, never married, Ketty Cooper, stands between the ladies.
Photo courtesy of Betty Blyer, 217 E. Main Street, Hegins, Pa., g/d/ of Harvey Stiely.

Heavy iron gears salvaged from the Monroe and Harvey Stiely mill. Water power must be very powerful to have turned these two gears which are only a small part of the millworks.

Two huge wooden gears of the Monroe and Harvey Stiely mill. These wooden wheels are over 7 feet in diameter and totally wooden. The teeth were made to be replaceable.

The Epidemic of 1859
And other mortalities for
Upper Mahantongo Township (1859–1860)

Contributed by Elaine (Maurer) Moran

In the book *There is Something About Rough and Ready* (Sunbury Press), Marilyn Malick Herb shared historical information about her great great grandfather (and my fifth great grandfather), Rev. Isaac Stiehly. The Reverend was an early pastor of Salem's (Herb's) Church in Rough and Ready, Schuylkill County, PA. Ms. Herb is the caretaker of his original records. They document the number of funeral services he performed. She observed the number of deaths among children were staggering. In her article "The Old Man" she provided four examples of juvenile deaths. Rev. Stiehly had recorded them in "fine German script" within a few short days of December, 1859. She wrote that "One can't help but wonder what illness was abroad that year."

Marilyn's article piqued my interest, and I decided to do some research. On the website Ancestry.com, I came across an 1860 Mortality Census Schedule for Upper Mahantongo Township, Schuylkill County, PA. It listed "Persons who Died during the Year ending 1st June, 1860, enumerated by F. Wertheimer, Ass't Marshal." (See Figure 1 below.) During that time period, a total of 13 people died. This did not seem that unusual until I realized that ten of the thirteen were children. The cause of death of eight of these children (which includes the four that Marilyn mentioned) is listed as "Scarlet Fever."

Figure 1: 1860 Mortality Schedule for Upper Mahantongo Township

Details below were extracted from the mortality census. Original spelling is retained.

Name of Person	Age	Sex	Month of Death	Occupation	Disease or Cause of Death	Number of Days Ill
Emillia Wetzel	9	F	Nov.	-	Scarlet Fever	16
Peter Steeley	9	M	Dec.	-	Scarlet Fever	21
David Paul	2	M	Nov.	-	Scarlet Fever	4
Caresta Tobias	1/12	F	Sept.	-	Unknown	9
Jerrom Hart	1	M	Aug.	-	Head Pluricy	120
Cassy Shadel	7	F	Jan.	-	Scarlet Fever	8
Amanda Ertman	11	F	Dec.	-	Scarlet Fever	6
Jane Ertman	9	F	Dec.	-	Scarlet Fever	6
Isaac Ertman	5	M	Dec.	-	Scarlet Fever	6
Emma Steeley	7/12	F	Dec.	-	Scarlet Fever	9
George Simmy	63	M	Jan.	Farmer	Consumption	14
Solomon Ertman	37	M	Oct.	Black Smith	Consumption	28
Ann Maria Maurer	72	F	June	-	Cough & inflammation	2

Upper Mahantongo Township is hidden away in the valley between mountains to the south, east, and north. Unfortunately, it was not hidden away from the ravages of scarlet fever. In the latter part of 1859 the shadow of death carried by scarlet fever hovered over the little rural village for three short months. But, before it moved away on its path to further destruction, it would take the lives of the eight children, forever affecting the families and the community left behind to mourn their loss.

Who were these children and who were their families? Who were the others who died that year?

My curiosity led me to search for more answers. From the mortality census, we learn that scarlet fever entered the village sometime in November of 1859, or at least this is when it first took the lives of area children. Two deaths occurred that month: Emillia Wetzel, 9 years old, and David Paul, 2 years old. The 1850 Census lists the household of Eliza Wetzel, 65, (House #143) of Upper Mahantongo Township, PA. In this same household lived Daniel Wetzel and Susanna Wetzel, both 30, Joseph Wetzel, 28, and Regena Wetzel, 26, and an Amelia Wetzel, 0 years old. It is uncertain whether this is the same child listed on the mortality schedule, though it is probable given the age and locality. In researching the Paul families enumerated in the census of 1860, I found Family #1029 listing Jacob Paul, aged 43, as the head of the household. No adult female is listed in the household, but children range in age from 16 to 4. It is probable that this was the family of David Paul given there are no other Paul families in Mahantongo Township where a child of David's age would logically fit. At two years old, he was too young to have appeared in the previous census, and he had died before the 1860 census was conducted. I could not locate any burial or cemetery records for Salem Church in Rough and Ready, nor neighboring Zion Lutheran Church in Erdman, for either Emillia/Amelia Wetzel or David Paul.

As if it weren't tragic enough to lose a single child, the family of Jacob W. Erdman and Catharine Seitz Erdman suffered the loss of three young children right before Christmas - all due to scarlet fever. They lost two daughters on the same day—December 17: Emanda, 11 years old, born June 18, 1848, and Jane, 9 years old, born January 5, 1850. Three days later, just four days before Christmas, they would lose their son, Isaac, 5 years old, born March 7, 1854. Both Rev. Stiehly's and Salem Church burial records list these children.

The census records indicate that Rev. Stiehly's own son, Petrus, was suffering from scarlet fever at the same time that the Reverend was conducting funeral services for the Erdman children. We can only imagine what Rev. Stiehly was thinking and feeling as he consoled the Erdman family. In the week following the death of young Isaac Erdman, Rev. Stiehly would suffer losses of his own.

On Christmas day, 1859, 9-year-old Petrus, son of Rev. Isaac Stiehly and his wife Anna Knorr Stiehly, would succumb to complications of scarlet fever after 21 days of illness. Unfortunately, it was not to end there for the Stiehly family. Three days later, on December 28th, the Stiehly family lost baby Emma, 7 months old, to scarlet fever. She was the daughter of Jared and Elizabeth Stiehly, and the granddaughter of Rev. Stiehly and Anna Knorr Stiehly. This is documented in Salem Church burial records. How Rev. Stiehly's faith must have been tested in those cold and dark days!

The census mortality record lists the death of 7-year-old Cassy Shadel in January of 1860, as the last death due to scarlet fever. The website Findagrave.com lists a Catherine Schadel born July 27, 1852, who died January 2, 1860, and is buried at Zion Lutheran Church in Erdman. It states that she is the daughter of Abraham Schadel and Froenica Schneider. This is probably the same child. Cassy/Cassie is a nickname for Catherine, and the date of death and age at time of death coincide with the census information.

Ten years before the scarlet fever epidemic in Upper Mahantongo Township, Louisa May Alcott wrote her famous book **Little Women** which includes words that help us relate to the fear and tragedy: "How dark the days seemed now, how sad and lonely the house, and how heavy were the hearts of the sisters as they worked and waited, while the shadow of death hovered over the once happy home." While this book is a work of fiction, the author pulls from her heart and puts into words the real grief she felt as her own sister suffered and died of complications of scarlet fever.

We can see why scarlet fever once struck fear in the hearts of people. It stole their children away! The streptococcus bacteria that cause scarlet fever spread easily and quickly, and in the 1800s there were epidemics. Scarlet fever can be easily treated with antibiotics today, but throughout the 1800s, children younger than 10 years old were especially at risk of death or serious complications from the toxic bacteria, including rheumatic fever which seriously weakened the heart. More information on scarlet fever can be found at:

http://www.humanillnesses.com/original/Pre-Sei/Scarlet-fever.html#ixzz3by06f7Ey

The families and the community must have breathed a deep sigh of relief and thanked God for his mercifulness when they were confident the scourge of scarlet fever had moved on. What a sad Christmas season for all of the families who were affected, not only in the infamous year of 1859, but during future Christmases as well when memories of their losses were relived!

While the epidemic was tragic in its scope, the deaths of the two other children who died that year are also worthy of note. Jerrom Hart, 1 year old, died after suffering 120 days from an illness described in the mortality census as "head pluricy". He was likely the son of James Hart and his wife Sarah who are enumerated in the 1860 Federal Census for Upper Mahantongo Township, Rough & Ready Post Office, conducted by the same person who conducted the mortality census, Wertheimer. In the household are listed a daughter Sarah, 9 years old, and a daughter Anna, 4 years old.

One-year-old Caresta Tobias who died in September of 1859 of unknown causes is the last of the children to be remembered. There are three young Tobias families listed on the 1860 U.S. Federal Census for Upper Mahantongo Township, Schuylkill County, PA.

- Family #1025 - John (38) and Sally (42) Tobias
- Family #1011 - Jacob (27) and Mary (27)
- Family #1007 Joseph (22) and Catherine (21)

All of the Tobias families have young children listed in the household except for Joseph and Catherine. From the census records, the family of Caresta cannot be determined with any certainty.

Three adults also died that year. One of them was Solomon Ertman, 37 years old, who died in October 1859. His occupation was listed as Blacksmith, and his illness was listed as Consumption. Today we know this bacterial disease as tuberculosis which is preventable and treatable. Solomon is listed in the 1850 Federal Census for Upper Mahantango Township as the head of Dwelling #179 with his wife Elizabeth, 30, and their children Polly, aged 4, and Lydia, aged 3. By the 1860 Federal Census for Upper Mahantongo Township, Elizabeth is the head of the household with Polly, Liddy, Daniel aged 5, and Elithabeth, aged 1 year. Also listed in the household is Henry Kline, 20 years old, with an occupation of Blacksmith. It appears that after Solomon died, Elizabeth was fortunate to have Henry continue the Blacksmith operation of her deceased husband, to support her and her young family after the death of their father.

George Simmy, a farmer, also died of Consumption, in January of 1860, at the age of 63. The Simmy family were of African American heritage, and were noted landowners as well as church and community leaders. Elsewhere in this book and in others, Steve E. Troutman writes of the Simmy family who were very early settlers in the Mahantongo Valley.

The oldest person listed on the 1860 mortality census was Ann Maria Maurer who died in June of 1859 at the age of 72. Her cause of death is listed as cough and inflammation after an illness of 2 days. I located a Maria Maurer, aged 64, in the 1850 Federal Census records for Upper Mahantongo Township. She was living in Dwelling #165 with the family of John H. Maurer, aged 24, farmer, Nelly, aged 25, David 6 months, and David P., aged 14. Nancy J. Rochelle Charlesworth confirmed that the Maria listed in this household is the same Ann Maria listed on the mortality schedule. She indicated that Ann Maria was her third great grandmother, and John H. and Nellie were her 2nd great grandparents. Records on the website Ancestry.com indicate that Ann Maria was born Anna Maria Zerbe on January 1, 1787, in Berks County, PA. She married Heinrich Maurer who predeceased her in 1845. Heinrich was the son of the Revolutionary War soldier Daniel Maurer and his wife Regina Wagner. More research would need to be done to determine the parents of Anna Maria Zerbe. Heinrich and Anna Maria had a number of children and many descendants. Nancy J. Rochelle Charlesworth sent me a 19-page descendant report for Heinrich and Anna Maria Maurer.

Earlier in this article, Marilyn Malick Herb is quoted as saying that the number of childhood deaths listed in Reverend Isaac Stiehly's burial records were staggering. Steve E. and Joan Troutman shared with me burial records of Rev. Isaac F. Stiehly. These documents covered an approximate 8 ½ year period of time from August 22, 1859 to Dec. 21, 1867. They are from the library of Dr. Glenn P. Schwalm and are contained in the Schuylkill County Pennsylvania Archives Vol. II by Phillip A. Rice and Jean A. Dellock published by Closson Press.

One might suspect that in a small rural community, in less than 9 years' time, there would be few deaths, especially of children. However, when I counted the number of children that he had buried during that time period, I learned that 246 had perished. Staggering is indeed an apt description!

While most did not list a cause of death, Rev. Stiehly recorded some of the details concerning burials he had conducted in his family Bible. Causes of these deaths were: poison, convulsions, typhoid fever, diphtheria, "laussinbin," slowed and continued fever for 9 days, diarrhea with blood stools, and brain fever (encephalitis).

The words that affected me the most were this translated passage from Rev. Stiehly's Bible: "Buried a daughter of Isaac Fisher and wife Sarah (nee Hain). Born on May 9, 1863, Tremont Twp., Schuylkill Co., PA. Baptized and named Sarah . . . Illness was "Scharlay Fubar" (Scarlet Fever) and suffered for 7 days. Died last Wednesday afternoon (December 21, 1864) at 4 o'clock. Aged: 1 y. 7m. 12 d." The dreaded Scarlet Fever had returned to the valley to plague yet another Christmas season.

I have to admit that prior to my research, I had a romanticized vision of the mid-19th century. I thought of that time as "the good old days" when life was more serene and less hurried. Now, I have a new appreciation for today's technology, for advances in medicine, and particularly for the antibiotics that allow our children and loved ones to survive the lethal infections and diseases of times past.

Salem's Church Cemetery Visit

On July 16, 2015, I visited Salem's Church cemetery in Rough and Ready with the intent of locating grave markers for those listed on the Upper Mahantongo Township mortality schedule of 1860. The day was bright and sunny, sharply contrasting with the sad evidence I sought.

I first located the stone of Emenda Erdman (Figure 2 below). Steve E. Troutman notes that Rev. Isaac Stiehly, the pastor who performed the burial rites, carved the stone and put his signature "fan" beneath the inscription. The stone graphically illustrates the tragedy of the epidemic.

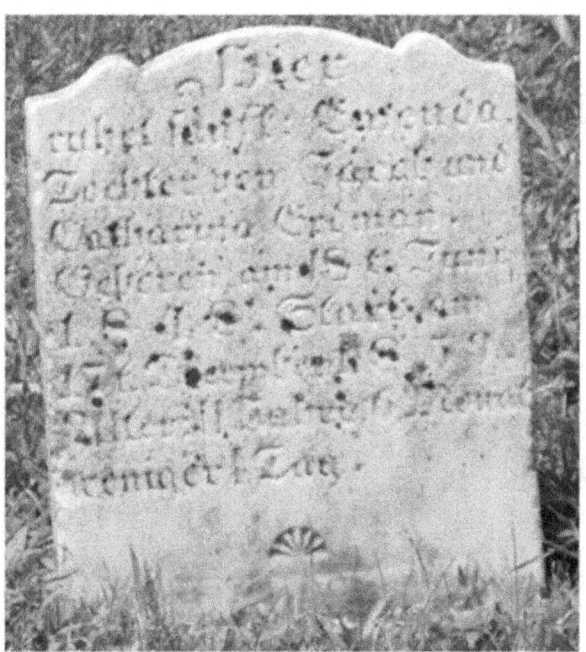

Figure 2: Emenda Erdman headstone

Steve notes that the veteran preacher, Isaac Stiehly, must have been deeply moved by this child's death. He included the German words "sanft" which means "gentle" and "weniger" which means "less than". Steve indicated that he has never seen these words engraved on another marker. Isaac covered the stone's face fully with his tribute to this little girl.

Located beside the stone of Emenda are nearly identical sized and shaped stones for her sister Jane, aged 9, who died on the same day, and her brother Isaac, 5, who died 4 days later (Figures 3 and 4 below).

Figure 3: Jane Erdman headstone

Figure 4: Isaac Erdman headstone

While Rev. Isaac Stiehly's signature fan was only visible at the bottom of the heavily worn stones of Emenda and Isaac, it was evident that all three of the Erdman children's stones had been carved by Isaac Stiehly.

To the right of Isaac Erdman's stone was another stone that was a little larger and whiter with a unique shape. (See Figure 5 right.) The inscription on the stone was obviously German, but the stone was well worn, and the words difficult to read. I examined the stone for quite some time in the glare of the bright sunshine before realizing that I was looking at the stone of Petrus Stiehly, Rev. Isaac and Anna Knorr Stiehly's son! The stone was unlike any of the stones carved by Isaac Stiehly. There was no fan carving—just the 9-year-old boy's name "Petrus" in relief below a small bell-shaped ornament at the top of the stone followed by the inscribed dates of his birth and death. Perhaps it had been too painful for Rev. Stiehly to carve into stone the details of his own son's short life and early death on that fateful Christmas day in 1859. The graves of the three Erdman children and that of Petrus Stiehly lie side by side in the order of their deaths starting 8 days before Christmas and concluding on Christmas day in 1859.

I next located the stone that marked George Simmy's grave. (Figure 6 right). It was easily recognizable as an Isaac Stiehly carved stone by its style and ornamentation, including Stiehly's signature "fan" at the top corners and bottom center of the stone. Of the many stones carved by Isaac Stiehly in this cemetery, the stone for George Simmy was one of the largest and most elaborately ornamented. It visually spoke to the respect and honor that Rev. Stiehly bestowed upon this important member of the church and community. The land upon which the church was built was once part of George Simmy's extensive land holdings in Upper Mahantongo Township. I found it interesting that the words carved on the stone were not in Rev. Stiehly's familiar fine German script, but in English. Possibly this was done to acknowledge Mr. Simmy's non-German heritage or his spoken language. The mortality schedule notes that Mr. Simmy was mulatto. Steve E. Troutman has written extensively of the Simmy family who were among the very first settlers to the region, in the late 18th century.

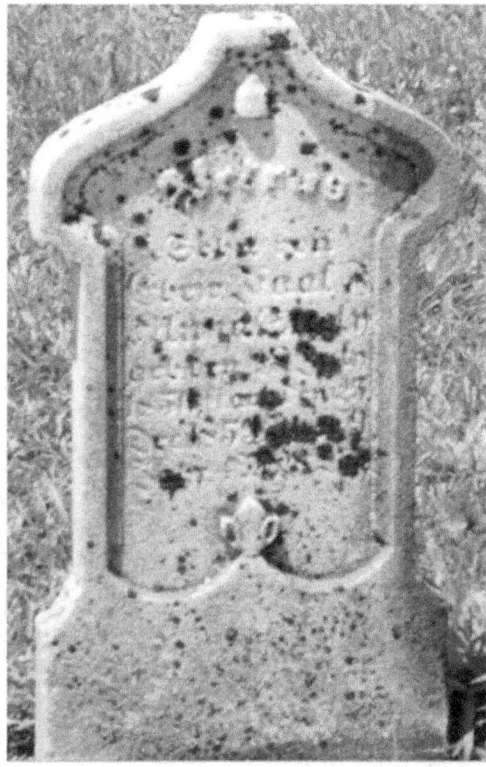

Figure 5: Petrus Stiehly headstone   *Figure 6: George Simmy headstone*

After researching for this article and visiting Salem's cemetery, I found myself mourning with the families and their living descendants for the loss of all these young children and other loved ones. While their lives were extinguished some 150 years ago, it is my hope that our research and interest in their histories will serve as an enduring testament to their lives.

Herb's Mill lately known as Erdman's Mill is located on Mahantongo Creek. Mahantongo Creek is east of this location. The mill dam was located east of this photo with the race constructed on the west side of the creek. The mill building stood east of the millhouse residence, between the tall trees. Mae (Smith) Erdman lived here when the mill was removed in 1981. Most local residents recall the name as Erdman's Mill.

The following is taken from an article by Donald Graves in the Weekender Pottsville Republican, August 26, 1989.
"May Erdman still lives in the miller's house occupied by her husband's family. She said the mill was worn out by the time it was torn down. 'The race went bad and the mill went bad,' she said. The Erdman mill was a timber-frame building on a stone foundation. Donald Stiely, who lives down stream from the Erdman mill, worked at the mill years ago. 'The mill stones were intact then,' he said, 'but the mill was operated by a tractor motor.'

Larona Heim's interview follows in the next pages.
She spent a lot of time at this Grist Mill and Mill House location. She is now deceased.

Larona Heim Remembers the Erdman's Mill, 31 March 2011.

Larona Heim lives near the Erdman's Mill, as it was known to the present generation and previous generations. This mill was earlier named Herb's Mill when the mill was operated by Henry Herb. The Herb family was prominent in the Rough and Ready area. Adam Herb operated the Rough and Ready General Store and the Salem Church located nearby was locally called Herb's Church. Adam and Henry are buried in the Salem Cemetery.

Adam Herb, (1787-1860) 73 y. 26 da., Married Magdalena Herb (15 Aug. 1792-22 May 1868) 75 y. 7 mo. 7 da. (Row 7)

Henry S. Herb, son of Adam and Magdalena Herb, (10 July 1826-18 May 1899), 72y. 10 mo., 8 da., Married Catherine, wife of Henry Herb, (24 June 1830-Dec. 1870), age 46 y. 6 mo. (Row 6)

Oscar and Ida Erdman operated the Erdman's Mill known by that name. Ida's father was a Knorr. Ida was a sister to Larona Heim's grandmother, Jenny Knorr, who never married. Jenny's daughter, Lila Marie Brown, married Henry "Tiny" Heim. Jenny and Marie and Henry Heim lived nearby the mill but on the opposite side of the creek. Fortunately for these sisters, Jenny and Ida, there was a bridge over the Mahantongo Creek and they could easily travel back and forth daily between the farm and the mill. Larona remembers her mother Marie was very close to her Aunt Ida and lived with them in the millhouse as a young grade school age girl. Oscar and Ida had a son Raymond, who was close in age to Marie, and they were good buddies. Marie lived with the Erdman's at the millhouse until she married. After her marriage to "Tiny" Heim, Marie moved back across the creek to her mother's home and lived there on her mother's homestead which had been a Knorr farm since the time of the first settlers.

The iron bridge which connected the mill and the old Knorr farm is now removed. After the 1972 flood, repairs were too costly and the bridge was abandoned and removed. Larona recalls this area was bustling with activity and was known as a place of gathering for the local folks. The gristmill dam was a short distance downstream from the iron bridge over Mahantongo Creek. A dam was constructed of logs and wooden planks, which created a waterfall. The milldam ponded the water which backed up underneath the bridge. A short distance farther upstream was the confluence of the Little Mahantongo Creek and the Mahantongo Creek. This joining place of the waters can be easily seen today from the township road. Many floods over time have changed the creek's location. The main flow of the water is now adjacent to the road where the mill race was previously located. Earlier the creek had been situated further east allowing the construction of the earthen race to be established where now no land exists. Larona recalled a "truck patch" for garden vegetables between the race and the township road. This land is also now washed away.

An ice house stood directly in front of the bridge on the west side of the township road. An excavated depression in the rock bank remains visible today. Harvesting ice from the milldam was a continuing process through the winter. The ice was packed in the ice house and covered with sawdust for insulation. This ice was the only method of cooling the food in the icebox during the summer months. Oscar Erdman had a sawmill south of the gristmill. Larona recalls that it was powered by a large one cylinder engine. This sawmill was the source of sawdust used in the ice house.

The millrace carried the water from the milldam to the gristmill where the water wheel was located underneath the mill on the east side. The race was not long in length so the milldam must have been high to provide the necessary drop in elevation to provide water power to turn the waterwheel. A millstone was used as a stepping stone at the doorway entrance to the gristmill. The grain was hoisted by rope and pulley to the third floor which was used as grain storage and an office. On the second floor the millstones were located which produced flour and corn meal as recalled by Larona. Animal feed was produced on the first floor level. A little brown dog named Jackie, was the miller's companion and was often seen sitting at the open mill doors on the second floor level. The dog watched the activity outside as grain was lifted up and feed and flour was loaded on wagons and trucks below. 1946 was an important year. They got electricity. No doubt electric lights were first installed and motors came later.

Oscar Erdman was an important person in the community. Not only was he the miller, but he also did "pow-wowing", or faith healing. Many people came to him seeking cures for their ailments. Oscar "pow-wowed" for Larona several times. Raymond Erdman, the son of Oscar, was one of the last to operate the mill. He married Mae Smith late in life. Mae was from up the valley, east of the Village of Franklin Square. A road named "Smith Road" exists today identifying the area where Mae originated. Raymond and Mae married in the late 1960's. They did not have any children. Raymond's widow, Mae, was the last of the Erdman family to own the mill. It was removed about 1981 as nature's elements had taken their toll and a lack of repairs caused the old building to collapse. The Erdman families are buried at the Salem Church Cemetery.

William Oscar Erdman (d. 22 May 1961) age 75 y. 7 mo. 29 da. Married Mrs. Oscar Erdman (d. 16 Jan. 1961) age 77 y. 4 mo. 19 da.

Raymond E. Erdman (d. 7 Nov. 1970) age 58. Married Mae H. Erdman (d. 21 May 1990) age 73.

Larona Heim married Bob Heim (now descease). They have children Karen, married to Dennis Heim, Kenneth "Butch" Heim, and Darlene who is married to David Roadcap.

The following photos were reproduced from slides taken by Steve E. Troutman, 4th of July, 1981. A previous conversation with May Erdman gave permission to remove two millstones from the collapsed Erdman Mill ruin. The mill walls fell down as Mother Nature took its toll on a building not maintained. The extra heavy timbers which framed the mill gears remained strong and held up the collapsed mill walls. The massive mill wheel grinding mechanism remained in place until the end of its existence. One grindstone seen here had fallen from the second story down onto and through the first floor. This stone can be seen in the photograph and is presently on display at the home of Joseph Michetti near Klingerstown.

Part III: The Mills of the Upper Mahantongo Valley

Antonio D. Michetti and Michael S. Troutman pose near the west wall of the Erdman's Mill.

Michael S. Troutman inspects a fallen grindstone.

Interior of the mill's second story, where grindstones were located. A round wooden tub which surrounded a set of grindstones is seen here on the left.

The fine workmanship of the mill builders is seen here with well mortised braces in strong planed timbers.

Part III: The Mills of the Upper Mahantongo Valley

The Herb-Erdman mill desk placed on a stool for a photo. The miller's journal was kept here. It was originally painted red, wall mounted, and supported by two front legs. Later it was painted green and was occupied by a family of mice for many years!

Herb-Erdman millstone used to grind cornmeal according to Mae Erdman.

Mrs. Mae (Smith) Erdman, July 4, 1981, in front of a small stone out building across the road from the millhouse.

Earl Troutman lifts the fallen millstone. Ruby Michetti watches. Steve Tressler is in the bucket. Michael Troutman, Tony, Rosa, and Angelina Michetti look on.

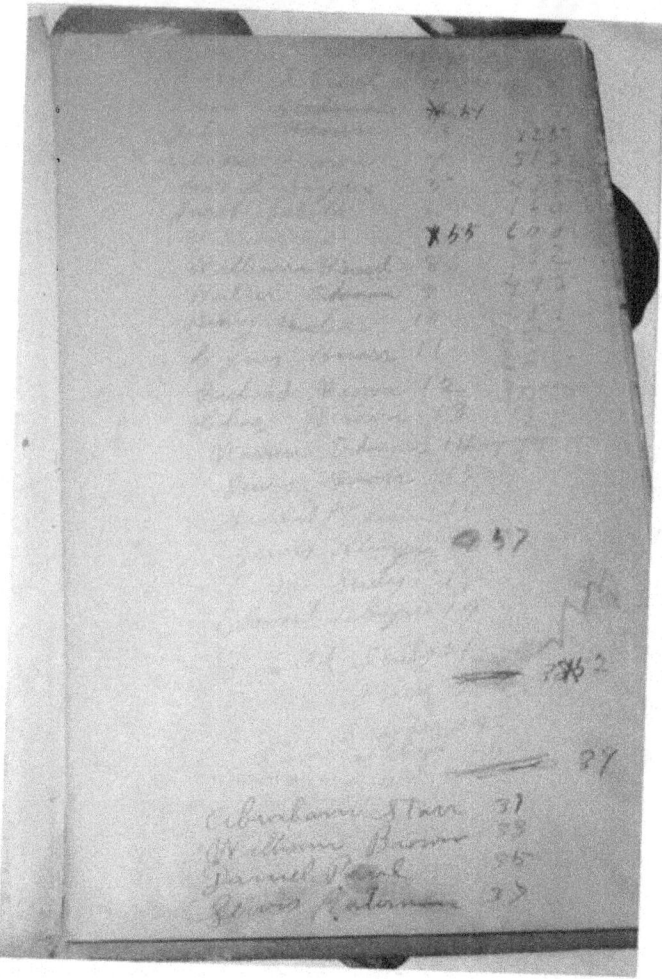

Above-
Elsworth Klinger account
17 entries total $13.24
Flour in 25 lb. Batch is .75
Cornmeal in 10 lb. Batch is .25
Middlings in 50 lb. Batch is .73

Oscar and Raymond Erdman in an automobile in front of the mill. Looking south.

Erdman's mill with Jackie the dog, looking out. Photo restored. Looking east. The Mahantongo Creek is behind the mill. Photo print date October 1960.

Henry Herb Gristmill-Oscar Erdman Gristmill

The Herb Family was in the gristmilling business. According to the 150th anniversary book of the Salem Church, the Salem Church was also known as Herb's Church, probably because it was in the vicinity of Adam Herb's store in Rough and Ready and Henry Herb's mill which operated on what was Mrs. Mae Erdman's property south of the church. This mill was located south of the junction of Mahantongo Creek and Little Mahantongo Creek. The mill dam was located on Mahantongo Creek and the millrace was established on the west side of the creek and carried the water a short distance south of the mill. This mill was in a very deteriorated condition, 30 years ago. One of the outside walls had collapsed, opening the interior to the outside elements. Mrs. Erdman lived in the millhouse next door. The large heavy millstones were originally located on the upper second floor level of the mill. I believe there were 3 sets of stones. One set had fallen down through the first floor to the earthen ground below. We used a chain and a tractor loader to pull the stone up and out of the building. The millstone was constructed of many stones held together by an iron band. It is presently on display in the yard at Joseph Michetti's residence, near Klingerstown. A smaller millstone, approximately 30 inches in diameter, was used to grind corn, as I was informed from Mrs. Erdman. Local residents recall the last name associated with this gristmill was Erdman's mill. The building is now removed.

Oscar and Ida Erdman rest in peace at Salem Cemetery in Rough and Ready.

Samuel Knorr Grist Mill, lately Stehr Brother's Mill

A color painting from a photo of Samuel Knorr's grist mill on Little Mahanotongo Creek

This mill is located at the county line between Northumberland and Schuylkill Counties and was built in 1808.

Interview with Alvin Stehr of Ridge Road, Klingerstown, PA, March 4, 2014.

The last mill to operate in the valley was lately known as Stehr Brother's Mill. It is located at the county line between Northumberland and Schuylkill Counties on Little Mahantongo Creek. This mill has a stone foundation on which the first floor brick walls were built. The second floor is constructed of timber framing with massive beams supporting the millstones and the necessary gearing to turn them. This still exists today.

Herbert Knorr sold this mill to Joseph Irvin Stehr in 1912. At that time the wooden water wheel still powered the mill. The mill dam was located where a nearby home is built today. Joseph replaced the wooden mill wheel with an iron wheel. Joseph I. Stehr had married into the Gahres family which had a long tradition of milling. His father-in-law introduced this profession to Joseph and he chose it to be his own. The Gahres mill is located south of Franklin Square on Creek Road. This is the Marjorie Gahres Boyer residence today and this mill is still known as "The Old Red Mill".

Joseph's sons Chester, Joe, and Alvin Stehr, continued their father's milling business. They replaced the rolling mill in 1950, which was sold for scrap, with a modern hammer mill. By this time the mill was powered by a petroleum fueled engine. Stehr Brothers, Inc. advertised their business as "In the heart of the Mahantongo Valley". The mill operated until October 10, 1992, when it was sold on public sale.

Part III: The Mills of the Upper Mahantongo Valley

Samuel Knorr Gristmill

Elmer Fetterolf Farm

An early Fetterolf farm in Schuylkill County just across the county line from Northumberland County, on the Little Mahantongo Creek, between Rough and Ready and Pitman. The red brick mill to the right side of the farm house was lately known as Stehr Brother's Mill. The large farm home was a double house. This farm could be the Peter Fetterolf pioneer homestead. Photo courtesy of Kenny Fetterolf, Rattlesnake Road, Leck Kill, Pa. Kenny Fetterolf lived here in his childhood.

Elmer Fetterolf Farm

Samuel Knorr Gristmill

Another early established gristmill on Little Mahantongo Creek, was located several miles upstream from Herb's Mill previously described. This mill was lately known as Stehr Brother's Mill. Presently it is the location of Titan Abrasives. This brick building has been restored and well taken care of. The mill was built by Samuel Knorr, (1811-1867) and should be referred to as the Samuel Knorr gristmill for historical purposes. Samuel Knorr's father was Heinrich Knorr, one of the three sons of Christian Knorr, who divided Peter Knorr's 300 acre tract near Rough and Ready. Henry, Peter, and John, were the sons of Peter Knorr. Peter's daughter, Anna, married Isaac Faust Stiely.

Aaron H. Knorr, (1833-1900) was the son of Samuel. In the 1860 census, he is listed as living next to his father, farming. His father Samuel is listed as a gristmiller. This mill location is near the county line. Jenny Knorr was from this mill family and married Elmer Fetterolf. They raised a large family at this location. Elmer became a very successful produce huckster, owning 5 farms during his lifetime. He was also a large shareholder in the Klingerstown Bank during the Great Depression and suffered severe financial loss as a result of the Bank's failure.

Part III: The Mills of the Upper Mahantongo Valley

Line Mountain Mills between Leck Kill and Pitman, PA

by Steve and Joan Troutman

Clement and Pauline Masser began housekeeping in a quaint mill-house between Leck Kill and Pitman, Pa. This was close by the home of Charles and Salome Masser, Clement's parents. Not many people realize that the roadside green shingled cottage was associated with a mill. June and Mark spend their early years in this dwelling. This location is presently just east of the Neal and Ruth Masser home. Here the little Mahantongo Creek flows through the Masser farm fields today which provided water power for many small mills of yesterday. Charles Masser's homestead was originally known as the Line Mountain Hotel. This stopping place later became the Line Mountain Post Office. Nearby was the Maurer's one room school and the Jacob's (Howerter's) Union church.

The mills that were built performed some tasks which are mostly unknown today. A linseed oil mill was located on this Masser farm south of Neal and Ruth Masser's home. Linseed oil from flax seed was used for paint and was burned in lamps. The crushed seeds were fed to the animals. Linseeds come from the flax plant.

Line Mountain Mill House

Donald Graves reported in his Pottsville Republican Weekender article of August 26, 1989.

"Felix Masser's farm near Pitman was the site of a linseed oil mill. Linseed oil, from flax seed was used for paint and was burned in lamps. The crushed seeds were fed to animals. The oil mill is identified on an 1830 county map. It later became a grist mill. The mill had already ceased operation by the time Masser's father, Charles, moved to the farm. Its timbers were used to build two wagon sheds which remain on his farm. His father removed the stone foundation and with it, built a cattle wall in front of his barn, which also remains. The wooden stairs of the mill now lead to the hay loft in Masser's barn.

The mill had two raceways, from the Little Mahantongo Creek and the other from a nearby mountain run that supplemented the creek water.

While the mill site is now farmed, the mill house remains on the north side of Route 4022. Like the mill, it is a timber frame house.

Masser knew the last miller, Adam Switzer, who told him he preferred to grind at night when the water level was higher. In addition to the grist mill, the farm also had a cider press and a sawmill on the site, according to Masser. 'We'd get wheat straw and sip the cider,' he said. The cider was stored in 50 gallon barrels.

The mill house stood until 2008.

The sawmill used a vertical saw blade which went up and down rather than the circular blades used today. There were more than 10 sawmills in the upper Mahantongo Valley, according to an 1875 map of the area."

Part III: The Mills of the Upper Mahantongo Valley

This gristmill stone rests in the barnyard of Niel Masser. Niel is the son of Felix Masser. The gristmill was established nearby along Little Mahantongo Creek. The foundation stones from this mill were re-set as the barnyard stone wall in front of the barn along the Pitman-Leck Kill highway. In the distance note the little green shingle house called the "millhouse".

Flax is raised for fiber and seeds. The fiber can be spun and woven into many products. Rope, delicate linen fabrics, laces, clothes, flour bags, tablecloths, and even summer sausage casings used by the butcher to smoke meats, were made of hand sewn linen. The flax plants stand up to 4 feet high with small branching stems near the top. They usually have blue flowers. Before flax can be processed, the seeds must be removed. Processing the flax fiber is a very long process including soaking in water, drying, breaking the stems, and combing the fibers to make cord and thread. Linen has a silky luster.

The linseed oil mill is identified on an 1830 county map. It later became a grist mill. The mill had already ceased operation by the time Charles Masser moved to the farm. Its timbers were used to build two wagon sheds which remain on the farm. Charles removed the stone foundation and with it built a cattle wall in front of his barn which remains. The wooden stairs of the mill now lead to the hay loft in Neal Masser's barn. The mill had 2 raceways, one from the Little Mahantongo Creek and the other from a nearby mountain run that supplemented the creek water. Adam Switzer was the last miller. He preferred to grind at night when the water level was higher. In addition to the grist mill, the farm also had a cider press and a saw mill on the site, according to Felix Masser, now deceased. "We'd get a wheat straw and sip the cider", he said. The cider was stored in 50 gallon barrels. The saw mill used a vertical saw blade that went up and down, rather than the circular blades used today.

J.K. Maurer operated a Hotel and Line Mountain Post Office at this location in 1875.

The Line Mountain Hotel was established by the Maurer Family. Later this dwelling was well known as the residence of Charles and Salome Masser. This photo from the album of Salome Masser and shows the home at the time of purchase.

Charles and Salome Masser do Business on the Front Porch

For a number of years a Pennsylvania German Fersommling was held at Kevin's Place in Lykens, PA. Sterman Masser was one of the organizers. The Pennsylvania German dialect was spoken at this gathering. Sterman gave the following story to the group after the evening meal.

Sterman's grandparents were Charles and Salome Masser of Leck Kill. They were prosperous farmers who raised fruit and vegetables for market. They had livestock as well, including pigs, chickens, and cows. Their large farm house had been earlier established as the Line Mountain Hotel and post office. It was easily assessable being situated at an intersection on the main road. Charles and Salome were some of the larger farmers in the area.

Charles and Salome often met with their neighbors on the front porch to conduct business related to the farm. Sometimes the Masser bull was with the neighbors cows for breeding purposes. Sometimes the Masser boar's services were needed for the neighbor's sow. This was common business and the neighbors often paid their bill on the front porch of the big farm house. Several steps led up to the long south facing porch, where a knock on the door was answered by Salome. Although Charles arranged the business, Salome was the "bill" collector.

One day a neighbor woman knocked on Salome's door. She was upset. She told Salome that her maid (the neighbor's hired woman) was with Charles Masser's "knecht" (hired man). Her maid was now with child and she wondered what Salome was going to do about this. Salome replied, "I know what to charge for the bull and I know what to charge for the boar, but I do not know what to charge for this!" No doubt, the neighbor lady left speechless.

Jacob and Catherine Masser, the grandparents of Charles Masser, depicted in charcoal.

The History of Northumberland Co., by Bell, p. 709, states: "The Line Mountain Hotel was built by Daniel Herb in 1808 and opened as a house of public entertainment in 1813. Among the landlords in the past have been Daniel Herb, Philip Maurer, Samuel Rothermel, and Isaiah Kiehl." Joan Masser Troutman indicated that this Hotel was later operated by J.K. Maurer. Joan's grandparents, Salome and Charles Masser, raised their family of 8 children here. The hotel was built next to the Howerter's Church and the Maurer's School. Although the old Line Mountain Hotel no longer exists, a similar house remains today. This brick house, the Daycock residence, is located approximately one mile west of where the old hotel earlier stood at the intersection of Rt. 125 and State Rt. 3010.

The History of Northumberland Co., by Bell, p. 710, states: "Samuel Rothermel's mill on Mahantongo Creek, at the line between Northumberland and Schuylkill Counties, was built in 1808 by Daniel Herb." The 1863 *Map of Schuylkill Co.*, by Scott, locates Herb's Mill east of the old hotel on the farm presently owned by Neil Masser. Among the grist mills identified downstream on the 1863 map is *Knarrs G. Mill*, (later Stehr Brother's); Samuel Knorr is named as the grist miller here on the 1860 Census. Note that this mill is built of bricks like the Line Mountain Hotel. Other mills identified include: another *Herb's G. Mill*, (last named Erdman's), *Rev. Isaac Stiely's G. Mill*, *Wiest's G. Mill* in Klingerstown, *Klinger's G. Mill* in the Klingerstown Gap, *Miller's G. Mill*, (later Monroe and Harvey Stiely). *Maurer's woolen mill*, (later Atkins) is near the Howerter's Church. Also identified in 1863 are *Herb's Hotel* (later Stine's Hotel), which is presently being removed in 2017. An earlier dwelling existed here with a large walk-in fireplace. *Fetterolf's sawmill* (on the Elwood Rothermel farm), was on Little Mahantongo Creek.

Jacob's Lutheran and Reformed Church and the Mills Nearby

Donald Graves, reporter for the Pottsville Republican Weekender of August 26, 1989, wrote the following:
"Old mills are fading into the past. The Mahantongo Valley of western Schuylkill County has lost much of its early self-sufficiency when farmers took their grain, flax, timber, and apples by wagon to nearby mills and brought flour, animal feed, linseed oil, lumber, and cider. The mills used the power of the Mahantongo and Little Mahantongo to turn vast machines of iron and wood.

A wool mill originally built by John Maurer (1783-1854) was on Little Mahantongo Creek. Later purchased by William Atkins, it processed sheep fleeces from valley farmers into blankets, trousers, and other items.
Henry Reiner owns the site where the mill was located. Reiner said the roof of the timber-frame mill had fallen in and the walls were collapsing by the time he tore it down years ago. The foundation stones were re-used in the foundation of a nearby bridge.
Water for the mill came from a dam in a grove of trees located behind the mill site. From the dam the water flowed to the mill in a mill race whose location is still outlined by a fence row. The mill's water power was later replaced by a massive, one cylinder, hit-and-miss motor."

Post card of Jacob's Lutheran and Reformed Church. Note the first meeting house-school roof on the left. Maurer's Hotel and post office was nearby as well as a grist mill, an oil mill, woolen mill, and a one room school house. The church burned in 9/23/1943.

William Atkins woolen mill was located south of Jacob's Church
The early oil mill was east of Jacob's Church.
Both these mills were located on Little Mahantongo Creek

Location of Atkins Woolen Mill

There was another mill near by on the Henry Reiner farm, also on the Little Mahantongo Creek. This mill was originally built by John Maurer (1783-1854) and processed sheep fleece from valley farmers into blankets, trousers, and other items. Later it was purchased by William Atkins. Henry Reiner said the roof of the timber-frame mill had fallen in and the walls were collapsing by the time he tore it down years ago. The foundation stones were used in the foundation of a near by bridge. Water for the mill came from a dam in a grove of trees behind the mill site. From the dam, the water flowed to the mill in a mill race whose location is still outlined by a fence row.

Perhaps this woolen mill was originally built to process linen cloth. The existence of a linseed oil mill near by, indicates that flax processing as well as wool processing must have been performed. In fact, the linseed oil mill would be earlier than the woolen mill. American pioneers often planted seed flax as their first crop. Domestic animal herds would have been established by a later generation of farmers and herdsmen.

The pioneers of the Mahantongo Valley of western Schuylkill County were very self-sufficient. The farmers took their grain, flax, timber, and apples by wagon to near by mills and brought home flour, animal feed, linseed oil, lumber, and cider.

The mill house stood until 2008.

William Atkins woolen mill was established along Little Mahantongo Creek in this lowland now farmed by the sons of Henry Reiner. Henry recalled the foundation stones from the mill were used to build the bridge over Little Mahantongo Creek. The scene is south of Jacob's Cemetery where at least five Revolutionary War soldiers are buried. They are named Reiner, Beisel, Klock, Howerter, and Diehl.

Peter Henninger established this mill later owned by the Gehres Family and remembered as the Gehres Mill. It is located south of the village of Franklin Square on Mahantongo Creek.

The following is taken and edited from an article by Donald Graves in the <u>Weekender Pottsville Republican,</u> August 26, 1989. He described the Old Red Mill.

"Just west of Route 125, on Mahantongo Creek, is a gristmill in the upper part of the valley. This is the mill that Joe Stehr operated before purchasing his own on the Little Mahantongo Creek. Margaret (Gahres) Dietrich(1) Boyer(2) lives in the miller's house which replaces an earlier house. Her great-grandfather, John Gahres, and her grandfather, Harry Gahres, both ran the mill. Before that it was operated by Peter Henninger in 1854, according to a sign on the property. Several millstones remain as well as a large iron wheel, a sifting machine, and other mill equipment. The mill made both flour and feed. Harold Carpenter, a neighboring farmer said the millrace crossed his farm with the milldam farther up the creek. In June or July, Carpenter said, the Gahreses would use scythes to cut the weeds in the millrace. They would also would also repair any breaks or washouts of the earthen race. While the gristmill stopped operation by the mid 1950's it continued as a cider mill until 1972. The press was powered by a tractor."

Marjorie (Gahres) Boyer interview, Feb. 17, 2011, at the mill house next door.
Parents-Irvin and Ida Gahres, Grandparents-Harry and Frona Gahres
Great-Grandparents-John and Lydia Gahres

Harry operated the mill in the late 1930's and manufactured animal feed.
John made flour for the earlier generations.
Both men used water for power.

The mill wheel is at the northeast corner of the mill and was fed by a water trough from the race. The water exited the mill through a pipe under the yard to the creek.

Haas Foundry—One Mile West of Franklin Square

An iron industry was established east of Rough and Ready, near the Village of Hepler. It was known as the Haas Foundry. Rev. Elden Ehrhart wrote the following in the book, <u>One Hundred Fiftieth Anniversary Celebration of Salem United Church of Christ</u>, in 1980:

"Samuel Y. Haas, who died in 1876, at the age of 39, was an inventive genius. He and his brother David, took over the Haas foundry at the line that presently separates Eldred and Upper Mahantongo Township. Everything and anything the people needed was made at this foundry; grain cradles, plowshares, steam engines, sawmills, etc. The first bicycle in the county, perhaps the state, was made in this shop by William Snyder in 1873. The first automobile in the county was made in here by one of the Haas brothers. Samuel had but three days of schooling, yet at an early age, according to the SHAMOKIN TIMES of April 1876, he showed remarkable inventive genius and mechanical skill. He was a watchmaker, machinist, painter, carpenter, worked with iron and brass, and could, as people said, do everything and yet never learned a trade. He taught and composed music. At the age of 14, he made a "French piano" which played eight tunes. At age 18, he made a steam engine and a small rotary engine. He felt it was foolishness to wind a watch every day, so he made a watch that ran for eight days without winding. He made a machine for finishing fence posts and boring holes to install them. He also invented a device to help start heavily loaded wagons and get them going when they were at rest. He was credited with many other inventions."

The Haas foundry building stood along Ridge Road, approximately one mile west of Franklin Square. The white out building on this photo stands within the foundry perimeter, according to Martha Peifer.

A wrought iron fence surrounds a garden near the Haas foundry building. One would think this fence was made here. Photo, July 2001.

Fisher's Foundry - Rebuck, PA

Fisher's Foundry, Rebuck, Pa. Slide photo 1972, by Steve E. Troutman. This photo is included in this series as an example of a local foundry. I have never seen a picture of the Haas Foundry near Franklin Square. The innkeeper at the nearby Drumheller's Hotel in Rebuck, Earl Drumheller, recalls this industrial building had rails hanging from the ceiling with rollers to move heavy castings on hooks. The widely known and popular Fisher Plough was constructed here of iron and wood. Many plough shares were made here by the iron workers. Who can provide more information on this extremely interesting local industry?

Wilson Erdman Mill - Haas, PA

For a photo of Wilson Erdman, see "The Erdman Boys" by Lorraine Andary

Donald Graves reported in the Pottsville Republican Weekender, August 26, 1989, as edited.

The Wilson Erdman Mill. Harold Hummel was interviewed as a former owner. When he bought the mill in 1941, it had already ceased its flour and feed operation. An iron water wheel was still in the mill as was a cider press. Both were later sold, he said, as were the grain bins, to other mills in the valley. At that time Hummel lived in one section of the miller's house. He said that the mill had an overshot wheel, with the millrace coming from a dam located on the Mahantongo Creek near a bridge on the Helfenstein Road. Another millrace came from a smaller creek to supplement the water power. Part of the raceway still exists near the mill which is now a private home.

The mill, a two story, timber frame building, was torn down to the stone foundation by Charles Smink, about 1960, according to Carl Gerhart, Smink's father-in-law. A millstone is the front step. Wilson Erdman and his sons were the last to operate the mill, according to Mark Swinehart, who lives near the mill. The mill was used for feed grinding in Swinehart's younger years. His father also got his apples pressed into cider there.

A large mill stone decorates the old mill location on Mill Hill Road.

The old mill in the Village of Haas is now remodeled into a residence.

Can You Identify this Mill?

Mystery Photo

Lawrence Knorr found this photo on E-Bay. It strongly resembles the Harvey Stiely Mill but there are architectural differences. It is labeled on the back in pencil, "Herb's Mill when started. Henry Herb's wife Polly, sold place to Irvin Erdman. Millwright-David Knorr. W.S. Anspach, photography. Esther Hepler (formerly Dietz)". Esther Dietz Hepler was a native of Rough and Ready.

Clues: David Knorr, is named as the grist millwright. He is the son of Johann Peter Knorr. Peter Knorr was the brother of Anna Knorr, wife of Isaac Stiely. David was a first cousin to Samuel Knorr who established the mill recently recalled as Stehr Brother's Mill. Samuel Knorr married Catherine Herb, daughter of Adam Herb who had the store in Rough and Ready. David Knorr did live past 1880. If he built this mill, it was likely around 1860??? He was born in 1809. David Knorr's residence in 1850 was south of the Salem Church in Rough and Ready, adjacent to the Peter Knorr residence. The 1850 Census of Upper Mahantongo Township lists David Knorr residence #216, Peter Knorr residence #217, Rev. Isaac F. Stiely residence #222. All these dwellings are nearby the Rev. Isaac Stiely Mill location.

Circa 1848, David Knorr lost his wife, Anna Maria (Kissinger) and remarried ca. 1860 Hannah Klinger. David and Hannah moved to Barry Township in Schuylkill County and raised a second family of 6 more children. He fathered 9 children with his first wife. Perhaps the mystery mill was in the Deep Creek Valley. Can anyone identify it?

Mystery Mill Identified

The mystery mill on the prior page has been identified! This mill was established by E.M. Stiely of Sacramento, PA. The mill was known as the Sacramento Roller Mills. It was established on the Deep Creek, approximately one mile west of Sacramento. The Harry Rissinger family owned and operated this mill, most recently, as Rissinger's Mill, located between Sacramento and Fearnot. Harry Rissinger, Jr. has a large flour bag, found in the mill, printed with the name E.M. Stiely, with the same mill scene pictured in this book on page 255. The decorated flour bag identifies the flour as "Winter Straight".

Harry Rissinger Jr. recalls there were many fish in the mill race. Fishermen would come to the mill to fish. They would open a trap door inside the mill, to step down to a wooden deck. This allowed access to the raceway water for easy fishing.

Elsworth M. Stiely (b. 4 Oct. 1863-d. after 1910) married Mary Knorr (b. 8 May 1863- d. after 1910). Elsworth M. Stiely is the son of Jared Stiely and Elizabeth Mayer. Elsworth is the grandson of Rev. Isaac Stiely. Leroy A. Stiely, lately deceased of Sacramento, is a descendant of this family. Mary Knorr, Elsworth Stiely's wife, is the daughter of John Knorr and Elizabeth (Ramberger) Knorr. There is a photo of Mary's mother, Elizabeth, on page 223 of the book entitled, *There is Something about Rough and Ready*, published by Sunbury Press. Elizabeth (Ramberger) Knorr is pictured in the photo with her son Emmon Knorr, Mary's brother, who lived east of the Steve E. Troutman residence.

The Stiely family genealogy listed above may be found in the book entitled, *The Relations of Isaac F. Stiely, Minister of the Mahantongo Valley*, by Lawrence Knorr, pages 63 and 74, published by Sunbury Press, Inc.

Part IV:

The Simmy Family—An African American Pioneer Family in the Mahantongo Valley

Double rainbow over Rough and Ready
View from William Simmy land, East toward Salem Church.
Northumberland and Schuylkill County, PA

An African American Pioneer Family in the Mahantongo Valley

William and Margret Simmy established a pioneer dwelling prior to 1790 at a location on the border of Northumberland and Schuylkill Counties, centrally located in the Mahantongo Valley. This area in Upper Mahantongo Township would later become known as Rough and Ready when a post office was established and named after President Zachary Taylor who died in office in 1850.

William Simmy's land was purchased from the Penn Family as recorded in the PA Archives in Harrisburg, PA. His Warrant dated 4th May, 1809, records his request to purchase 230 acres. This was prior to the existence of Schuylkill County. Schuylkill County was formed out of Berks County in 1811. William Simmy was the first pioneer settler to clear this parcel of land in the wilderness of what was then northern Berks County. The land is as stated on his application for ownership "on the waters of Mahantongo Creek in Mahantongo Township, part in the county of Northumberland and part in the county of Berks, including his improvement consisting of a dwelling house and about 30 acres of cultivated land. The land was first improved in the month of April 1790 and not before that. Crops of grain produced and raised upon the said land that William Simmy and his family actually reside thereon, witness our hands and seals, this 4th day of May, 1809, Michael Druckenmiller and Samuel Keim."

A Survey of the land was completed by 12th of May, 1809.

The Patent was issued 13th of September, 1810. This is the deed recorded in Patent Book H #3, page 704, to William Simmy.

William Simmy (ca. 1760-1833) and his family as well as Tobias Enty (ca. 1762-) and his family settled as close neighbors in what is presently Upper Mahantongo Township, Schuylkill County, PA. It is thought that they emigrated to Pennsylvania prior to 1790 from islands in the Caribbean region. The British colony of Barbados and the French colony of Haiti had imported a large slave population from Africa. These Negroes, black slaves, grew the sugar cane and produced the sugar. The white plantation owners intermingled with the slaves and a mulatto population became established on the sugar plantations. These "colored" offspring were given improved social status and given the names of European kings. The Simmy given names of William and George attest to this practice. Many mulatto people as descendants of the slave owners were given their freedom and inheritance.

During this time period in the mid to late 1700's, the British colony of Pennsylvania was anxious to promote settlement in the wilderness to establish a buffer of sorts between the native American Indians and the heavily populated counties south of the Blue Mountains. Therefore land was not expensive and attractive for purchase to these Caribbean immigrants with agricultural ambition. It was the tradition at that time to give a name to the land one purchased. William Simmy named his land, the plantation he established here in Pennsylvania, "Industry Awarded". His close friend Tobias Enty settled neighbors to the Simmys, on land adjacent as recorded in the early census records of 1810, naming Simmy and Enty as free black men. Prior to the Simmy and Enty families in the Mahantongo Valley, both families are recorded in census records as living in the eastern portion of the Deep Creek Valley, near the Kimmel's Church in Barry Township, now Schuylkill County, PA.

For more information of this remarkable story about Black emigration to the United States from the Caribbean region, see the book , "Sugar in the Blood," by Andrea Stuart, 2012, www.aaknopf.com, a division of Random House Inc., New York.

Part IV: The Simmy Family—An African American Pioneer Family in the Mahantongo Valley

Simmy Family Homestead near Rough and Ready in the Mahantongo Valley, Spring 1835 By Deanna Wiseman, 2014

Something about the Deanne Wiseman's Painting of the Simmy Homestead

by Steve E. Troutman

The name of the painting is "The William and Margret Simmy Homestead in the Mahantongo Valley".

It is springtime in 1835. The month of May has arrived on the Simmy homestead. The members of the Simmy family have come together to help their brother George with his spring chores. The Simmy apple orchard is in blossom. The horse and buggy is seen driving down the lane as morning errands need to be completed. Potatoes are being planted. On top of the hill a field is being prepared for spring grain planting. The sons and daughters of William and Margret are pictured here working together where they grew up as children. Old William, their father, had just died a year prior. Some of the Simmy grandchildren are playing in the creek. A cow and her calf along with a small flock of chickens roam the hillsides. William and Margret's pioneer home is pictured. It is a log house and a log barn. When William Simmy first cleared the land to build his log house, a 22 foot by 15 foot dwelling, he probably cut the trees higher up on the hill above the cabin location. Thereby, he would have had easier movement of the logs downhill to his building site. It is of interest to the writer that this land first cleared by felling trees in the wilderness must have been where the current residence of Steve and Joan Troutman is located today on Ridge Road. The location of Ridge Road marks the southern boundary of William Simmy's 230 acres.

William Simmy Sr. died 6th of May, in 1833. His wife, Margret, predeceased him. A Simmy burial plot is recorded in the county history entitled, Genealogical and Biographical Annals of Northumberland County, by Floyd, page 752. William and Margret's grave markers are pictured in the painting by Deanne Wiseman. The burial plot no longer exists but it is recalled by several local residents including the late Hilda Klinger and Ray Davis.

The Children of William and Margaret Simmy

William Simmy Jr. (1786-1862) married Catherine Enty

William Simmy Jr. (1786-1862) is the oldest son. He is pictured farming the hilltop field above the house and barn. William Jr. is preparing to plant oats. William Simmy Jr. married and had only one daughter, Catherine who married Joshua Enty Jr. William Simmy Jr., at this time, owned and lived on the farm now known as the property of Steve Dietz, located south of the Salem Church.

Residence of Steve Dietz, Upper Mahantongo Township, Schuylkill County, Pa. William Simmy's log cabin stood adjacent to this dwelling in the open space to the south. Jim Dietz recalls the garden and log cabin were used by his grandmother for food preparation.

Part IV: The Simmy Family—An African American Pioneer Family in the Mahantongo Valley

A lovely foot bridge crosses the Mahantongo Creek at the Dietz home.

View from the Simmy mill dam location looking north toward the William Simmy log cabin site. This log cabin was located near the Steve Dietz farm house. It is now removed. William Simmy is buried on the Ernest Klinger family farm on the "pine hill", in Rough and Ready.

William Simmy, Jr. lived in the log cabin on this farm, which is the Steve Dietz Farm, and may be buried on the William Simmy Sr. cemetery plot on the Ernst Klinger Farm.

The Simmy millrace can be easily found now surrounded by large trees. The mill was built downstream from this location near the dam and carried water to the mill before it exited to the creek again.

The presence of this mill race on the farm owned by William Simmy Jr. establishes the existence of a mill at this location on the Mahantongo Creek.

The 1850 Census of Upper Mahantongo Twp., Schuylkill County, PA, lists the residence as household No. #6, William Simmy Jr., farmer. Household No. 1, the first place recorded by the census taker in this township in 1850 lists widow Elizabeth Kleine, age 60. The Kleine-Kline name is associated with the sawmill profession. Perhaps the Kleine family who lived nearby was involved in the building of this mill race and mill.

Henry Kleine was a very early settler near the Salem Church where he warranted 200 acres of land in 1792. David Hess purchased 104 acres from Henry Kleine in 1825. This parcel became known as "Hessedahl," or Hess Valley. This valley is approximately one mile west of the Salem Church, now part of Klinger Farms. For more on this pioneer Kleine family see the book "There is Something About Rough and Ready," page 207. We will discuss more of the Kleine family of saw mill operators in the following pages. The presence of this mill race predicates the concepts that William Simmy Jr. was also a saw mill operator. Jim Dietz, a long time local resident, suggests that a grist mill was also operated at this location.

Part IV: The Simmy Family—An African American Pioneer Family in the Mahantongo Valley

Margret (ca. 1790-) married Farmer Jones

The oldest daughter Margret Simmy (ca. 1790 -) married Farmer Jones. Margret and her sister, Mary Elizabeth, named below, had purchased the eastern portion of their father's 230 acre estate on public sale, in September of 1834, less than one year prior to this painting timeline. This would be the portion where Ernest and Sandy Klinger live today. Five years later, in 1840, Farmer Jones, is named on the census records as living in Jackson Township, Northumberland County, PA.

Margaret (Simmy) Jones

Mary Elizabeth Simmy married Joshua Enty Sr.

Daughter Mary Elizabeth (1792-1865) married Joshua Enty Sr. (1775-1842). Mary's baptism is recorded in Klinger's Lutheran Church in Erdman, PA. The daughters are seen here planting potatoes in the plowed soil of the meadow land.

The children playing in the creek represent the grandchildren and great grandchildren of pioneer settlers William and Margret. One of the children could be grandson Elijah S. Enty, son of Joshua Enty Sr. and Mary Elizabeth (Simmy) Enty. Elijah was born ca. 1830 and died 25th of February in 1907. During the Civil War Elijah S. Enty served in the 43rd Colored Troops as a Sergeant and was discharged in 1865 being shot through the hand. Elijah's middle initial, S., stands for his mother's maiden name of Simmy.

Another of the children playing in the creek could represent the great grandchildren of William and Margret. Their daughter, Mary Elizabeth Simmy, married Joshua Enty Sr. as named above. Joshua Enty Jr. (B. 1811) married Catherine aka. Kitty Simmy, daughter of William Simmy Jr. Joshua and Kitty were first cousins. They had two sons, Jonathan (1844-1864) and Gabriel (1846-1914), both Civil War Soldiers who served in the 43rd US Colored Troops. Elijah S. Enty as named above, was wounded at Petersburg, Virginia. Jonathan Enty (1844-1864) died in action at Petersburg. Gabriel Enty (1846-1914) was discharged in 1865 as wounded in the right hand at Petersburg, Virginia. More Enty family who served and died in the Civil War are identified on the website, www.mahantongoheritage.org, including three of the sons of Tobias Enty. Joshua Enty Jr. and Kitty are named on the 1850 census as living in Lower Mahantongo Township, which at that time was located south of the Mahantongo Mountain, in the area now known as the Hegins Valley.

150TH Anniversary Civil War stamps were issued by the US Postal Service. This scene depicts Negro soldiers serving in the Union Army with their artillery.

Part IV: The Simmy Family—An African American Pioneer Family in the Mahantongo Valley

George Simmy going to market

George Simmy, son of William Simmy Sr.

George Simmy (1796-1860) youngest in the family, is on the horse and buggy headed for Hepler or Klingerstown, which were nearby villages where stores existed in 1835. George is the son who purchased the western portion of his father's 230 acres on public sale, where the Simmy homestead house and barn was located. George purchased the landscape as seen in this painting. George continued to live here on the homestead even as an old bachelor. Ray Davis recalls the story he became blind in his old age but would walk with a cane to the general store and post office in Rough and Ready. The 1850 census of Upper Mahantongo Township lists George Zimmy in household No.262, age 50, farmer, race Mulatto. There is another family named in this household No. 262, John and Sophia Wolfgang. John is age 30 and Sophia Wolfgang, age 25. Daniel, Elizabeth and Maria are the Wolfgang children, ages 5, 3, and 2. Evidently, George, needed help on the farm.

George Simmy's neighbors are of interest. Jacob Kleine, age 50, is at household No. 265, occupation, saw mill. Widow Kline has her residence shown on the 1875 map of Upper Mahanoy Twp., Northumberland Co, PA. The location of this home is not far from George Simmy on top of the hill above Hessedahl, previously owned by Henry Kline. Aaron Mattern has built a new home at this location near the intersection of Mattern Road and Heim's Hill Road.

John Knorr, in household No. 268, age 37, has his occupation named as saw mill also. Jacob Kleine and John Knorr must have operated the saw mill near George Simmy's land. The 1875 map of Upper Mahantongo Township, Schuylkill Co., PA shows this saw mill near the residence of Abraham Erdman, the present day residence of Brian and Shiela Klinger. This map also shows a blacksmith shop which was operated by Michael Runch, age 40, as named on the 1850 Census, in household No. 266. Today this location is the residence of Ronald

Maurer. No doubt, Michael the blacksmith, was kept busy doing repairs to the Kleine–Knorr water powered saw mill. The mill was located on Beissel's Run less than one mile west of the Salem Church. John Knorr and Isaac H. Knorr later purchased 97 acres from George Simmy in 1853. George Simmy was blind at the time of this land transaction as noted in the deed transfer. This is presently the home farm of Ernest and Sandy Klinger. See "There is Something About Rough and Ready," page 203.

George Simmy is also recorded as selling the land upon which the Salem Church is established. This congregation was organized in 1824 by Rev. Isaac Stiely and a building was erected in 1830. A deed dated April 22, 1854, recording the land transfer between George Simmy of Upper Mahantongo and the members of Salem Church of Lutheran and Presbyterian (Reformed) Congregations is the only extant deed in existence. Rev. Isaac Stiely's funeral records lists the funeral text and burials of William Jr. and George Simmy. See "There is Something About Rough and Ready," pages 4, 210 and 211.

The estate of George Simmy is recorded in the Schuylkill County Court House in Pottsville, PA. He seems to be without a family of his own. No wife or children are named. The administrators of George Simmy's estate list many financial transactions of George Simmy who loaned money to others in his community. An indenture (deed) dated 29 December 1859, recorded in the Schuylkill County Courthouse, describes the transfer of land from George Simmy to Abraham W. Erdman, his neighbor for a consideration of $10. This is the land where Brian and Shiela Klinger live today, west of the Salem Church. George Simmy is named in the family bible of Abraham and Mary Erdman as a close family friend. See "There is Something About Rough and Ready, page 204.

William Simmy Sr. and Margaret Simmy Homestead

Part IV: The Simmy Family—An African American Pioneer Family in the Mahantongo Valley

This painting is the end result of many hours of research and study. The physical evidence that remains of the pioneer home includes the 15 by 22 foot stone home foundation now partially filled in by debris. The base of a red brick chimney can be seen on the east side of the house foundation under the grass. This brick chimney was a later addition. I think the pioneer home had an outside stone chimney for a fireplace on the west side. The house had a cellar door evidenced by the void in the stone foundation on the north side. The house cellar space would have been used to store the apples grown in the Simmy orchard. The first floor main entry door was probably located on the south side. The hand dug well is easily found. It is a perfect circle of stones immediately west of the house. It was between the house and the barn. It is now filled in with stones to keep animals from falling in as the area was once a pasture for cows. I think the stones from the fireplace chimney were used to fill the well. A few very large rocks mark the barn location. The house and barn were of log construction as stated on the estate records at the time of sale of William Simmy Sr.'s property in 1833. Metal artifacts found around the house include lead musket balls and a small mule or donkey shoe found while digging for a burial place for a pet dog next to the barn location. Civil War artifacts found include clothing buttons and a military belt buckle. Artillery was the soldier's profession according to the type of button. These are pictured in the book, "There is Something about Rough and Ready," available from Sunbury Press of Mechanicsburg, PA.

Today, the general area has changed. In 1959, Ralph Klinger had a large pond built to the east of the Simmy homestead. Troutman Brothers of Klingerstown built the dam. Earl Troutman and Clarence Brosius of Klingerstown were some of the equipment operators.

The Simmy Homestead was undisturbed by the pond construction. In the springtime daffodils and blue bells bloom. They arrive every year about Easter time. They are a remembrance of people from the past and their efforts to beautify their place in the world.

Simmy Homestead view, 2014

Simmy Foundation and an Iron Pot

View from William Simmy land, East toward Salem Church.
Tobias Enty lived at the foot of the hill, now the Teeter residence.

Simmy Court House Records

William Simmy Sr., died May 6, 1833, md. Margaret

On August 17, 2012, Joan E. Troutman made a trip to Pottsville, Pa. The Schuylkill County Court House was her destination. Joan was researching the Simmy family from Rough and Ready. Pages were located pertaining to William Simmy and his family, including William Simmy Jr., George, Mary Enty, and Margaret Jones. William Simmy Sr. land records are first recorded as referenced in Patent Book H, Vol. 3, page 704, dated 13 September, 1810. This record is held in the Archives of the Pennsylvania Historical Museum Commission. This patent is the first deed awarded by the Penn Family for this land. Contact was made with the PA Historical Museum Commission concerning the issuing of patents. Other official records issued before receiving a patent include warrants and surveys. Documents from the Schuylkill County Court House refer to the existence of William Simmy's patent issued in 1810. At this time, in the early years of Pennsylvania, the frontier was here in the Mahantongo Valley. The Penns as land owners were anxious to promote settlement here in the wilderness to establish a buffer of sorts, between the native American Indians and the heavily populated counties south of the Blue Mountains. Therefore, land was not expensive to encourage settlement. Locally in Klingerstown, a grist mill was completed by the Alexander Klinger family. This mill was constructed with a similar vision. The Klingers hoped that settlement in the area would be promoted if a mill were built. Their goal was to sell land also.

13th of May, 1832, Deed Record, between William Simmy Sr. and Jacob Starr, of Upper Mahantongo Twp. William Simmy in consideration of the sum of $110.90 to him paid by the said Jacob Stare, containing 11 acres, 16 perches land. (Jacob Starr is an ancestor of Richard Ney who resides on this property today.)

Estate of William Simmy, Upper Mahantongo Twp., 1833, 1st day of December.
William Simmy Jr., the eldest son, and heir of William Simmy Sr., late of the county of Schuylkill.
William Simmy Sr., the elder, died intestate on or about the 6th day of May, A.D. 1833, leaving no widow, but 4 children George, Mary, Margaret, now intermarried with Farmer Jones, and your petitioner, (Wm. Simmy Jr.) A tract of land situate partly in the county of Northumberland and partly, and the dwelling house thereon, in Upper Mahantongo in the said county of Schuylkill, bounded by lands of George Erdman, Peter Ressinger, Jacob Starr, and others containing 200 acres or there about.

12 men are appointed to make a inquisition as to the value of William Simmy's patented land. They include: Henry Maurer, George Maurer, John Wagner, Adam Herb, Peter Schlegel, Isaac Knorr, Jacob Bechtel, Benjamin Leffler, George Erdman, Jacob Dressler, Abraham Erdman, and Jacob Starr, 12 free and honest lawful men. The 12 men divided William Simmy's patented land into parcels A,B, and C.

24th March, 1834, Schuylkill County Court
William Simmy and George Simmy of Upper Mahantongo Twp. both heirs of William Simmy Sr. promise to pay to the other children of the said deceased their part of the valuation money, diagram "C" bounded by George Erdman, Frederick Rabuck, David Hess, containing 41 acres and 37 perches, it being appraised at the sum of $7.91 3/4 for each and every acre, amounting to the sum of $326.50. This is the property where Kurt and Jamie Snyder reside.

Orphans' Court of Schuylkill County, 21 July, 1834

William Simmy and George Maurer both of Upper Mahantongo Twp. in Schuylkill County are bound under the Commonwealth of Pa. in the sum of $4000. The real Estate of William Simmy deceased. To wit, that part marked "A" bounded by the lands of Isaac Schaffer, George Erdman, other lands of said deceased, David Hess, and Peter Reisinger, Jacob Bechtel, and Jacob Starr containing 90 acres and 108 perches, and that part of the estate marked "B," bounded by the lands of David Hess, other land of said deceased and lands of George Erdman containing 90 acres and 122 perches.

William Simmy Jr. is named administrator, signed and sealed William Simmy and George Maurer.

Public Sale

Saturday, the 13th day of September, 1834 at 10 o'clock in the forenoon on the premises, William Simmy sale. 2 tracts of land, the first bounded by land of Isaac Schaffer, George Erdman, other lands of the said deceased David Hess, Peter Rissinger, Jacob Bechtel, and Jacob Starr containing 90 acres, 108 perches. (Ernest Klinger's farm residence is on this tract). The second tract bounded by lands of David Hess, other lands of said deceased and lands of George Erdman containing 90 acres, 122 perches, consisting of a log dwelling house, a log barn, and an orchard. (The Steve E. Troutman residence is on this tract).

Orphans' Court at Orwigsburg, 21 October, 1834

William Simmy, the administrator of William Simmy late, of Upper Mahantongo Twp. makes report that tract #1 was purchased by Joshua Enty and Farmer Jones, as marked with the letter "A" in the draft for the sum of $8.25 per acre. Tract #2, marked with the letter "B" purchased by George Simmy for the sum of $9.00 per acre.

The 1834 survey of the patented lands of William Simmy name adjoining land owners of interest including the name David Hess. There has been much speculation concerning the origin of this local name Hessedahl. Now we know that David Hess lived in his pioneer home further up the valley north of William Simmy. George W. Erdman is also named as adjoining on the south. George's father, Andreas Erdman, married Rachel Williamson, also of the local area, where Darwin Mauser and Benigna's Creek Winery are today. The Rabuck lands named to the west of William Simmy is lately recalled as the Egdar Clark farm. Parcel C is recalled as the Ivan Boyer property, most recently, Kurt Snyder residence. Today these parcels, A, B, and C are known as Klinger farms of Rough and Ready.

Henry Kline's Land Transferred to David Hess, adjoining land owner to the North of William Simmy.

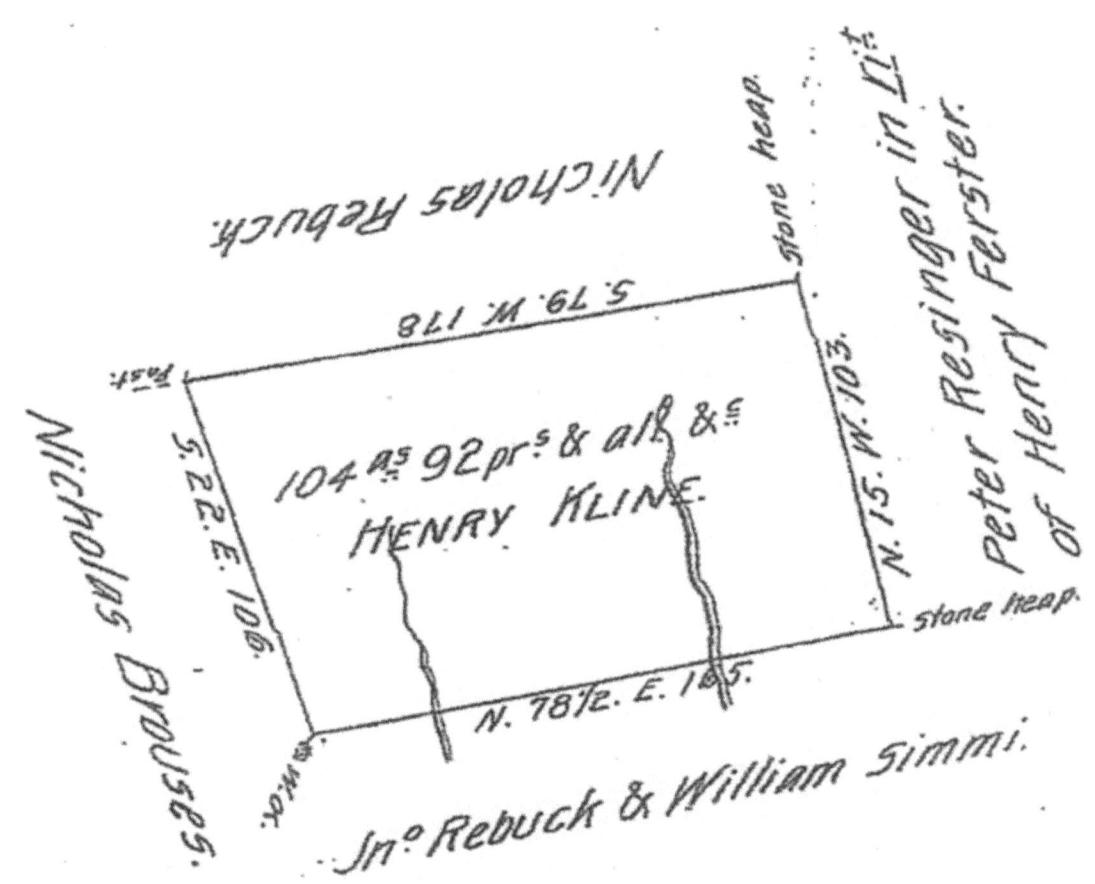

Situate in Upper Mahanoy Township (on a branch of the Mahantongo Creek, near Berks, now Schuylkill County Line). in Northumberland County. Surveyed 27th day of August 1825, unto Henry Kline by virtue of his Warrant dated 31st August 1792 containing one hundred and four acres, 92 perches and allowance of six per cent.

To Gabriel Heister, Esqr, surveyor General William Laird, OS.

Henry Kline applied for land adjoining William Simme, land warrant #236 surveyed August 27, 1875, which returned 104 acres 90 perches as patented to David Hess. Henry Kline had previously applied for 200 acres of land situate in Berks County, adjoining land of Henry Firster, and vacant lands on a branch of Mahantongo Creek. Henry Kline said tract of land is vacant and this is no improvement there on. Witness our hands August 29th, 1792, signed David Kennedy, James May and Peter Nagle.

David Hess's Patent dated 31 December 1825, conveyed Henry Kline's right in and to the same to David Hess. Witness Joshua Dickerson, Secretary of the Land office, 28th Day of February 1827.

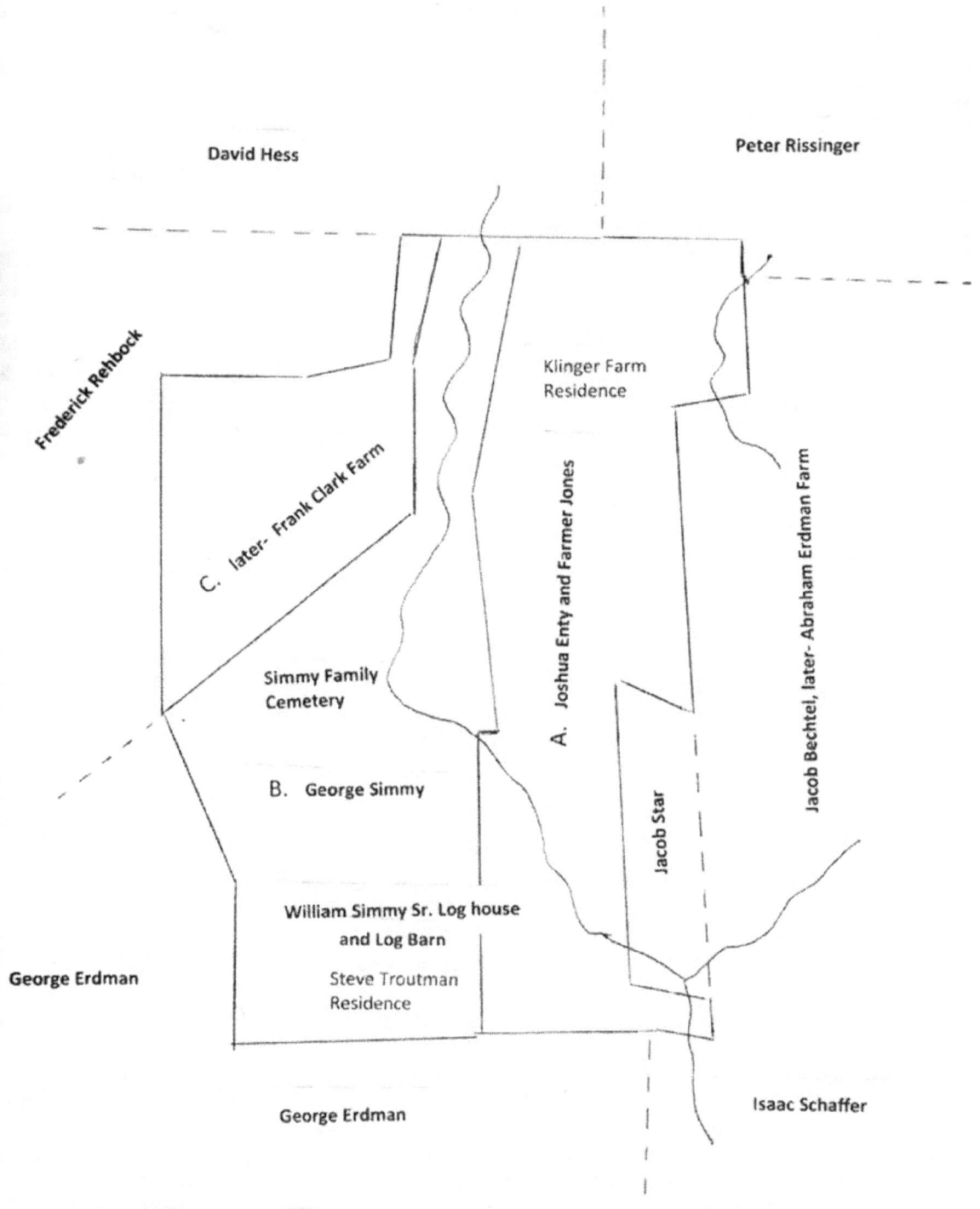

William Simmy Sr., 1810 Pioneer Homestead divided in 1834

Part IV: The Simmy Family—An African American Pioneer Family in the Mahantongo Valley

William Simmy Sr. patent of 230 acres in Rough and Ready

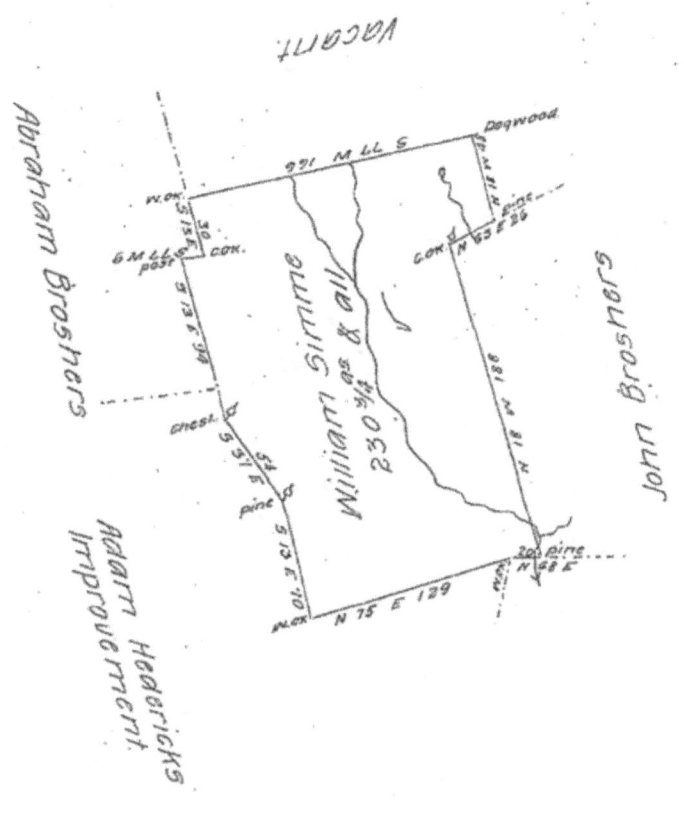

Situate on the waters of Mahontonga in Mahontongo Township part in the County of Northumberland and part in the County of Berks surveyed on the 22 day of May 1809 for William Simme by virtue of his warrant bearing date on the 12 day of May 1809 Containing two hundred and thirty acres & three quarters with the usual allowance of six P Cent &c

Henry Donnel D.S.

To Andrew Porter Esqr.
Surveyor General

The Penns' Manor of Spread Eagle and the Grist Mills of the Upper Mahantongo Valley

The land of William Simmy Sr. divided into three tracts at time of estate sale

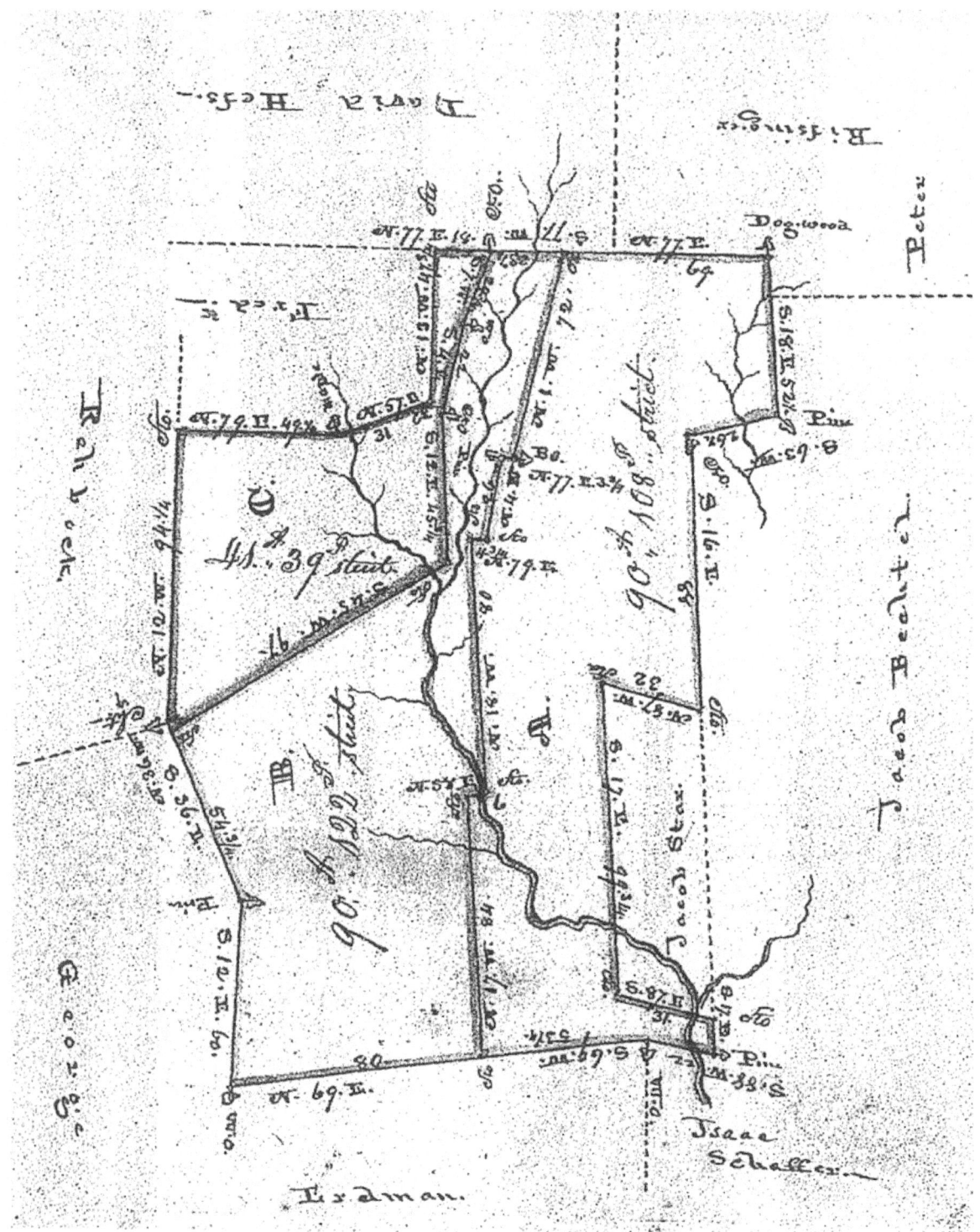

Part IV: The Simmy Family—An African American Pioneer Family in the Mahantongo Valley

The land of William Simmy Sr. divided into three tracts at time of estate sale

Situate in Upper Mahontongo Township, Schuylkill County. Containing by Resurvey 222A 109P. strict measure. It being the Major Part of the same larger tract of land, which was Originally Surveyed unto William Simme. by Virtue of a Warrant granted to him, dated the 12th day of May A.D. 1809, and afterwards confirmed to him by a Patent, dated the 13th day of September, A.D. 1810. Vide Patent Book. H. Vol. 3 Page 704 &—

Resurveyed as the Estate of the said William Simme, now decd. at the request of the heir of the said decd. and divided in the presence of a Jury. March 11th A.D. 1834— By.

```
A. Contains ---- 90A 108P. strict.        Bieber
B. Contains ---- 90. 122. do
C. Contains ---- 41. 39. do
                 222. 109. strict
```

William Simmy Jr. b. November 20, 1786, d. May 6, 1862, married Catherine.

William Simmy Jr. lived approximately 3 miles east of his father's patented land along Mahantongo Creek, south of Salem Church. Today this farm is the residence of Steve Dietz. William Simmy Jr. established a mill on this farm as evidenced by the mill race bordering the creek. Perhaps it was a grist mill or a saw mill. At the time of his passing, May 6, 1862, an extensive estate settlement was recorded. William Simmy Jr. died on the same month and day, as his father.

Schuylkill County Court, 1st day of November, 1862
In the matter of the estate of William Simmy deceased, the petition of Samuel Ente, eldest son of Catherine Ente, late Catherine Simmy, and only daughter and child of William Simmy late of Upper Mahantongo Twp., Schuylkill County, deceased. Said Samuel Ente, being a grandson of said William Simmy deceased, Benjamin B. Crabb and Mary Ann his wife, late Mary Ann Ente and daughter of said Catherine Ente, deceased, and granddaughter of said William Simmy, deceased, Samuel Jones and Sarah, his wife, late Sarah Ann Ente, another daughter of said Catherine Ente, deceased, and granddaughter of William Simmy deceased, and William Heitzman, guardian of Jonathan Ente, a minor son of said Catherine Ente, deceased and grandson of said William Simmy deceased. Was presented setting forth that said William Simmy lately died intestate leaving neither widow nor children surviving him but leaving as his heirs, his deceased daughter Catherine, who in her lifetime was intermarried with Joshua Ente. Mary Ann married Benjamin B. Crabb, Samuel Ente, Sarah Ann married Samuel Jones, Jonathan Ente who is a minor and petitioners Gabriel Ente, Edward Ente, Catherine Ente, and Silas Ente, the last four named in their minority. Note by the compiler that one Joshua Ente was earlier married to Mary Simmy, the daughter of William Simmy Sr.

A certain farm and tract of land situate in the township of aforesaid bounded by lands of Adam Herb, Benjamin Baum, Reuben Wherry, Isaac Kline, Michael Dietz and others containing 100 acres, more of less. Your petitioners pray your honor, to award an inquest to make partitions of the premises and with respect to the true evaluation thereof, affirmation of 12 good and lawful men.

Schuylkill County Court House, 13 February, 1863 (See survey map)
An inquisition taken upon the premises late the estate of William Simmy in the township of Upper Mahantongo appointed 12 men, Augustus B. Katherman, Charles Maurer, John H. Maurer, Joseph Fetherolf, George Moyer, Adam Herb, Simon Wearry, Solomon Wearry, David Wearry, Henry Herb, Michael Dietz, and David H. Maurer. Who say upon their oaths concerning the premises.

Parcel #1. A certain 1 story log house, part log and part frame barn and tract of land containing 88 acres and 106 perches valued and appraised at $19.50 per acre.

Parcel #2. A certain tract of woodland containing 11 acres and 8 perches valued and appraised at the sum of $10.20 per acre. Survey completed Feb. 11, 1863, by Val. Savidge.
Orphans' Court, Schuylkill County, William Simmy Jr. Estate
Having first given due and timely notice by hand bills and advertisements, during the last 20 days, as directed by order, on the first day of August, 1863, at the public house Daniel S. Herb, in Upper Mahantongo Twp., at 1 o'clock in the afternoon exposed the real estate to public sale at auction. Whereupon David Klinger and Harrison Fetterolf became the purchasers for the price of $1695, they being the highest and best bidders.

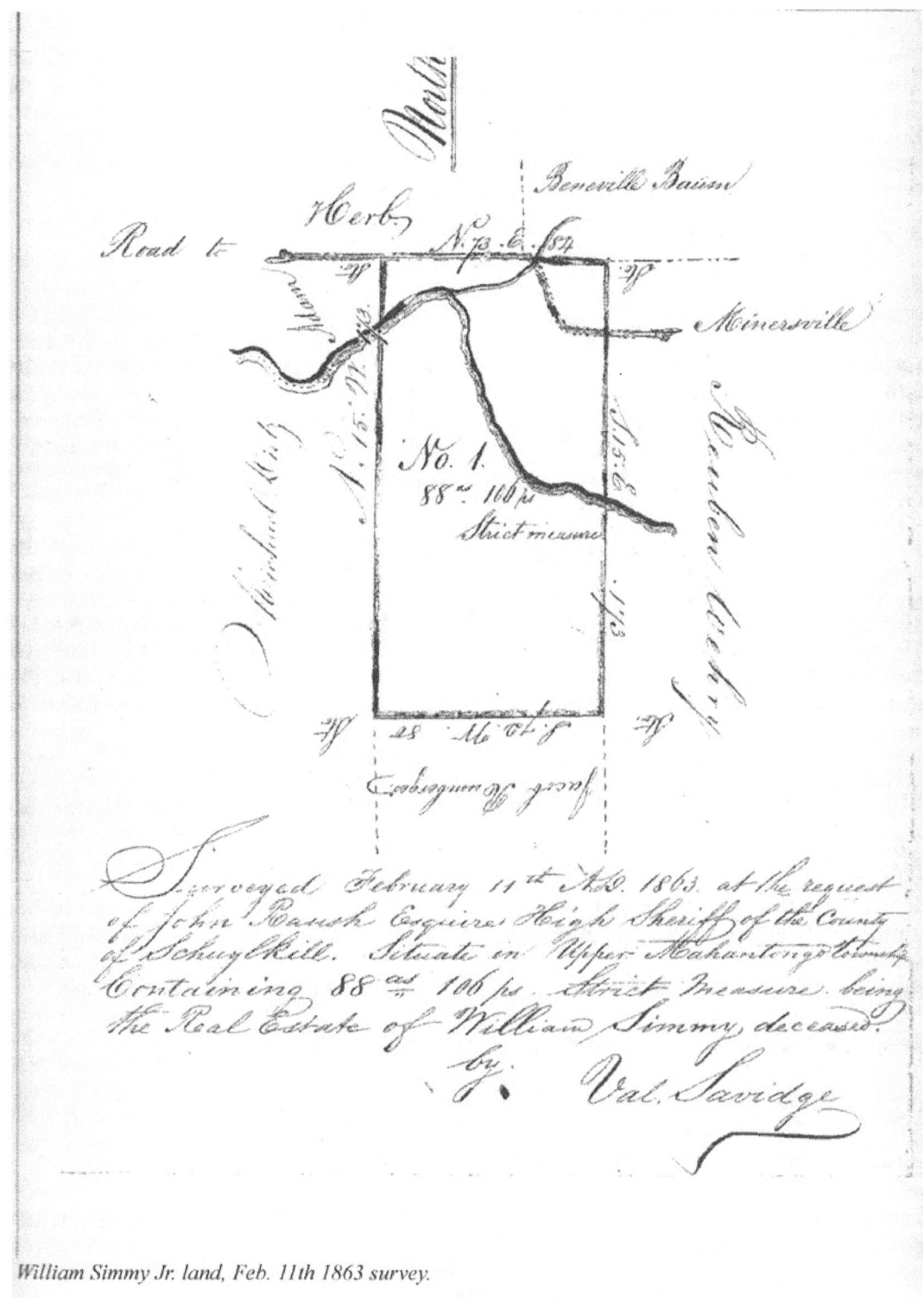

William Simmy Jr. land, Feb. 11th 1863 survey.

Other names of interest in the administration papers include: Isaac S. Knorr, collector of state and county taxes, David W. Paul, who was assigned an interest in Samuel Ente's inheritance.

Catherine Simmy married Joshua Ente, who was named executor of William Simmy Jr.'s estate. Their son, Samuel, the eldest child, challenged the administration of his father,(Joshua Ente), of the William Simmy Jr. estate, stating mismanagement of the affairs.

Schuylkill County Court, November 1, 1862
In the matter of the appointment of Joshua Ente, administrator
Samuel Ente, the grandson of William Simmy Jr. said that Joshua Ente, (his father), is mismanaging and wasting said estate and property of said deceased for his own use. We request that said Joshua Ente be removed from further administration and a suitable person appointed in his place.

Schuylkill County Court, Feb. 15, 1866
To the sheriff . . . Greetings. We command you that you attach Joshua Ente, administrator of William Simmy, if he can be found, and keep him safely so that you have his body before our judges at the Orphans' Court to be held in Pottsville, on the first Monday of March next, to answer us of a certain contempt by him to us done, in not complying with a certain rule issued by our court on the 22 of December, 1865. Witness the Honorable James Ryon, Esq.

George Simmy, July 4, 1796- January 8, 1860

George Simmy, at the time of his death, seems to be without a family of his own. There is no mention of a wife or children in his estate settlement begun in June of 1860. The administrators of George Simmy's estate are county appointed men Frailey and Shrope. They appraised goods, chattels, and credits of George Simmy, late of the township of Upper Mahantongo Township, Schuylkill County, Pa. Their administration lists many financial transactions between George Simmy, who loaned money to others in his community. Interesting notes include:

Note of Johannes H. Knorr and Isaac S. Knorr to George Simmy for $107.17 ¼, dated April 1, 1853, payable April 1, 1862, pertaining to title claim interest property unto Abraham W. Erdman for value received. Witness my hand and seal the 30th day of December, 1859, signed George Simmy, witness present , Isaac H. Knorr.

Note of same as above to George Simmy, payable April 1, 1861, dated April 1, 1853.

Note of same to same, payable April 1, 1860, dated April 1, 1853.

Note of same to same, payable April 1, 1859, dated April 1, 1853.

Note of same to same, payable April 1, 1863, dated April 1, 1853.

Note to Henry Knorr and Isaac H. Knorr to George Simmy for $150, with interest, in one year from dated March 29, 1856.

Note to Beneville H. Beisel and David H. Beisel to George for $100, with interest, in one year after date, dated March 2, 1855. $6 interest paid each year for 1856, 57, 58.

Note to Isaac F. Stiely to George Simmy for $100, with interest, dated the 1st of April, 1856, payable 1 year after date. Interest paid on this note until 1859, at $6 per year.

Part IV: The Simmy Family—An African American Pioneer Family in the Mahantongo Valley

Note to Gabriel Reinard and Carlous Reinard to George Simmy for $100, dated November 2, 1859, payable 11 month after date.

Note to George Henninger, or order by David Fetter for $30 with interest, dated April 1, 1859, payable 1 year after date.

Note to Moses Wolfgang and Samuel Ressler for $100. Payable 1 year after date, dated April 1, 1856. Interest paid for 2 years, $12.

Note to Emanuel Christ for $24 to George Simmy, April 1, 1857, payable 1 May, 1857.

Note to Isaac Kline for $15 to George Simmy, January 6, 1856 payable 6 months after date. Interest paid 1857, on the within note, $7.

George Simmy Deed Transfers
This indenture made the 31 March, 1853, between George Simmy of Upper Mahantongo Twp., State of PA, of the first part and John Knorr of Upper Mahntongo Twp., Schuylkill Co. and state aforesaid of the other part. Witness that the said George Simmy for and in consideration of the sum of $2,140.46 lawful money of the United States of America unto him will and truly paid by the said John Knorr. . . . that tract of land situate in Upper Mahantongo Twp. by other lands of John Smith, John Yoder, George Keim, other lands of George Simmy, and Jacob Stare, containing 97 acres and 69 perches. It being part of the same premises which Jacob Bechtel and Catherine, his wife, by indenture bearing date, the 12th day of April, 1847, did grant unto the said George Simmy, (partly hereto) his heirs forever. The indenture recorded in the office for the recording at Orwigsburg, in Book #28, page 44, together with all the houses, buildings, barns, waters, etc., is now granted to the said John Knorr and his heirs and assigns forever. Signed George Simmy, in the presence of us, witness, Heinrich K. Romberger and Isaac H. Knorr. The above named George Simmy, being blind, the same was carefully read to him in the presence of us. This is presently the residence of Ernest Klinger.

On the 31st day of March, 1853, George Simmy appeared personally before the Justice of the Peace, and desired the same might be recorded as to law. Witness my hand and seal aforesaid. Isaac H. Knorr, recorded and examined May 17, 1853.

George Simmy Deed Transfer
This indenture made the 29th day of December, 1859, between George Simmy of Upper Mahantongo Twp., Schuylkill Co., PA of the first part, and Abraham W. Erdman of the same township, county, and state, aforesaid, farmer of the second part. Witness that the said George Simmy for and consideration of the sum of $10 lawful money of the United States of America, well and truly paid, by the same, Abraham W. Erdman at the delivery of these presence. This being the same parcel from 1847 conveyed to Jacob Bechtel, and Catherine Bechtel, late Catherine Brocius. Whereas, Jacob Bechtel, and Catherine, his wife, by their indenture dated 12 April, 1847, did grant and confirm the same tract of land unto George Simmy and his heirs forever. In witness whereof the said parties of these present have set their hand and seal, Isaac H. Knorr, and Isaac _ Knorr. Signed and sealed, George Simmy.
This is presently the residence of Brian and Shiela Klinger.

Be it known that on the 29th day of December, 1859, before me the subscriber for the county, personally appeared above named George Simmy and due form of law acknowledged the above indenture to be his deed and desired the same might be recorded according to law. Witness my hand and seal, Isaac H. Knorr. Recorded and examined January 11, 1860, Levi Hubey, recorder.

Editors Note: Many of the Simmy family mentioned in these court records are of unknown burial locations. William Simmy Sr. and wife Margaret, William Simmy Jr. and his wife Catherine, as well their children, who died prior to 1860, may be buried in a family plot adjacent to William Simmy Sr's pioneer home. This family plot is named in *The Northumberland County History by Floyd* p. 752, as located on the Ammon Knorr farm, now Klinger Farms. The cemetery was in an apple orchard north of the Steve and Joan Troutman residence, which is pasture today.

William Simmy Jr. lived on Mahantongo Creek. An 1863 survey map shows 88 acres with adjoining land owners. Following information is pertaining to these neighbors. (See survey map)

Reuben Wehry
Reuben Wehry and his sons Josiah and James Monroe Wehry made furniture that is displayed in the Faye Kopp Room at the Mahantongo Heritage Center, 75 Grove Road, Pitman, Pa. Working in the last half of the 19th century, he is most famous within family history for building the steeple for Salem Union Church at Rough and Ready. Pieces of furniture in the Hermitage collection were made by his son, Josiah Wehry and later his other son James Monroe Wehry. Information from Johannes and Christian Zinzendorf. Reuben Wehry, 1820-1890, married Lovina Knorr, 1828-1911. They are buried at Salem Cemetery. The Joe Kopp farm, nearby, is recalled as being the Wehry homestead.

Beneville Baum
Beneville Baum was born Sept. 2, baptized October 15, 1825, page 57, Zion (Klinger's) Church Record. He was the son of Heinrich and Salome Gundrum Baum. The Henry Baum farm is now Troutman Brothers in Klingestown. Beneville is the ancestor of Cindy Baum, contributor to this book. Beneville married Susanna Maurer, 1822-1899. They are buried at Salem. Almond Oxenrider lives on Beneville Baum's farm today.

Jacob Ramberger
Jacob Ramberger, 1802-1854, married Catherine Klinger, 1802-1871. Jacob is the son of Heinrich buried at Hill Lutheran Church, Berrysburg, Pa. Jacob and Catherine's home was unusual in design for an early Mahantongo Valley dwelling. Johannes and Christian Zinzendorf dismantled the Ramberger dwelling which was of a log constructed lower story, with an upper story of fachware, timber frame style. Fachware is typical old German construction. Portions of the dwelling are at the Hermitage in Pitman. The Jim Dietz residence occupies the Ramberger farm today.

Michael Dietz
Michael Dietz, 1806-1882, married Hannah Klinger. This would be the property west of William Simmy Jr., where the Sherry family lives today. Conversation with Janice Dietz, in September of 2012, confirmed that the Sherry property adjoining their farm was indeed the Michael Dietz place. Steve Dietz and his father, Ronald Dietz, are descendant from Michael Dietz. Janice recalled the old house on the Dietz place was removed several years ago. The Sherry's burned it down. George and Lizzie Wolfgang owned this farm prior to the Sherry's ownership. This was George, the blacksmith, from Rough and Ready.

Part IV: The Simmy Family—An African American Pioneer Family in the Mahantongo Valley

Simmy and Associated Colored Family Vital Records

The Simmy families from the area of Rough and Ready, Schuylkill County and Northumberland County, Pa. with supplemental records of neighboring black families from the Upper and Lower Mahantongo Valleys

The Mahantongo Valley of central Pa. is divided by a county line through the middle of the valley, separating Northumberland and Schuylkill Counties.
Early reference to Lower Mahantongo refers to the Deep Creek Valley, Barry Township, south of the Mahantongo Mountain.
Early reference to Upper Mahantongo refers to the Mahantongo Valley designated today, as north of Mahantongo Mountain and south of the Line Mountain.

Zion (Klinger's) Church Record by Irvin R. Klinger, p. 11-Baptisimal Records
Ma. Elisabeth, da. of Will Simey and w. Marg.
b. March 24. bapt. June 3, 1792. sp. Elisabeth Stutzmenin

William and Margaret Simey Family
1. William Simey Jr. (20 November 1786)-(6 May 1862)
2. Margaret (1790-) md. Farmer Jones
3. Mary Elisabeth (24 March 1792)-(abt. 1865) (See baptismal record above) md. Joshua Enty son of Tobias Enty (1742-1842)
4. George Simmy (4 July 1796)- (8 Jan. 1860)

Census
1790	Northumberland County. Pa. William Simms white
1810	Upper Mahanoy Twp, North'd. Co. William Simmy 11 Free colored persons
1810	Next door to Simmy Andy Toby (black) 7 Free colored persons
1820	Upper Mahanoy Twp., William Simmy 1 white female (45+) 1 colored male (26-44)
1820	William Simmy Jr. *(1786-1862)* 1 white female (26-44) 1 colored male (26-44) *1786-1862* 1 colored female (45+) *Margaret his mother?* Household next to Hepler households of John, Christopher, Henry, George, and Peter. William Smith household is between William Simmy and Wm. Simmy Jr. Total persons in Upper Mahantongo Twp. is 863. (3 free colored males) (2 free colored females) and (3 other persons except Indians)
1820	Lower Mahantongo Twp., *Deep Creek Valley* Joshua Enty 9 colored persons in household next to Michael Artz (white) Abraham Enty 8 colored persons next to Philip Dieter (white) Tobias Enty (1742-1842) son Joshua Enty married Mary Elisabeth Simmy (1792-abt. 1865) Other children of Tobias Enty include Edward, William, (14 April 1887), Barry Twp., Schuylkill Co., and Elija H. Enty (25 Feb. 1907) Barry Twp., Schuylkill County.
1830	Upper Mahanoy William Simmy 6 free colored persons
1840	Upper Mahantongo William Simmy *1786-1862* 1 colored male (55-99) 1 white female (40-49) 1 white male (5-9)
1840	Upper Mahantongo John Ernst 1 colored male (36-55) 1 colored female (10-24) 1 colored female (24-36) Total 4 free colored males, 5 free colored females, 9 free colored persons in township. John Ernst is 6 doors away from Jacob Hepler, George Hepler, and Christopher Hepler. John Ernst is 2 doors away from Samuel and Abraham Zimmerman.

Census Joshua Enty md. Mary Elisabeth Simmy

1840   Upper Mahantongo Joshua Enty 5 colored persons - 1 male (under 10), 1 male (24-36) 2 females (under 10) 1 female (10-24) Next door to William Simmy and widow Ramberger. David Stein, *Stein's Hotel*, is 9 doors away. 1850 Upper Mahantongo William Simmy *1786-1862* (age 60) mulatto, Mary Crick (age 29), colored. William Simmy is a farmer with neighbors Henry Ramberger, occupation miner, and Sophia Ramberger and Benevil (farmer) and Susanna Baum. In 2012, William Simmy residence is the Steve Dietz home, Henry Ramberger residence is on the Marlin Paul farm and Benevil Baum residence is on the Ammon Oxenrider farm.
William Simmy farm value listed as $2800.

1850   Upper Mahantongo George Zimmy (mulatto) is recorded in household 260 with family of John and Sophia Wolfgang. George Zimmy is named as farmer with appraised value of land $3000. By 1853, George is blind. (See page 203) and needed assistance. The Wolfgang's family probably lived with George Simmy.

1852   Pa. land warrants 1733-1987 lists William Simmy—26.12 A. warranted 7 April 1852, Schuylkill Co., Pa.

1860   Upper Mahantongo William Simmy *1786-1862* mulatto (73) Rosena Koons (19) colored Lydia Enty (2) mulatto George Crapp mulatto (5) All born in Pennsylvania

1860   Jordan Twp., Northumberland Co. Samuel Jones, mulatto, age 32, with Sarah, age 20, Maria Jones, age 55, (widow with $1000 real estate), William, age 20, and Catherine, age 15, all are listed as mulatto.

1860   Upper Mahantongo Twp. Charles Lookman, age 60, a mulatto farm laborer, living in the Daniel Herb household.

1864   Jonathan Enty (1844-1864) was declared missing in action at Petersburg, Virginia, 30 July 1864, while serving with the 43rd US Colored Troops, (USCT). He was a farm laborer from the Fountain area, Schuylkill Co.

Rev. Isaac Stiely has recorded William Simmy's funeral which he performed in 1862. Rev. Stiely's burial record #1543 lists Simmy, William, (20 November 1786) (6 May 1862) 75y. 5mo. 16da. Text: Haebreer 9:27, "And as it is appointed unto men once to die, but after this the judgment." William Simmy is not buried at Salem Church. He is not buried in any local church graveyards. He is probably buried in the Simmy family plot on the Ernest Klinger farm next to the Simmy homestead.

US Federal Census Mortality Schedules (1850-1885)
George Simmy, mulatto, died of consumption 1860, January, age 63, Upper Mahantongo Twp., Schuylkill County, Pa.

George Simmy who lived near the Simmy burial plot on the Simmis land is buried at Salem Cemetery in Rough and Ready. Rev. Isaac Stiely burial record # 1408, lists Simmy, George, (4 July 1796) (8 Jan. 1860) 63y. 6mo. 4da. Afro-Amer., text: Galeschta 4:1-28, which concerns the concept of slavery. Gelatians 4: 7, "So through God you are no longer a slave, but a son, and if a son then an heir." The Simmis burial plot is now on the Ernest Klinger farm.

Deed dated April 22, 1854 "Between Peter Schlegel and George Simmy, both of Upper Mahantongo Twp., of one part, and members of Salem Church of the Lutheran and Prysbyterian Congregation of the other part for the sum of $10.50." Peter Schlegel and Jacob Wehry were appointed by the congregation to purchase land for the establishment of a church building.

George Simmy also transferred land to Abraham and Mary (Troutman) Erdman. They lived where Brian and Shiela Klinger reside today west of the Salem Church. George Simmy must have been a good friend of the Erdmans because he is buried between Abraham and Mary in the Salem Church yard.

Susan H. Mc Carthy is a descendant of Abraham Erdman. She resides at 3813 Candlelight Drive, Camp Hill, Pa. 17111. She has in her possession a family Bible record of Memoranda naming George Simmy, colored, 1791-1860. The birth date is in error, but it is the same man. Also listed are the children of Abraham and Mary Erdman, including, Senari, Ellis, William, Central, Abby, Maretta, Mrs. Howater, Mrs. Schlegel, and Mary.

Maretta is the same person Martha M. Erdman born August 26, 1861, died October 26, 1925. She married Jacob Paul Hornberger born January 30, 1861, died October 20, 1934. Jacob's middle name is his mother's maiden name.

Physical Evidence of the Simmy's

Dale Erdman and son, Justin, searched the Simmy homestead on the Ernest Klinger farm with a metal detector in May of 2012. They discovered metal originally adorning a US military uniform. Items found include a box plate closure which is stamped US. This box was a type of shoulder pouch used to carry ammunition. It was made of leather and was used to carry gun powder and balls for a percussion cap rifle. They also found a rare one-piece coat button identified as pre-Civil War. Civil War buttons were typically manufactured in 2 pieces. This button made of metal is well preserved and carries the image of an eagle and the letter "A". "A" is for Artillery. I = Infantry, C = Cavalry, R = Rifleman, D = Dragoons. They also found many ammunition balls close by the house foundation. Some were perfectly round, being "dropped" balls, and most were deformed, from being used. Dale said "Simmy must have been shooting rabbits from the front porch!"

Dale and Justin's research from Mexican-American War records show:
1845 – W.R.Simms (file 5538)
1856 – Will K. Sims (file 59)
The above men wrote letters to the Adjutant General after military service, perhaps in request of pension.

It is a coincidence that the Village of Rough and Ready is named after Zachary Taylor, US President from 1848-1850. He was the hero of the Mexican-American War.

Steve found other physical evidence over 20 years ago. A small pony or donkey shoe was found in good condition. The Simmy home location was being used as a pet cemetery. Simmy must have had animals for farm use, perhaps to pull a cart.

Early Families that Migrated from the Mahantongo Valley

Isaac Shaffer is named on page 274 as an adjoining land owner to William Simmy Sr. in 1834 in Upper Mahantongo Township. The Tobias Enty family also lived adjoining to William Simmy Sr. as recorded in the census records from 1810 in Upper Mahantongo Township. The Isaac Shaffer family and some of the Tobias Enty family left Upper Mahantongo Township soon after 1834 and are recorded as living in Jefferson County, PA where they were once again neighbors. See the appendix entitled, "Early Families that Migrated from the Mahantongo Valley". This narrative provides additional information about the 1830-1840 migration of Mahantongo Valley settlers to their new homes in Jefferson, Armstrong, and Clarion counties. See Appendix pages 329 and 330.

Jody (Klinger) Teeter's residence on Ridge Road was earlier the Ammon Knorr farm, at the intersection with Hoffman Road.

The Aaron and Jody Teeter residence was the location of the Enty Residence in the early 1800's. Other previous residents include Abraham Starr (Civil War Veteran) and Nathan Erdman and Lamar and Larona Klinger. J. Starr and A. Starr named 1875 map

Part IV: The Simmy Family—An African American Pioneer Family in the Mahantongo Valley

Present residence of the Richard Ney Family

The Ney Homestead location was the Jacob Starr property in the early 1800's as purchased from William Simmy, Sr.

The present residence of Brian and Sheila Klinger, it was also the residence of Abraham and Mary (Troutman) Erdman, who purchased this land from George Simmy. George is buried between Abraham and Mary Erdman at Salem Church.

Brian Klinger's Residence, Winter of 2015

Part IV: The Simmy Family—An African American Pioneer Family in the Mahantongo Valley

Earnest and Sandy Klinger Farm Prior residents include the Smith's who also owned the Mattern Farm in the background. This land was originally William Simmy, Sr.

Klinger Farms as viewed from the residence of Kurt and Jaime Snyder. The Snyder residence was earlier Frank Clark and Ivan Boyer. The Frank Clark Farm was originally part of the lands of William Simmy, Sr.

Dennis Mattern Residence in 2015, earlier owners include the Smith's, John Knorr, and William Simmy, Sr.

The new residence of Aaron Mattern in 2015. This was the earlier residence of Widow Kline on the north side of Hessedale. Isaac Kline and David Hesse settled south of this new residence.

Part IV: The Simmy Family—An African American Pioneer Family in the Mahantongo Valley

A new Amish one room school is being built on the David Ray Stoltzfuss Farm in Rough and Ready on Boyer Road. The Stoltzfuss Farm was earlier the residence of Edgar Clark, and Barbara and Tyrone Whery.

Peter Zerfing Residence in the early 1800's. Zerfing's one room school was nearby on Hoffman Road. Most recently the Walter and Betty Dietrich residence which is presently owned by Michael Reiner. "Humpty" Bordner lived here as well.

Zerfing's School, October 9, 1914, Upper Mahantongo Township, Schuylkill County, PA

The children stand with the teacher as a group. Three rows were identified, although the rows are not straight.

Row 1: Girl holding sign; Bessie (Ramberger) Clark; Kathryn (Ramberger) Wiest; unknown girl; unknown boy.

Row 2: Minnie (Ramberger) Drumheller; Raymond Ramberger; Kate Wiest, in white dress, holding her hands together. This is George Deibert's mother; Emma Smith, small dark complexed child with a bow in her hair; unknown girl, with white buttons on dress; Helen (Ramberger) Davis; Unknown girl with polka dot dress; unknown girl; tall unknown girl; Clarence Wiest, small boy with dark jacket; Naomi, raised on Willie Erdman farm, which is now Mike Deibert farm. She married Charles Starr, standing next to her in back row.

Row 3: Unknown boy; unknown girl with two ribbons in her hair, plaid shirt, probably a Hoffman; Annie Mae (Ramberger) Rothermel, Mary Starr, black hair bow, married Howard Maurer; Erdman girl, black hair bow; teacher; Willie Klinger, nickname, Knickerty Knackerty; Charles Starr; unknown boy.

For more information on the Ramberger children identified on this photo, see the book, "There is Something about Rough and Ready," pages 107-115.

Part IV: The Simmy Family—An African American Pioneer Family in the Mahantongo Valley

Interview with Larona (Wiest) (Klinger) Smink, August 6, 2015

at Her Home on Ridge Road, East of Franklin Square, PA

Larona was born in Rough and Ready, the daughter of Clarence (Clippy) Wiest and Irene (Reed) Wiest. Her homestead has been earlier referred to in this book as the "Abraham Erdman residence". This farm is approximately ½ mile west of the Salem Church. It is the current residence of Brian and Shiela Klinger. Brian is the son of Larona (Wiest) Klinger and Lamar Klinger. Lamar grew up on the adjacent Klinger farm, ½ mile north of Larona's homestead. Here indeed is the marriage between a girl and the boy next door. Lamar Klinger died young leaving Larona with 4 children. Many years later Larona married Henry (Charlie) Smink of the Pitman area.

Clarence (Clippy) Wiest was born and raised in Rough and Ready on the farm now the residence of Chris and Missy Lenker. Irene Reed was born in Rough and Ready and raised on the Reed farm north of the Salem Church, now the residence of Steve and Ginny Haas. This farm has been referred to earlier in this book as the "Peter Schlegel farm". For more information about the various people who lived on these farms see the book, "There is Something about Rough and Ready". It is published by Sunbury Press.

One of the pictures in the Larona's photo collection is the Zerfing School picture from 1914. (See photo accompanying this article.) This one room school was located on Hoffman Farm Road close by Larona's childhood home and her later residence along Ridge Road where she raised her family. The photo is in her possession because her father, Clarence, attended this school. Clarence's homestead was approximately 1 mile west of the school house on Creek Town Road. There was a path across the fields from Clarence's homestead, up the hill, past the Jacob Ramberger farm, and down the hill to Zerfing School. There are 4 Ramberger children in the photo with Clarence. Note the building construction with vertical wooden boards and battens.

The homestead of Clarence Wiest was on the north side of Mahantongo Creek. A swinging bridge crossed the creek nearby. The bridge was maintained by the township and allowed foot traffic over the creek. On the south side of the creek was the blacksmith shop. Clair Hoffman was the blacksmith. His shop was an attraction for the boys of the area. The building still stands today on Vista Road, near the residence of Audrey Straub. See page 137 of the aforementioned Rough and Ready history book for a photo of the blacksmith shop. This is where Clarence got his nickname of "Clippy" Wiest. It seems as though the boys had a hair clipper and wanted to try it out. This clipper was operated by hand. Evidently Clarence cut the most hair and so earning his nickname, "Clippy," referring to the hair cuts he gave his friends. Clair Hoffman later moved his blacksmith shop across the creek. He took up residence on Hoffman Farm Road with his wife, Mary Starr. His given name was Harvey Clair Hoffman and his wife's given name was Mary Jane Starr. This location is the current residence of the Gene and Beverly Reiner family. The old blacksmith shop on Vista Road became a residence. Gurney Starr, who was married to Clarence's sister, Minnie (Wiest) Starr, remodeled the blacksmith's building for their home.

Larona, like her father, attended Zerfing School. When she was 5 years old, the teacher had a room and boarded at her parent's home, Clarence and Irene Wiest. This was conveniently less than one mile from the school. The teacher's name was Ellen Deichert Pianna, from Tower City. She was the teacher in 1941 when Larona was only 5 years old. The teacher wanted Larona to come to her school, even though she was one year younger than most. And so she did attend although Larona said the older kids made her nervous. There were some boys, Rothermels and Hoffmans, who did not behave well. Larona said things were thrown by the boys in the school room over her head and this upset her! Water for the school was carried from the house next door, which was the residence of Will Fetter. Presently this house is owned by Mike Reiner. In years past, the Zerfing family lived here and gave the land for the school. The Fetter's did not have children. Larona often visited with them as a young girl, while her father, Clarence, farmed the fields with his mules. Sometime later, a tragic fire engulfed the barn on the Clarence Wiest farm. The mules perished in the fire. Larona spent two years in grades one and two at Zerfings. She attended Klingerstown School for third grade. (Author's note: Evidently the school closed in 1943.) Some of the school students at Zerfings crossed the Mahantongo Creek on a swinging bridge. There were two swinging bridges about ½ mile apart. These bridges were constructed of four cables, anchored to concrete abutments with steps. Wooden boards provided a walkway. The two bridges were still useable in 1975 when Steve and Joan Troutman moved to Rough and Ready to their current residence on Ridge Road.

Larona recalled the neighbors of her childhood years. Oscar Starr lived on the next farm toward the Salem Church. The old house was removed and a new one was built there. Howard Maurer and his son, Ronald (Ketzer) Maurer, were the next generations. As a young lady, Larona spent time at Howard's babysitting little Ronald. Guy and Stella (Kreitzer) Klinger lived where Louise Rothermel has her residence today. Guy Klinger built this house nearby Larona's homestead. (His father, Allen, was a brother of Verna Klinger who married Stanley Romberger. Stanley and Verna were the grandparents of Steve E. Troutman. Stanley and Verna lived one mile west of Klingerstown. Barbara (Klinger) Ramberger, daughter of Guy Klinger, picked strawberries for Clippy.) Larona and her mother visited the Jacob Ramberger farm, ½ miles west of Larona's homestead. This Ramberger farm is now gone. It would have been visible from the residence of Steve and Joan Troutman. There is a book available which describes several Ramberger farms in the Rough and Ready area from yesterday. Extensive Ramberger genealogy is included in the book, "The Rambergers of Rough and Ready," by Troutman and Adams, available from Sunbury Press. Larona and her mother, Irene (Reed) Wiest, visited the residence of Clara Ramberger and Helen (Ramberger) Davis to quilt. This was on the Jacob Ramberger farm. Larona was a young girl at the time and she learned to quilt with these ladies. Quilting sessions were held during the winter months, every few weeks. These sessions took place in the parlor of the Ramberger home. There were many flowers surrounding the house, including blue bells and Easter lilies. After Larona was married with children, she returned to the Ramberger place to take pictures of her children in the blue bells. Larona and her husband, Lamar Klinger, always admired this location as a peaceful spot.

Larona told the story of Abraham Brooks. Abe Brooks became well known in the Rough and Ready/Hepler area. He was a poor Jew who came into the valley with just a bundle on his back. He be-friended Clarence Wiest and Tiny Heim. Abe worked for John Reed on the farm where Steve Haas lives now. The Reeds were Larona's grandparents. Abe was business minded. Clarence Wiest had an automobile and drove Abe to buy eggs from area farmers. They traveled quite far. They went down the valley to Millersburg and crossed the Susquehanna River on the ferry to Liverpool. On the west side of the river, they bought eggs from the Snyder County farmers. On one of the ferry boat crossings, their automobile slipped into the river, and had to be pulled out. They returned to Rough and Ready with their unbroken eggs. At the beginning of the next week, Abe and Clarence traveled to Frackville and Girardville to sell their eggs on market. Abe was successful with this business.

Abe married Jane Fetterolf from Rough and Ready. They had 2 daughters and 3 sons as Larona recalls. One son became a dentist, another son became a doctor, and the girls became school teachers. Abe's son Maynard Brooks, never married. He worked at the Pottsville Court House and continued to live on the homestead. Larona and her mother Irene, worked for

Maynard Brooks doing the washing of laundry and housecleaning. Maynard raised sheep on his farm and Larona's husband, Lamar Klinger, sheared his sheep. The Brooks farm is now the residence of Steve Jones near the Mahantongo Elementary School. Larona ended her story by saying, "Abe was poor when he came, and well to do in his old age."

Clair Hoffman Farm House

Current residence of Gene Reiner who built a new home on this location. Earlier residents include Clair Hoffman, and George Klinger.

Clair Hoffman's Blacksmith shop, on Visa Road, south of his farm on Hoffman Road.

Clair Hoffman's Blacksmith shop at his residence on Hoffman Road.

Part IV: The Simmy Family—An African American Pioneer Family in the Mahantongo Valley

Present residence of Ronald Maurer. This was earlier a Starr residence. A blacksmith shop is identified at this location on the Schuylkill County 1875 map.

The Kline's and the Knorr's operated a water powered sawmill at this location on the intersection of Mattern Hill Road and Ridge Road. This mill is marked on the Schuylkill County 1875 map. Many local farm buildings were built using wood cut at this location.

Something More about the Simmey, Enty, and Crabb Families

Tim Conrad (tconrad@ptd.net) is a historian for the Simmey and Enty families. He remarked, "Someone had an old write up on the Wehry family and it included this about my ancestor, Jacob Maurer."

Testimony in Maurer versus Simmy, 29 Oct. 1828. David Weary stated "I am related to Maurer. He is married to my father's sister. She is dead". Insinuated that Jacob Maurer treated his wife badly and that she committed suicide. "He is so miserable . . . caused the death of his wife." Jacob Maurer had first married Maria Magdalena Wehry. D. Wary is recorded on the 1875 map of Schuylkill County, Upper Mahantongo Township, as living at the prior William Simmy Sr. residence. In 1828 when the court record of Maurer versus Simmy was written William Simmy Sr. would have been alive. William Simmy Sr. died in 1833. William Simmy Jr., born in 1786, would have been 42 years old at the time of this testimony. Perhaps this was a dispute over land ownership or services provided. Both the families of William Simmy Sr. and William Simmy Jr. were assisted by Maurer men who served to administer Simmy property. Henry and George Maurer are named as some of the 12 free honest men during William Simmy Sr's. estate settlement in 1833. John H. Maurer, David H. Maurer, and interestingly enough, David Wearry, are named as some of the 12 free honest men during William Simmy Jr's. estate settlement in 1863.

Tim Conrad has in his possession a book signed by Gabriel Enty which was owned by the Claude Yoder family of Pitman, PA. The book is entitled, "The Complete Letter Writer," published by Leavitt and Company of New York. Gabriel Enty inscribed this book at the time of his purchase. "Gabriel Enty from Mathintongo (Mahantongo), Baught this book in Pottsville, Pennsylvania, July 5 AD, 1866, price 40 cents." Gabriel also wrote on the inside of the front cover, "Gabriel Enty Steal not this book for fear of shame for here you see the owner's name Gabriel Enty."

Gabriel Enty (1846-1914) and his older brother Jonathan Enty (1844-1864) and older sister, Mary Ann Enty (1832-) (md. Benjamin Crabb) were born in the Mahantongo Valley. The Enty men served during the Civil War with the 43rd Colored Troops. At the time of his purchase of the above mentioned book, Gabriel's older brother Jonathan, had been killed in the Civil War. Jonathan left a wife, Mary E. Wilson, with a young son Aaron Enty. Jonathan Enty went missing in action at Petersburg, Virginia during the Civil War. He was presumed dead.

Norm Gasbarro (civilwar.gratzpa.org) has posted a Civil War blog on the Enty family in the Civil War. He has published enlistment records which pertain to Gabriel and his older brother Jonathan. The record for Gabriel Enty follows.

Gabriel Enty-43 U.S.C.T.

43 Reg't. U.S. Colored Inf.

Age, *18 years*; Height, *5 feet 7 ½ inches*; Complexion, *Dark*; Eyes, *DK*; Hair, *DK*; Where born, *Northumberland County, PA*; Occupation, *Black smith*; Enlistment, *March 22, 1864*; Where, *Pottsville, PA*; By Whom, *Capt. Lower*; Term, *3 years*; Remarks, appointed a Corpl April 1, 1864; Wounded on duty, July 24, 1864; Discharged, June 8, 1865 at hospital by reason of G.S. Wounds (gun shot); signed, J.H. Schooley, copyist.

Jonathan and Gabriel Enty both had a dark complexion and were about the same height. At the time of his enrollment, Gabriel was living in Heginstown (Hegins, PA), and working as a black smith, a trade he learned from his brother-in-law, Benjamin Crabb. During Gabriel's service he was wounded in the right hand and was discharged on 8th of June, 1865, on a Surgeon's certificate of Disability. He was wounded at Petersburg, Virginia while throwing up breastworks (shoveling ground) and it resulted in a partial loss of the use of the right hand. After his discharge from the Army, Gabriel worked various jobs. It was during this time, soon after his discharge, that he purchased the above mentioned book. He was a coal miner living in Shamokin in 1870. He was a black smith living in Harrisburg in 1878. He later worked in Wilkes- Barre through 1904. In his old age he was cared for at the State Soldier's Home in Erie, PA. At that time he stated he was divorced, being the father of 8 children, 5 of whom were still living. Gabriel is buried in the Wilkes -Barre City Cemetery in Luzerne County, PA. This biography information courtesy of Norm Gasbarro, Gratz, PA.

Jonathan and Gabriel Enty had an older sister Mary Ann Enty. She was married to Benjamin Crabb who was a black smith from Gratz, PA. There was a long family association between the Simmy, Enty, and Crabb families for several generations. The US Federal Census records from 1860 record the household of William Simmy, Jr., and it lists the family members. This household was located at the current residence of Steve and Janice Dietz, south of the Rough and Ready church. The dwelling is recorded in Upper Mahantongo Township, Schuylkill County, race, Mulatto, post office, Rough and Ready. The following family members are listed: William Simmy (Jr.), age 73; Rosena Koons, age 19; Liddy Enty, age 2; George Crapp (Crabb), age 5.12 (5 months, 12 days?). Author's note: William Simmy Jr.'s wife Catherine, was deceased at a young age. Catherine, the daughter of William Simmy Jr. and Cathrine, married Joshua Enty. Perhaps Liddy Enty is Catherine and Joshua's daughter, living with her grandfather. Rosena Koons is probably the maid.

The Crabb family is described in the book, "A Comprehensive History of the Town of Gratz, PA," published by the Gratz Historical Society, 1997. Pages 340 and 341 are the source of the following text:

The Crabb family lived here for many years, arriving in Gratz about 1824. Peter Crabb, b. ca. 1787 and wife Mary Magdalena, b. ca. 1804, purchased lot 47. A log house was constructed, this being the current residence of Mrs. Shirley Byle. Benjamin Crabb was the second son of a family of 8 children.

Benjamin (1824) md. Mary Ann Enty (1832) of Schuylkill County. After the Civil War, Benjamin lived in Sacramento where he was employed as a blacksmith, working for Edward Wiest at the Hotel. In 1870, Benjamin, his wife and 4 children, lived in Gratz, and he worked as a black smith. They lived in part of the house his brother Jeremiah occupied. In 1880 Benjamin was living in Gratz and continued as a black smith. Another section of the Benjamin Crabb residence was occupied by George Crabb, age 49, and his wife Mary A. Crabb, age 48. George Crabb was also a blacksmith. Benjamin lived in Berrysburg, perhaps earlier in his life. From Gratz he moved to Fountain in Schuylkill County, later to Porter Twp. In Porter Township Benjamin and his brother, Jeremiah were partners in a blacksmith shop. It was located along the old Williams Valley Road between Reinerton and Muir. Benjamin and Mary Ann (Enty) Crabb had children Ellen, Jeremiah, William, Laura, and Benjamin W.

The Simmy, Enty, Crabb Genealogy

William and Margaret Simmy had 4 children born in Upper Mahantongo Township, Schuylkill Co., near the Northumberland County border. One child, Mary Elizabeth, (24 March, 1792-ca. 1865) has her birth recorded in the baptism record of Zion Lutheran Church, in Erdman, PA. Mary Elizabeth's baptism is dated June 3, 1792, sponsor Elisabeth Stutzmenin. Parents are named William and Margaret Simmy. The mother, Margaret Simmy is named one other time in this baptism record, on 10/28/1792 when Margaret (Mrs. William Simmy) was named the baptisimal sponsor of William, the son of John and Catherine Jacobs, b. 5/27/1792. This baptisimal information, courtesy of Elaine Moran.

Joshua Enty, Sr. (1775-1842) md. Mary Elisabeth Simmy (1792-1865). Daughter of William Simmy, Sr. Joshua Enty, Jr. (1810-1850) md. Catherine Simmy (1812-1850). Daughter of William Simmy, Jr.

Some of their children include: Mary Ann (1832-) md. Benjamin Crabb (1824-); Jonathan Enty (1844-1864) and Gabriel Enty (1846-1914). Both served in the Civil War.

Enty Family Research by Elaine Moran
The Enty Family, by Arthur Donald Enty

Edited from the original article published in the book entitled Jefferson County Pennsylvania History 1982 Published by Jefferson County Historical and Genealogical Society, Inc. Printed by Walsworth Publishing Co., Marceline, MO, page 149.

The name ENTY is unique to America. All Entys are related and sprang from one Tobias Enty, a Black merchant seaman from the Bahama Islands sailing under an English Flag. Tobias arrived in Philadelphia in 1783 when the black plague was epidemic. (Editor's note: In 1793, the yellow fever plague was epidemic. Arthur Enty may have been referring to this epidemic.) Black labor was in great demand and highly paid to bury the dead. Tobias left his ship, changed his name from Henty to Enty, and started the Enty Clan. He married a German woman named Elsa, served in the U.S. Army in the War of 1812 for which the Government awarded him a large tract of land in Schuylkill County, and raised a family of seven sons and one daughter. Tobias, my great, great, great Grandfather, died in 1842. Tobias' sons, Peter and Edward, and Grandson, Abram II, migrated to Jefferson County in 1834. Peter was an expert geologist/miner. They visited the Brice family in Templeton, Armstrong County on their way to Jefferson County. The Brice's were an old, established Black family having settled there in 1804. They met the Pauls in Jefferson County, another established Black family. Marriages/families ensued and the three families are closely entwined even today. Peter settled in Pansy, Abram, above Worthville, and Edward, on a farm across the creek from Langville. Family cemeteries are located atop a hill there which we call Jim Paul Hill and another is on the road between Pansy and Langville. Most of the Entys today are of the Peter Enty lineage. Peter died in 1875. Peter had a large family (16 children); Many are buried in the family cemeteries.

Entys have served in the US Military in every conflict since the War of 1812. Nearly all able-bodied Entys and Brices fought in the Civil War with the Pennsylvania Colored Volunteers. More than a dozen gave their lives in that great war. They served with pride, honor, and glory; e.g., Ben Enty marched to the Sea with Sherman and they dug tunnels under Petersburg, VA and blew up that stronghold. The Entys, Brices, and Pauls were proud hard working farmers and miners. They were deeply religious, owned properties, voted, loved, married, and raised their families as free men and women. They loved sports, hunting, fishing, and still do. We are rightfully proud of them and their accomplishment.

The following information provided through the website, *Africans in America*: Philadelphia's yellow fever epidemic of 1793 was the largest in the history of the United States, claiming the lives of nearly 4000 people. This plague caused the skin to turn yellow and the person's vomit to be black. Refugees from the Revolution in St. Dominque arrived in Philadelphia throughout the 1790s. Saint Dominque was a French colony on the Caribbean island of Hispaniola, from 1659-1804. It is widely believed that refugees from St. Dominque were responsible for bringing yellow fever to Philadelphia in 1793. In late summer, as the number of deaths began to climb, 20,000 citizens fled to the countryside, including George Washington, Thomas Jefferson, and other members of the federal government (at that time headquartered in Philadelphia). At the urging of Benjamin Rush, the support of Philadelphia's free black community was enlisted ... The Black community dedicated themselves to working with the sick and dying ... as nurses, cart drivers, and grave diggers. Despite Rush's belief that Blacks could not contract the disease, 240 of them died of the fever. As the weather cooled, the disease subsided, and the deaths stopped.

Appendix

Maps Pages 300-306 Courtesy of:
The Atlas of Schuylkill County, PA by R.W. Beers and Company
Published by: F.W. Beers and Company, 36 Vesey St., New York, 1875

Maps pages 307-310 Courtesy of:
Northumberland County Sec #10 and #11, 1858
Pennsylvania State Archives

Maps pages 311-318 Courtesy of:
Northumberland County Sec #13, #14 and #15, 1875
Pennsylvania State Archives

Documents pages 319-324 Courtesy of:
Pennsylvania Archives, Harrisburg, PA
Dan Stutzman
stutzman.d.m.@gmail.com

Documents pages 325 and 326 Courtesy of:
Mr. E. Terry of the PA Historical and Museum Commission, 1984.

Survey Draft for Robert Clark, page 327

Survey Draft for Heinrich Shadle to George Shadle, page 328

Families who Migrated from the Mahantongo Valley to Jefferson, Armstrong, and Clarion Counties, page 329

Pioneer Colored Settlers in Jefferson County, PA, page 330

The Penns' Manor of Spread Eagle and the Grist Mills of the Upper Mahantongo Valley

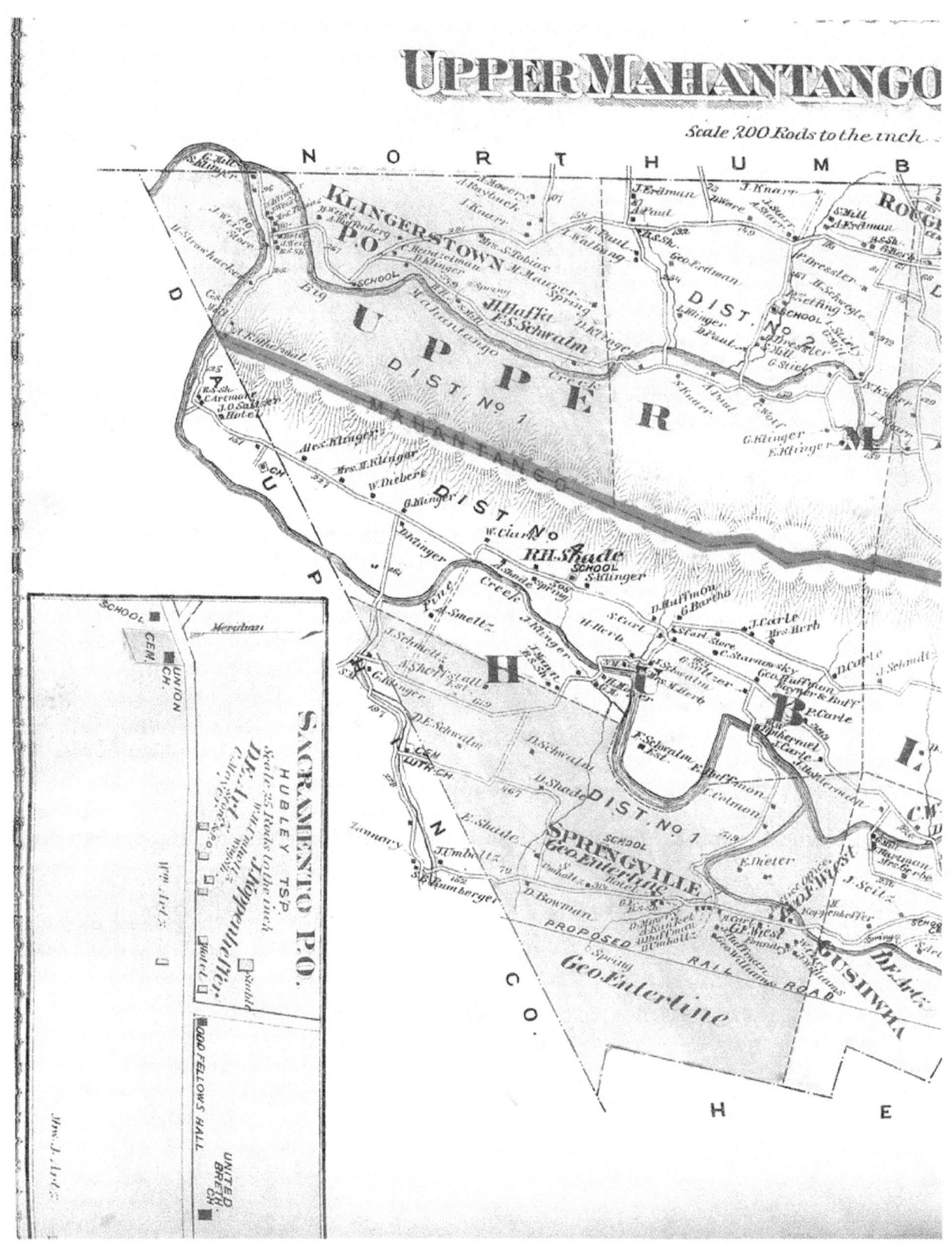

The Penns' Manor of Spread Eagle and the Grist Mills of the Upper Mahantongo Valley

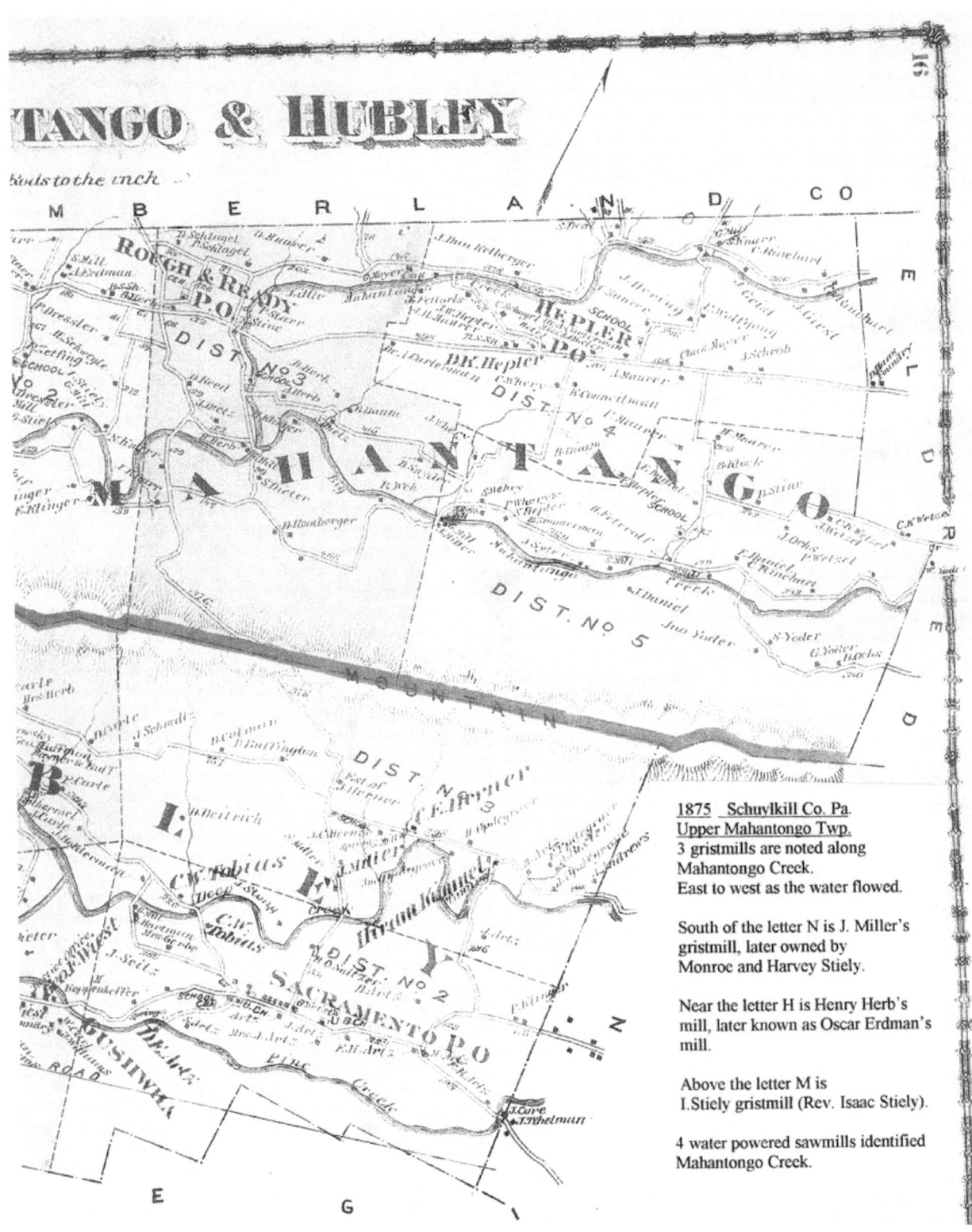

1875 Schuylkill Co. Pa.
Upper Mahantongo Twp.
3 gristmills are noted along Mahantongo Creek.
East to west as the water flowed.

South of the letter N is J. Miller's gristmill, later owned by Monroe and Harvey Stiely.

Near the letter H is Henry Herb's mill, later known as Oscar Erdman's mill.

Above the letter M is I. Stiely gristmill (Rev. Isaac Stiely).

4 water powered sawmills identified Mahantongo Creek.

Appendix

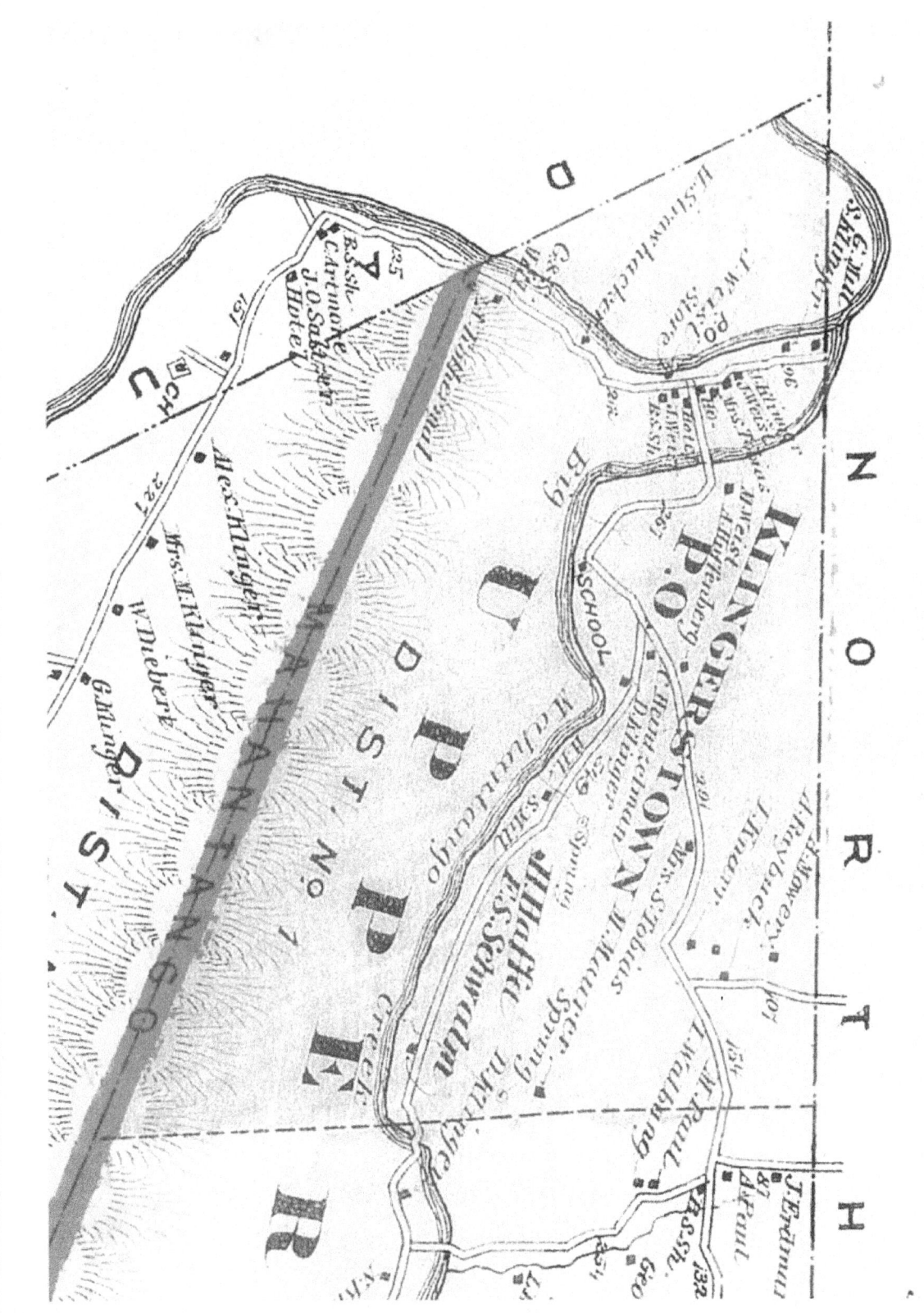

The Penns' Manor of Spread Eagle and the Grist Mills of the Upper Mahantongo Valley

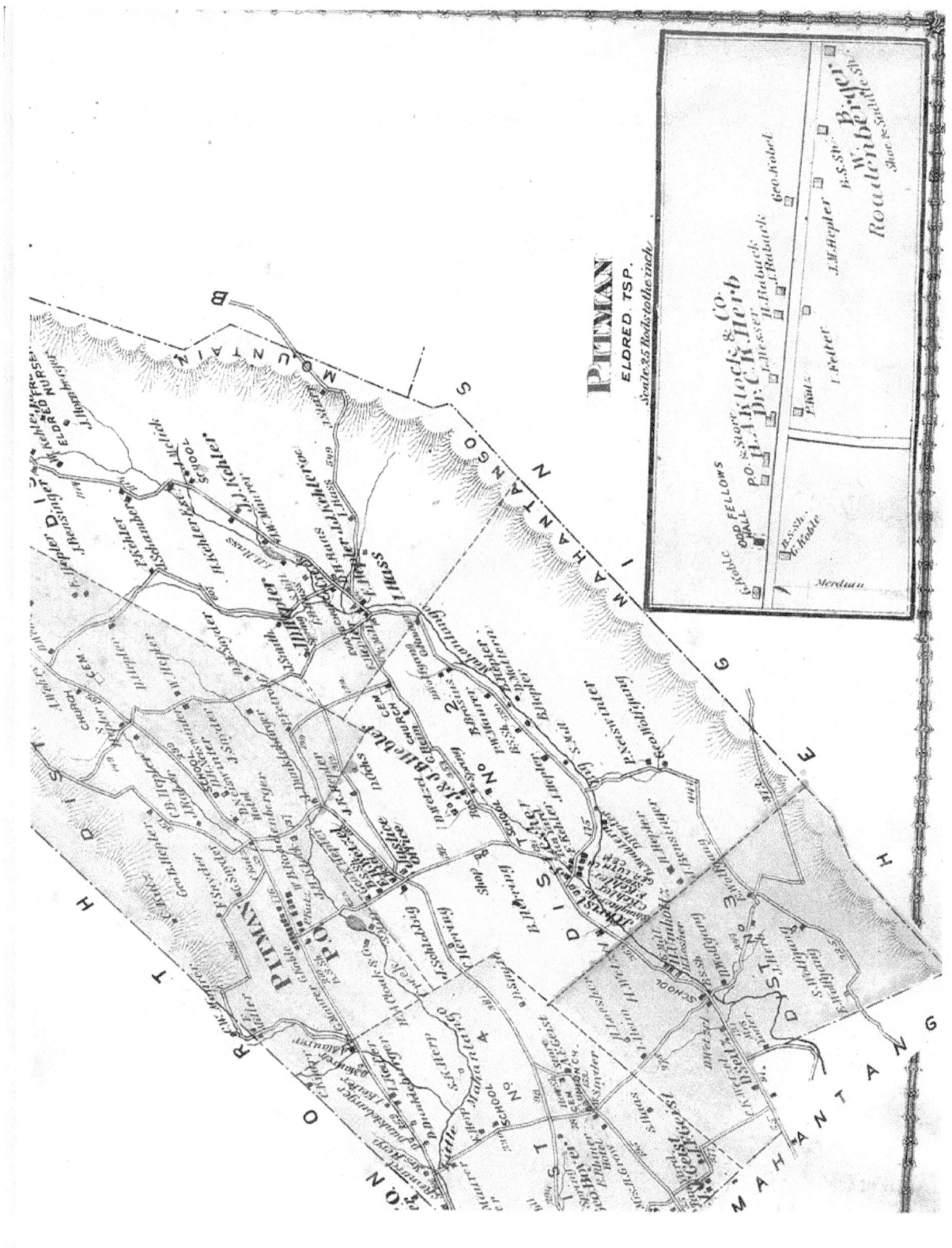

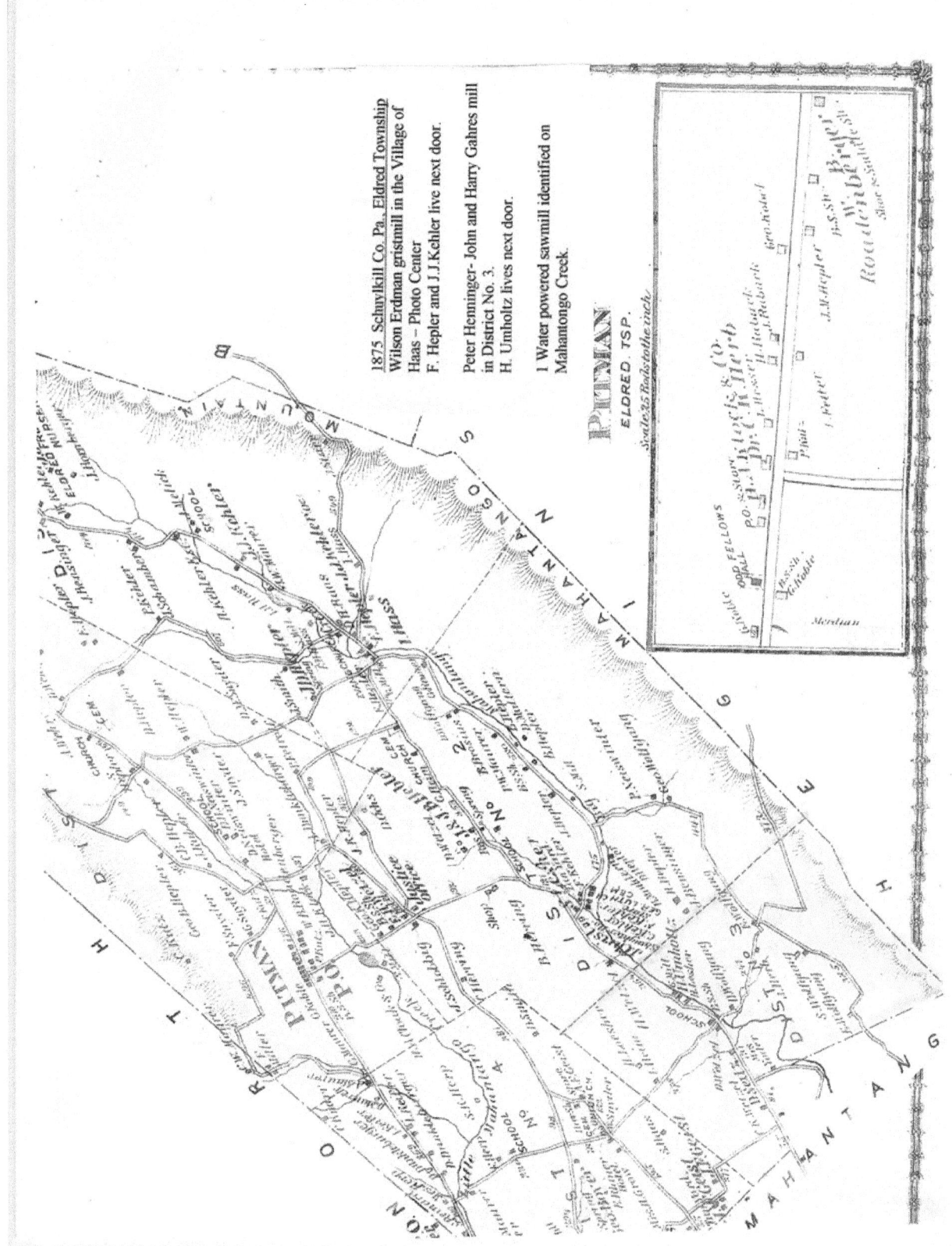

1875 Schuylkill Co. Pa. Eldred Township Wilson Erdman gristmill in the Village of Haas – Photo Center
F. Hepler and J.J. Kehler live next door.

Peter Henninger- John and Harry Gahres mill in District No. 3.
H. Umholtz lives next door.

1 Water powered sawmill identified on Mahantongo Creek.

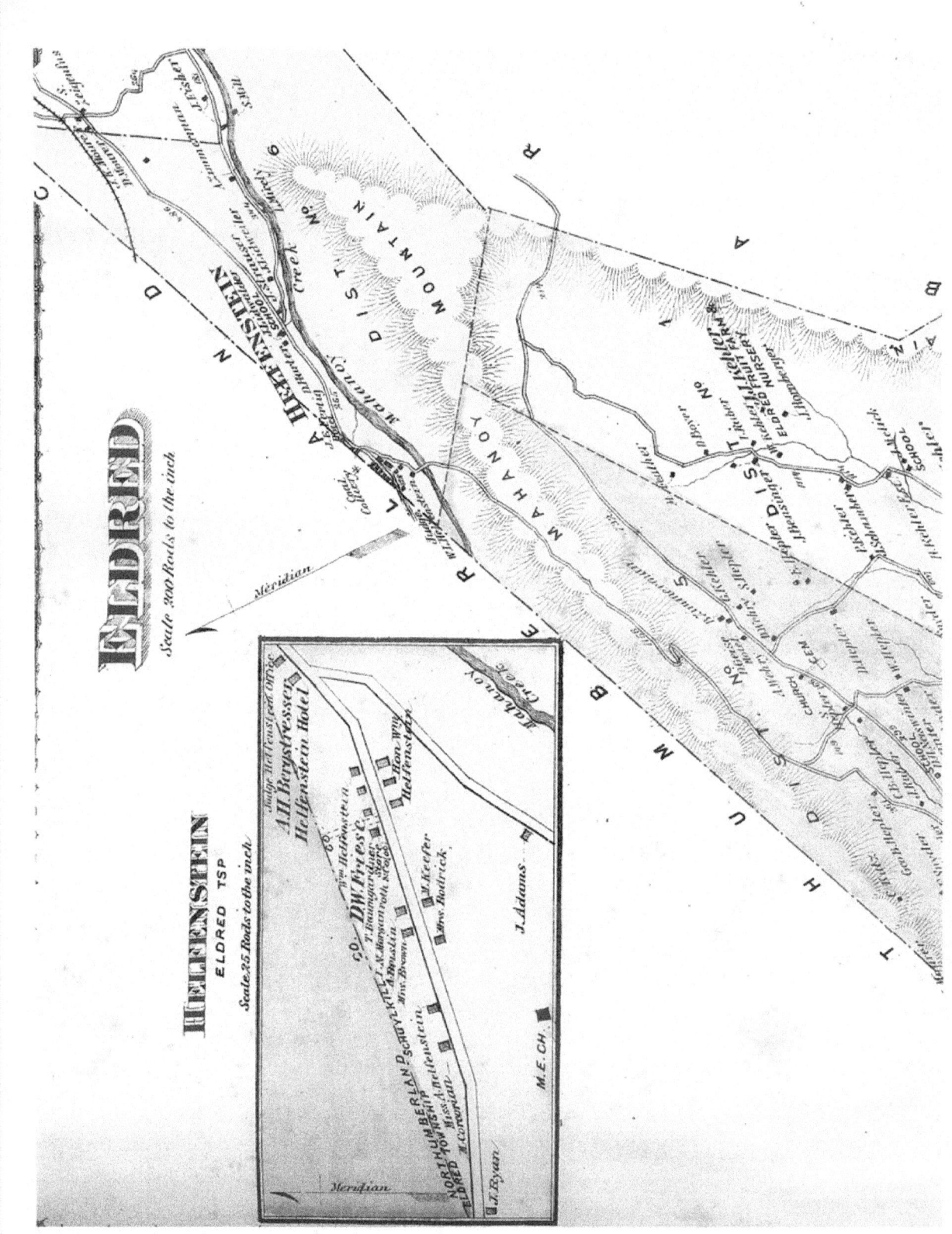

Appendix

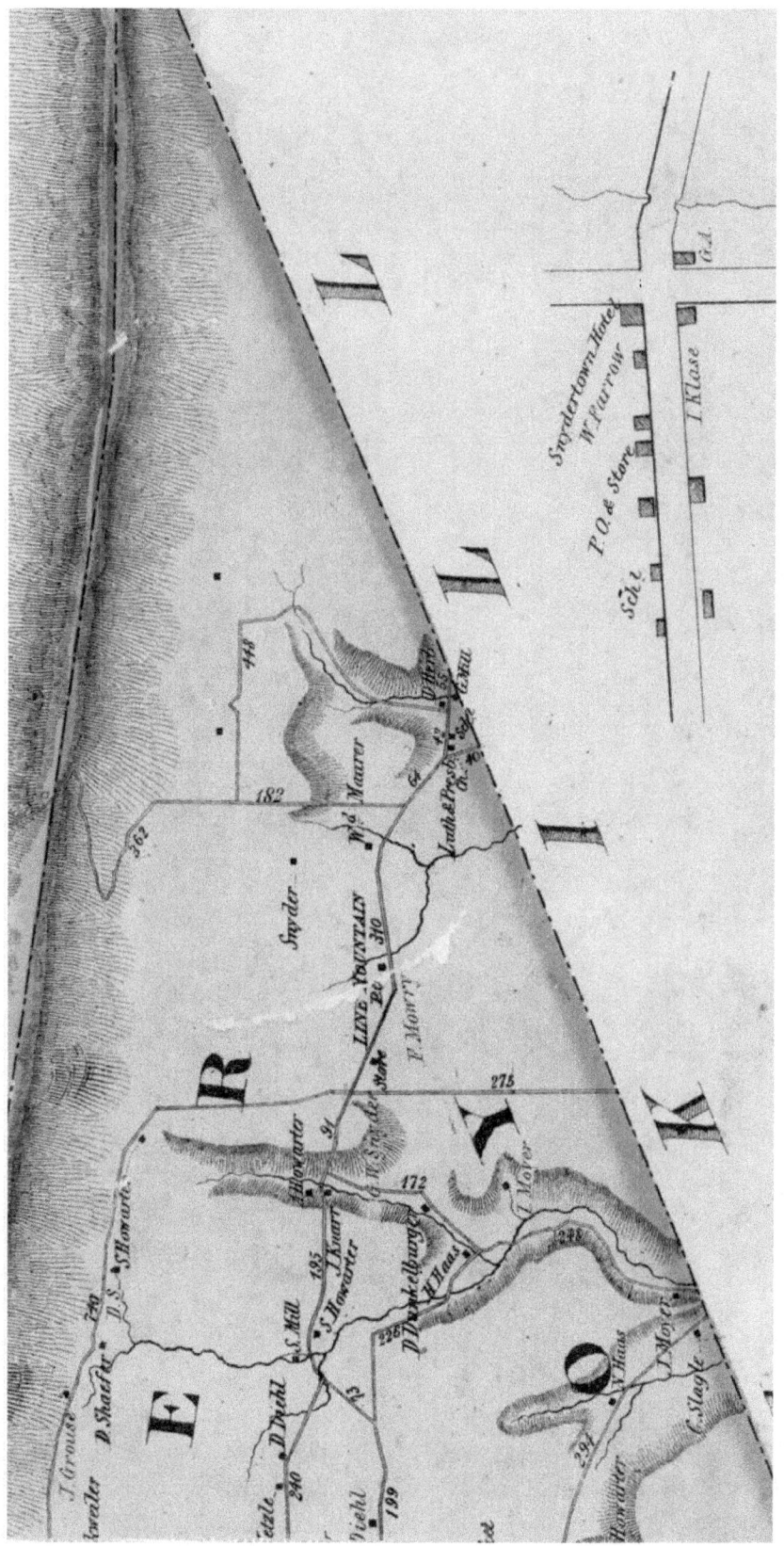

The Penns' Manor of Spread Eagle and the Grist Mills of the Upper Mahantongo Valley

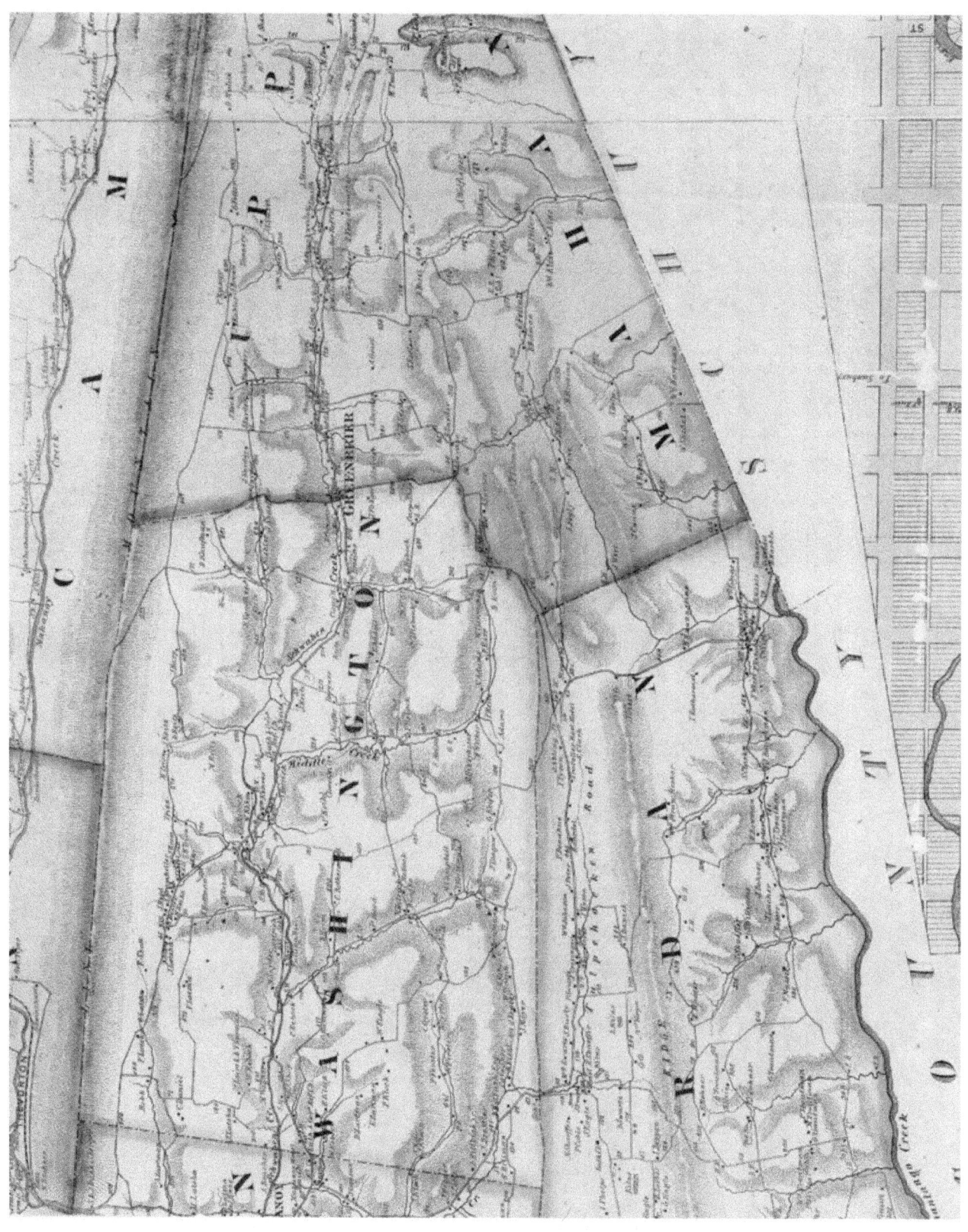

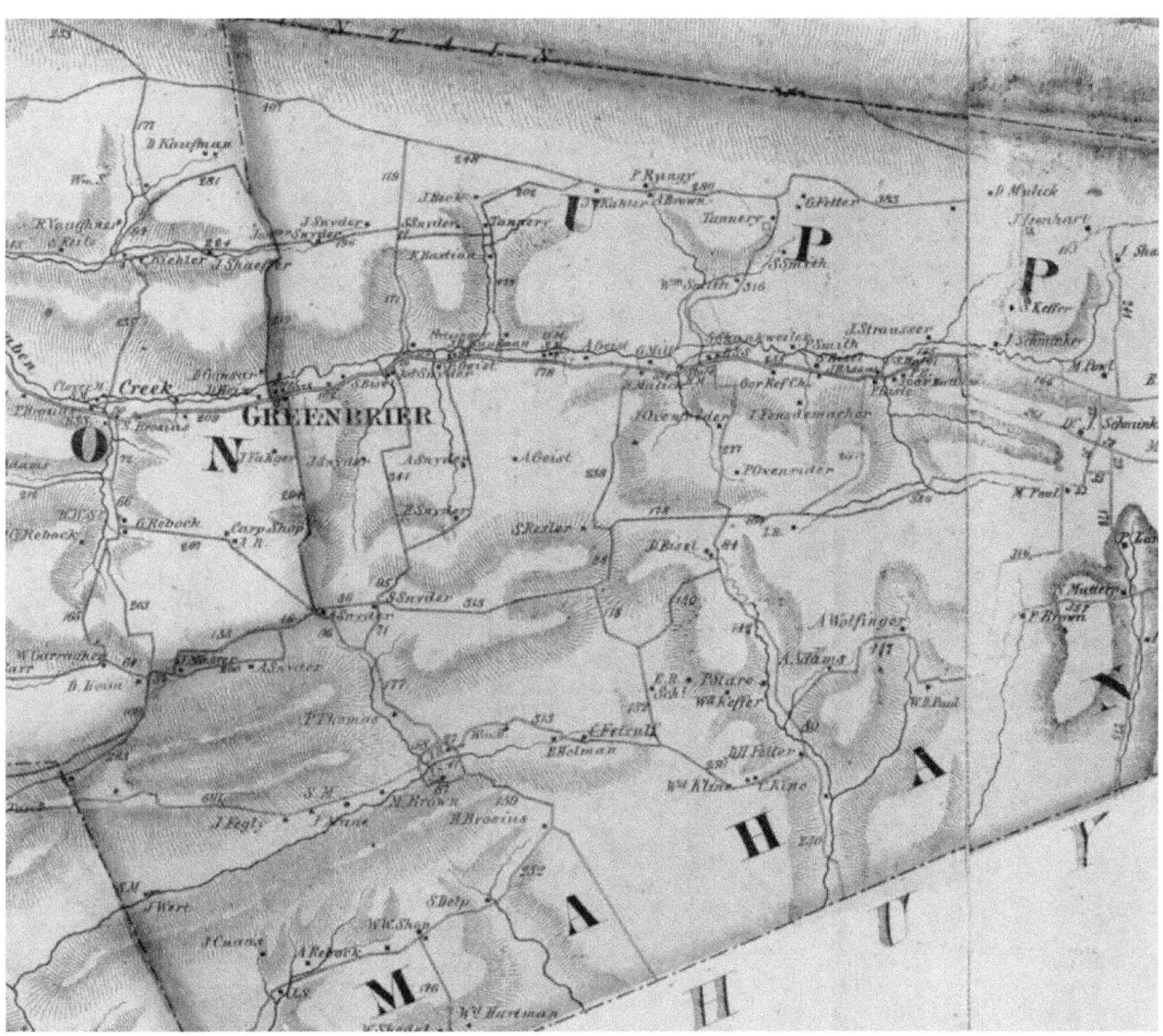

The Penns' Manor of Spread Eagle and the Grist Mills of the Upper Mahantongo Valley

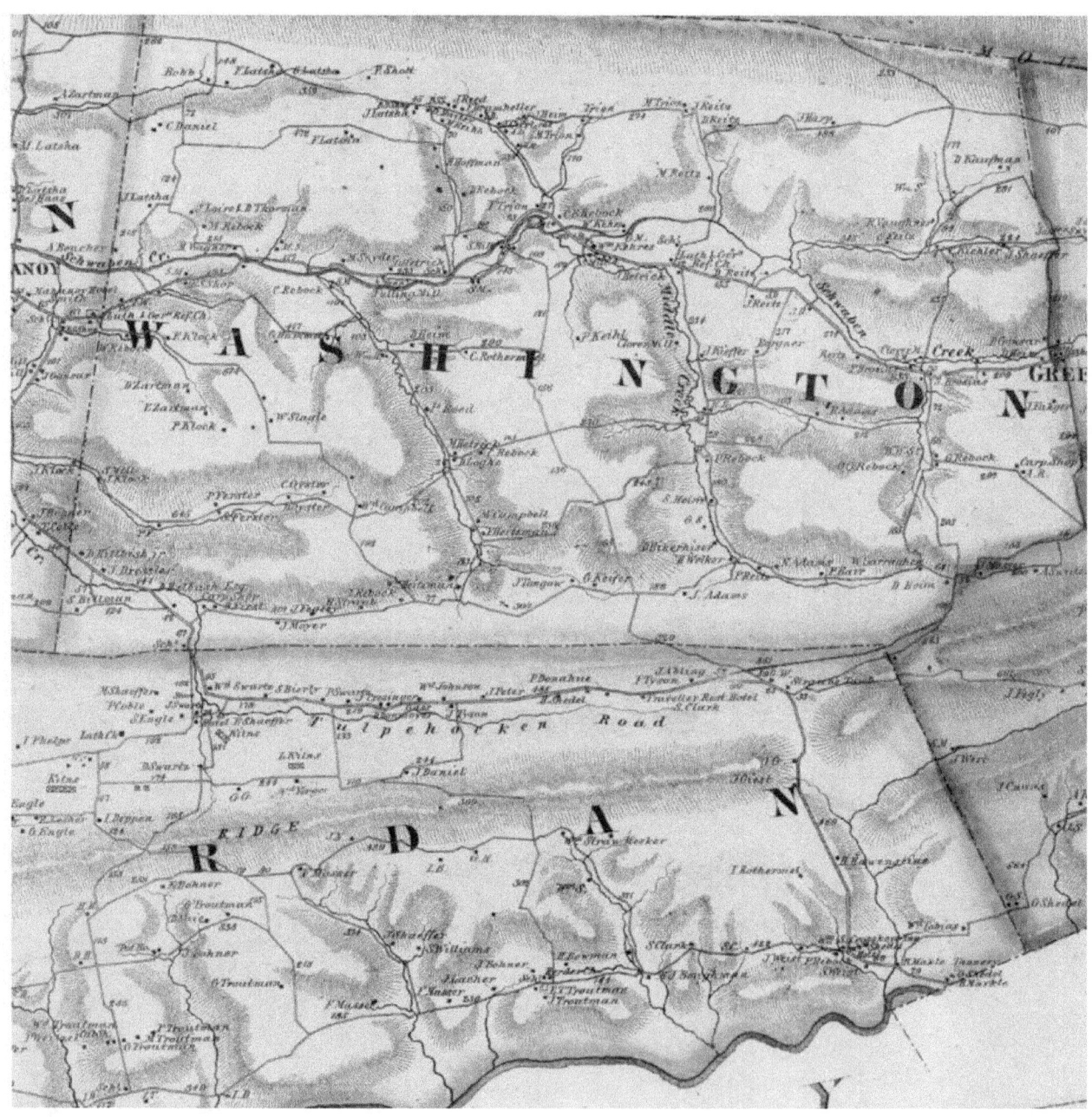

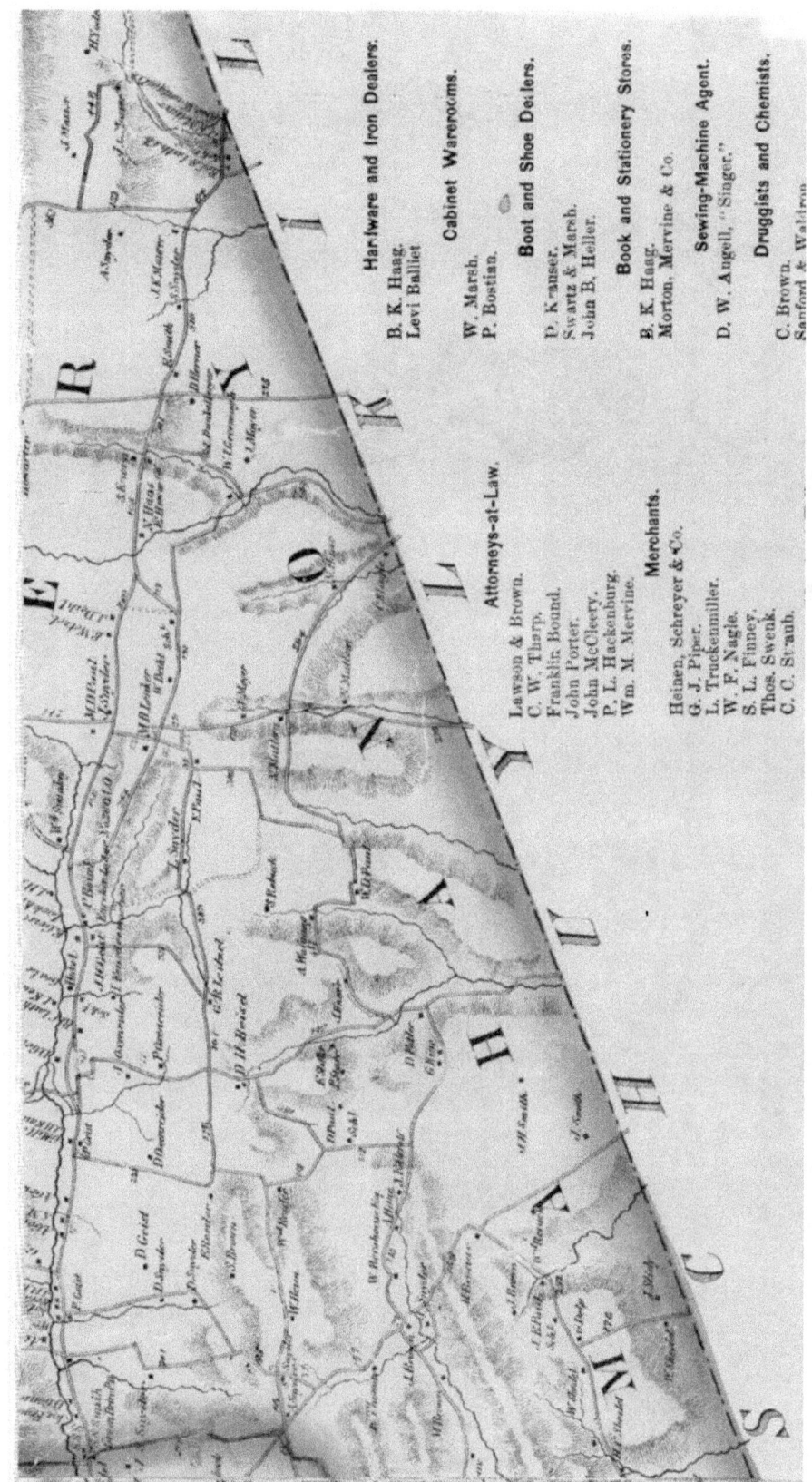

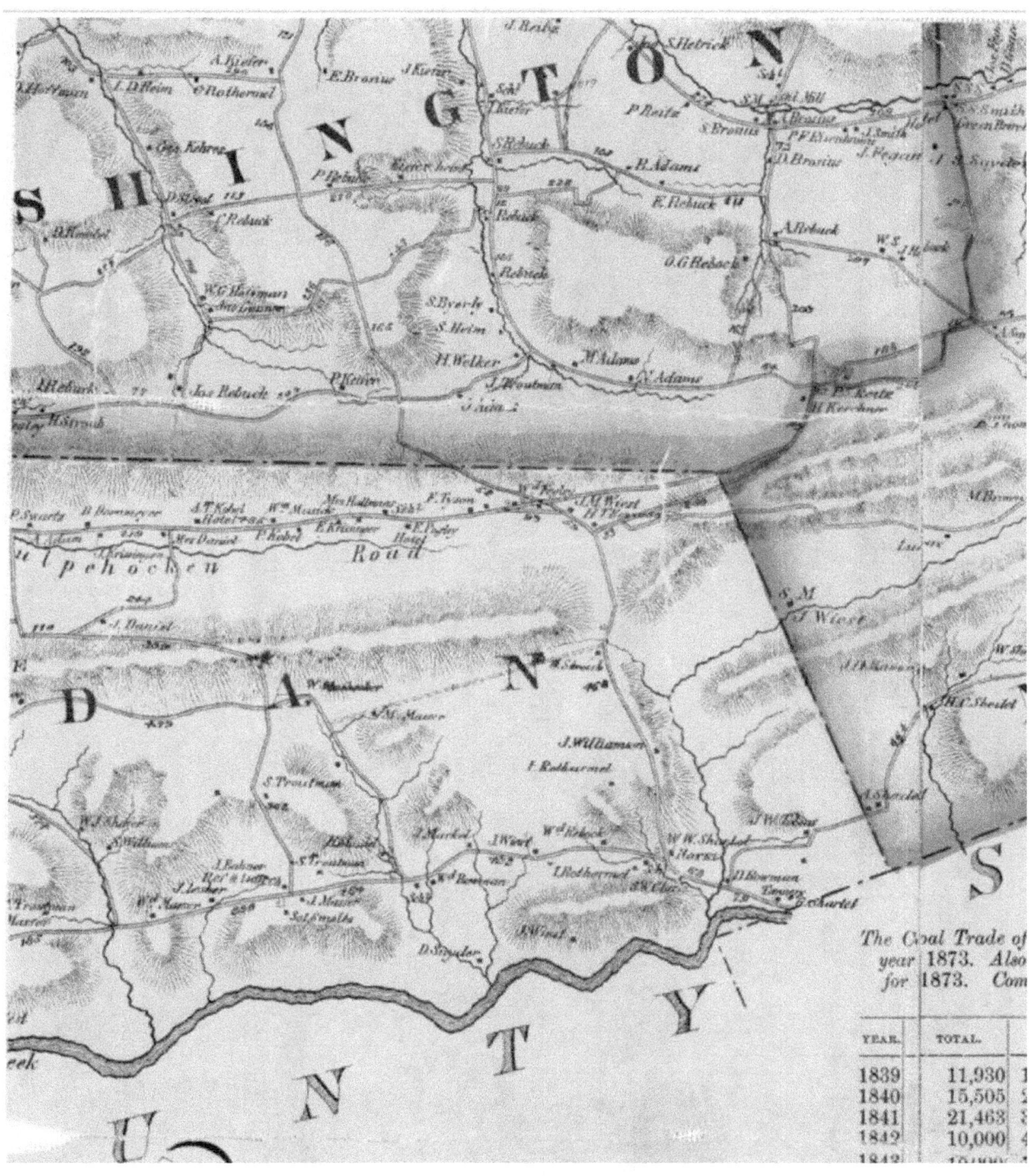

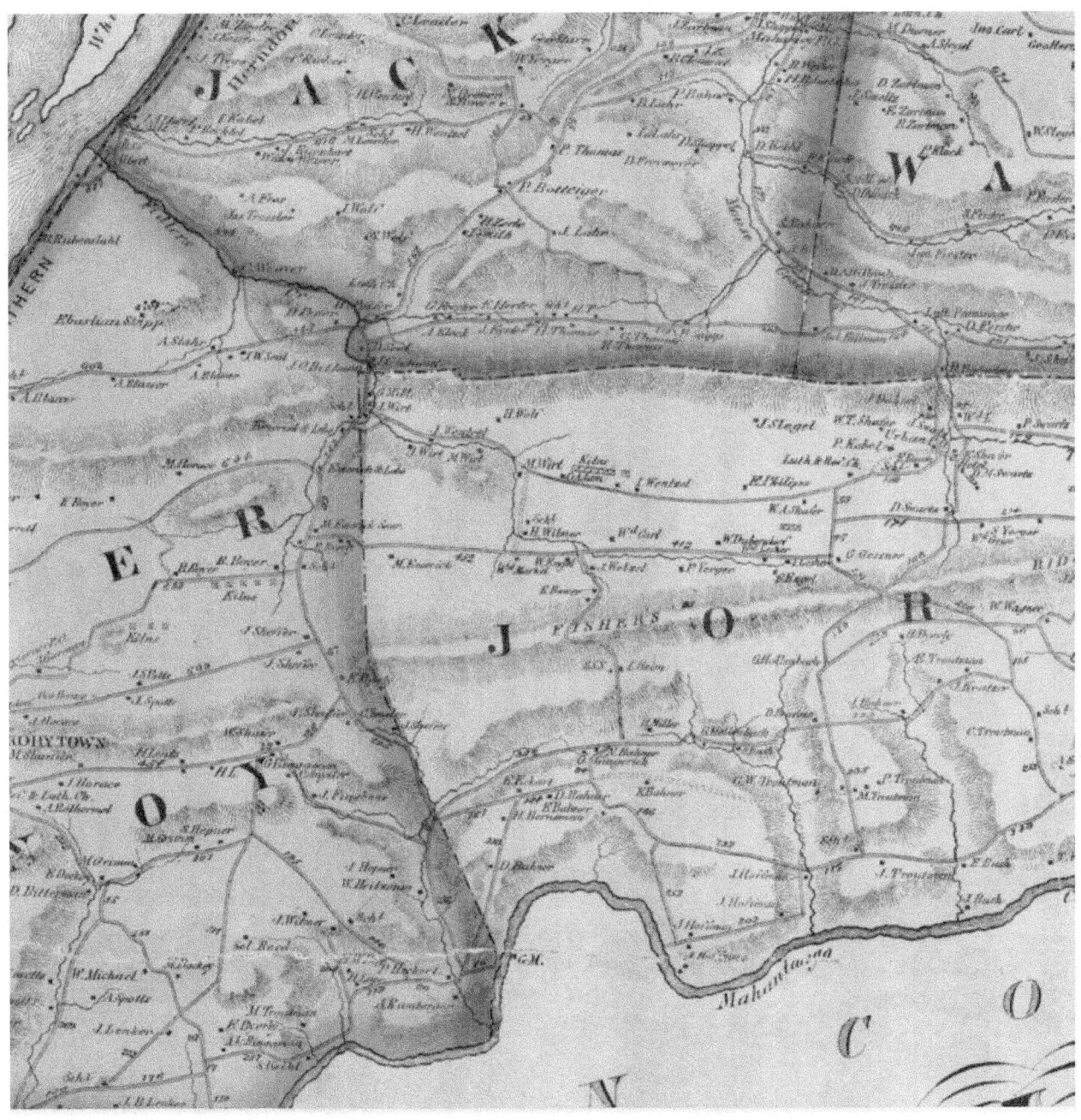

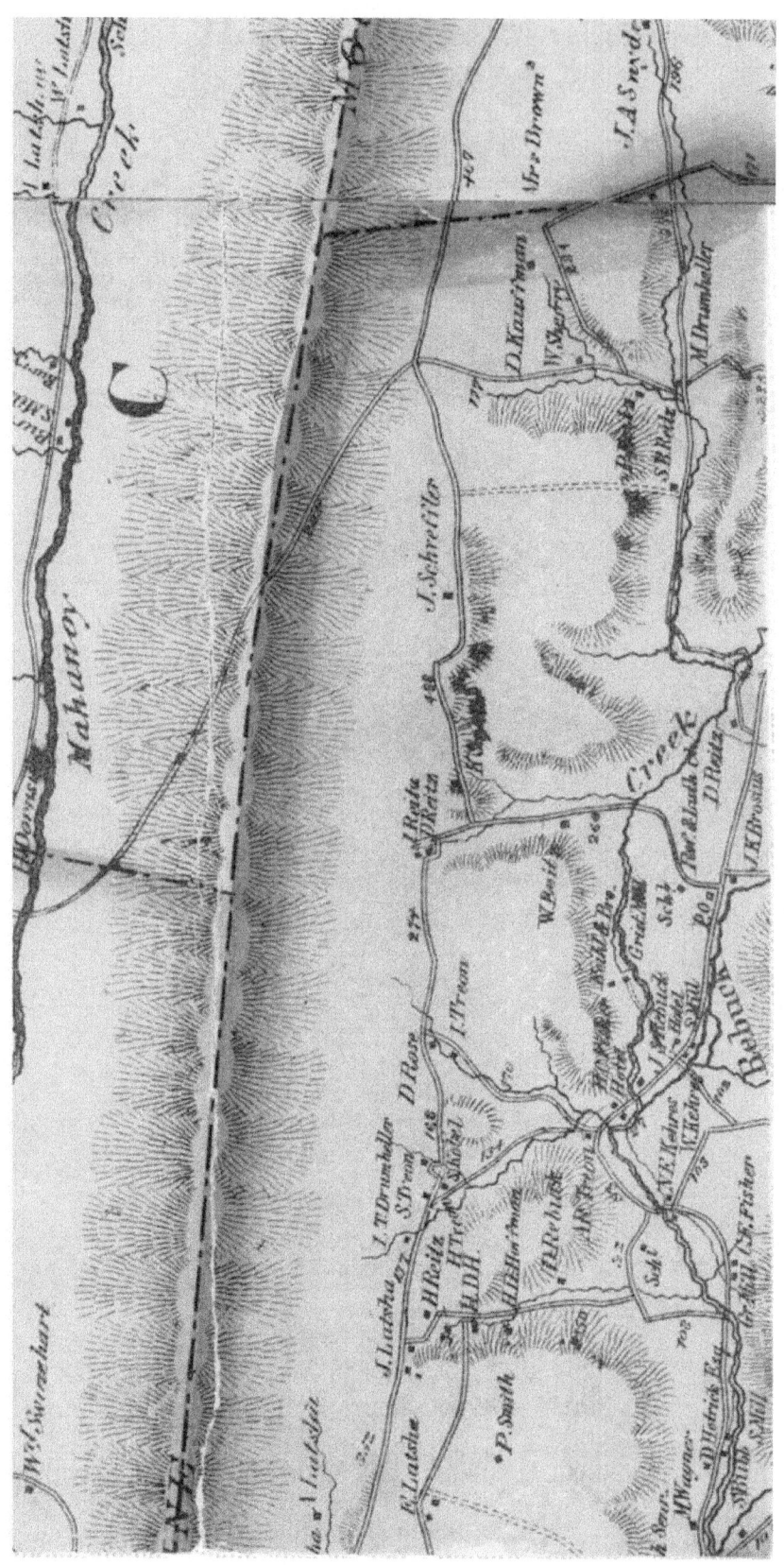

Appendix

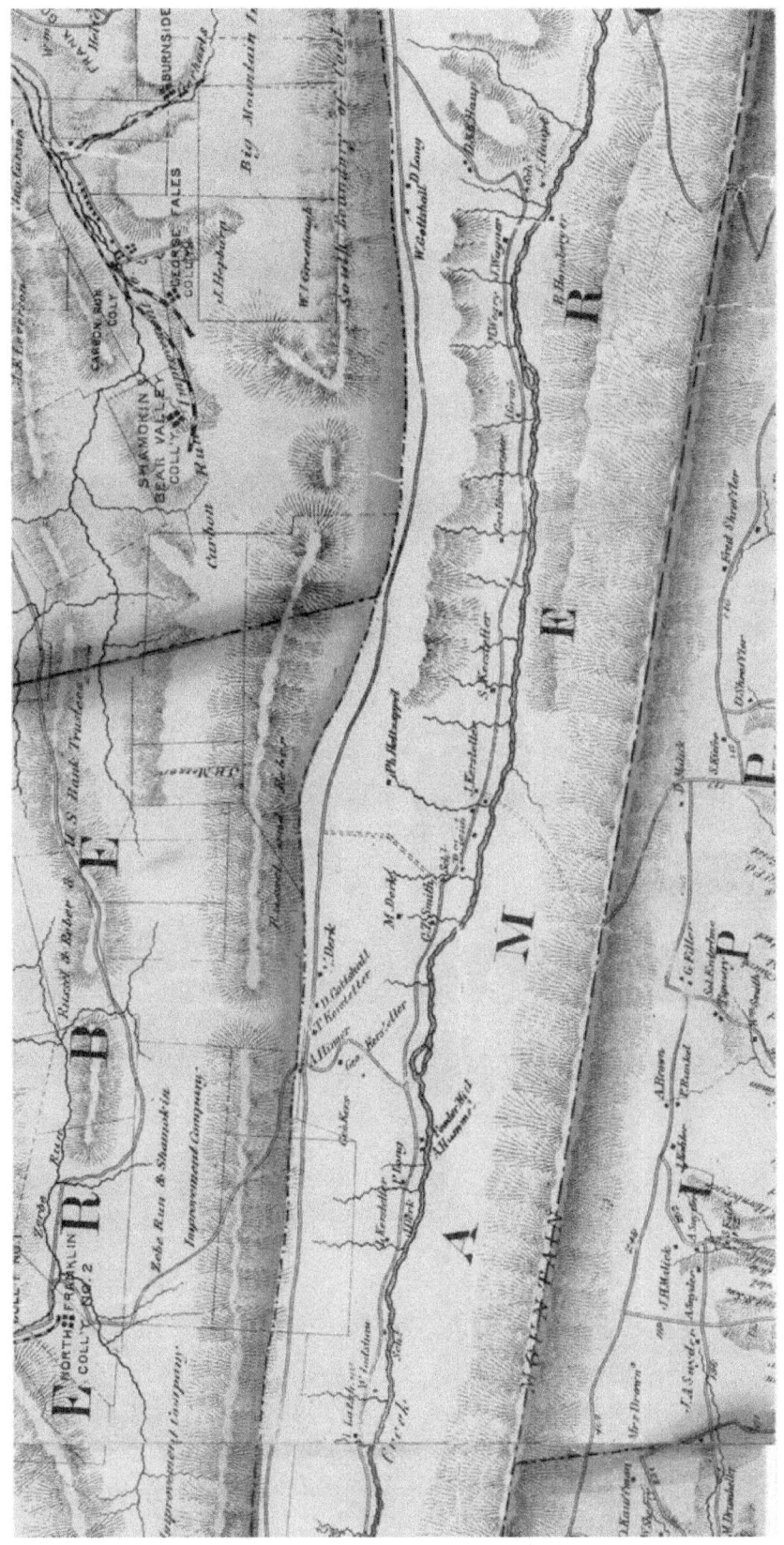

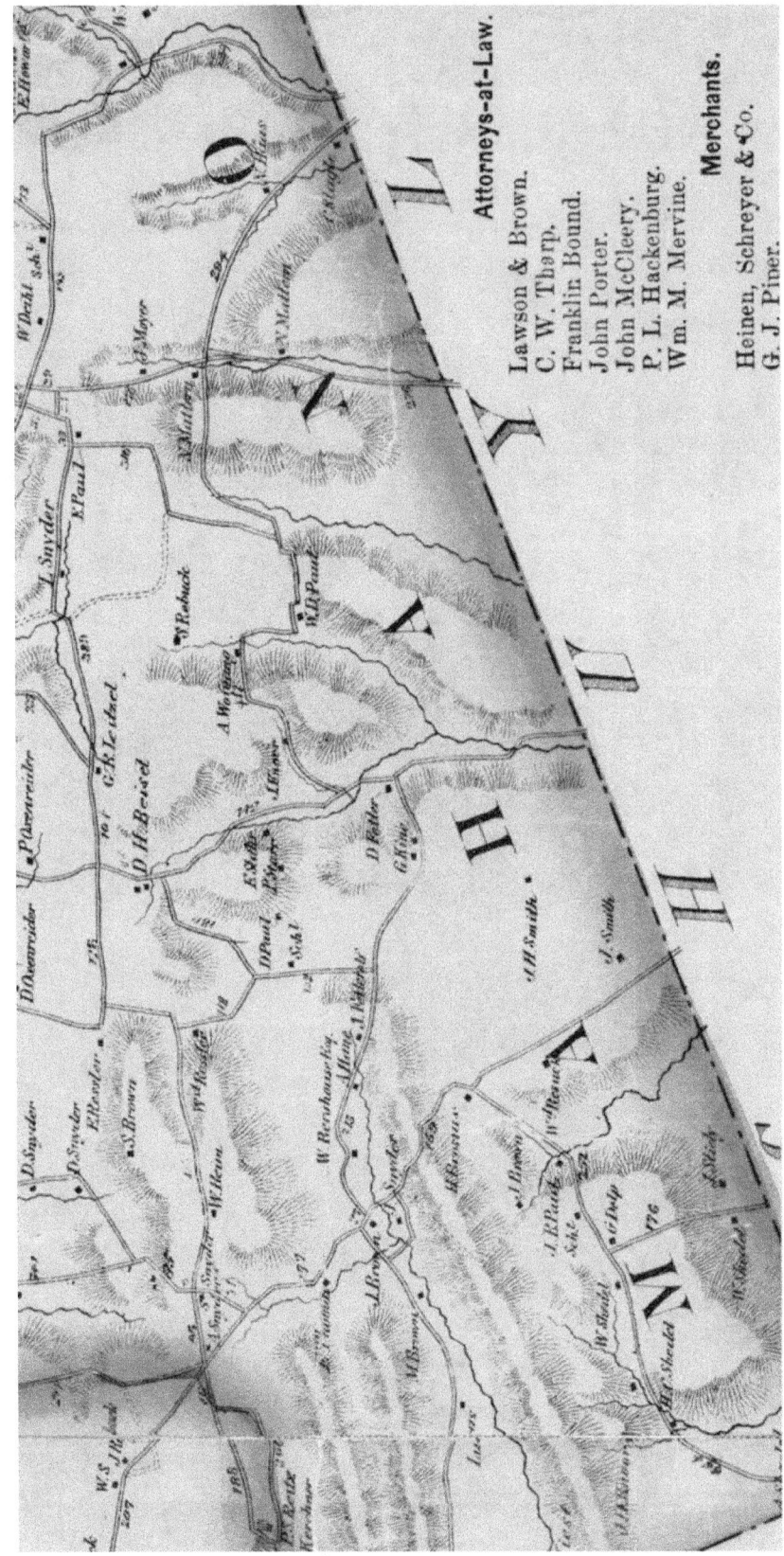

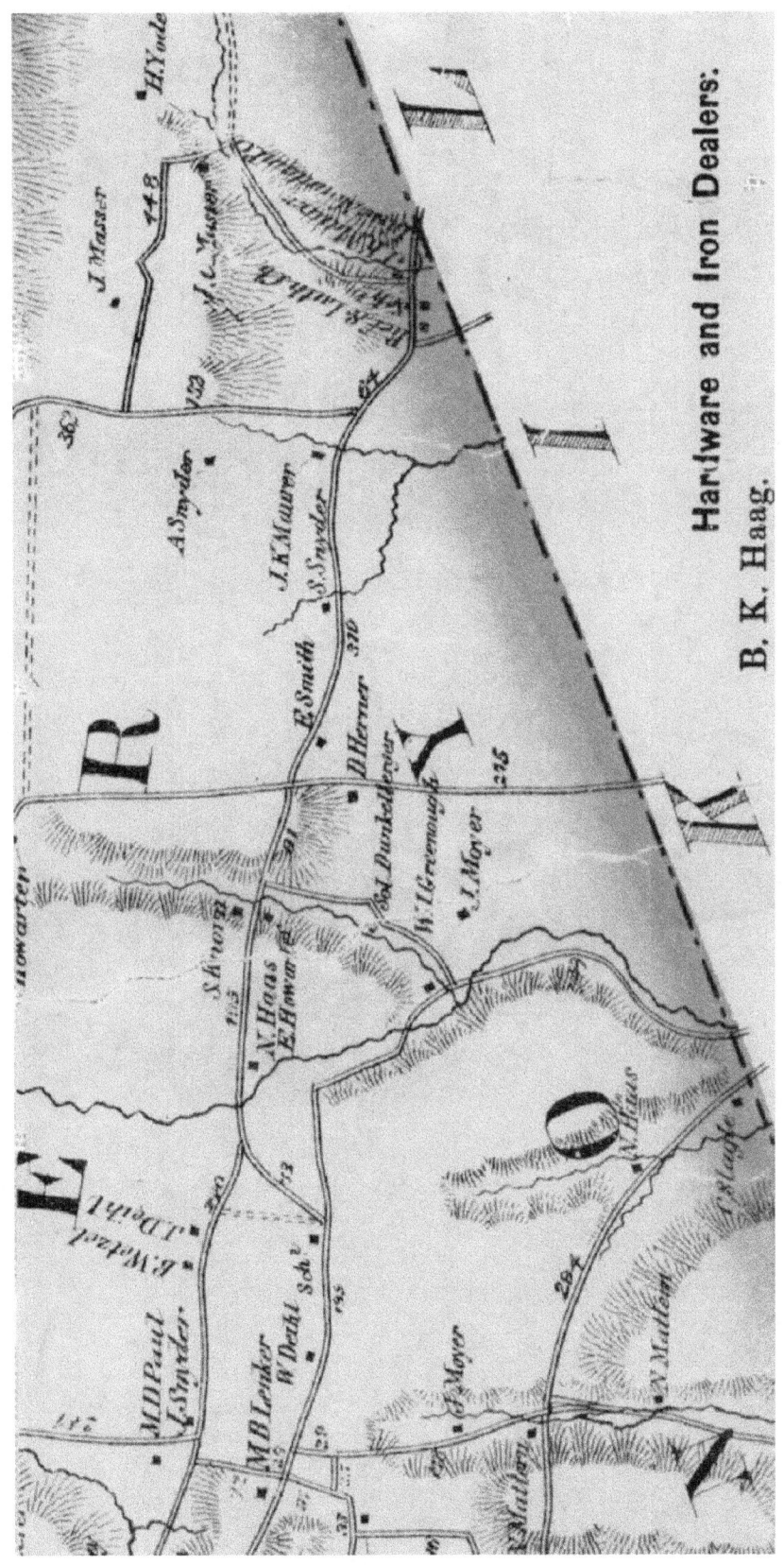

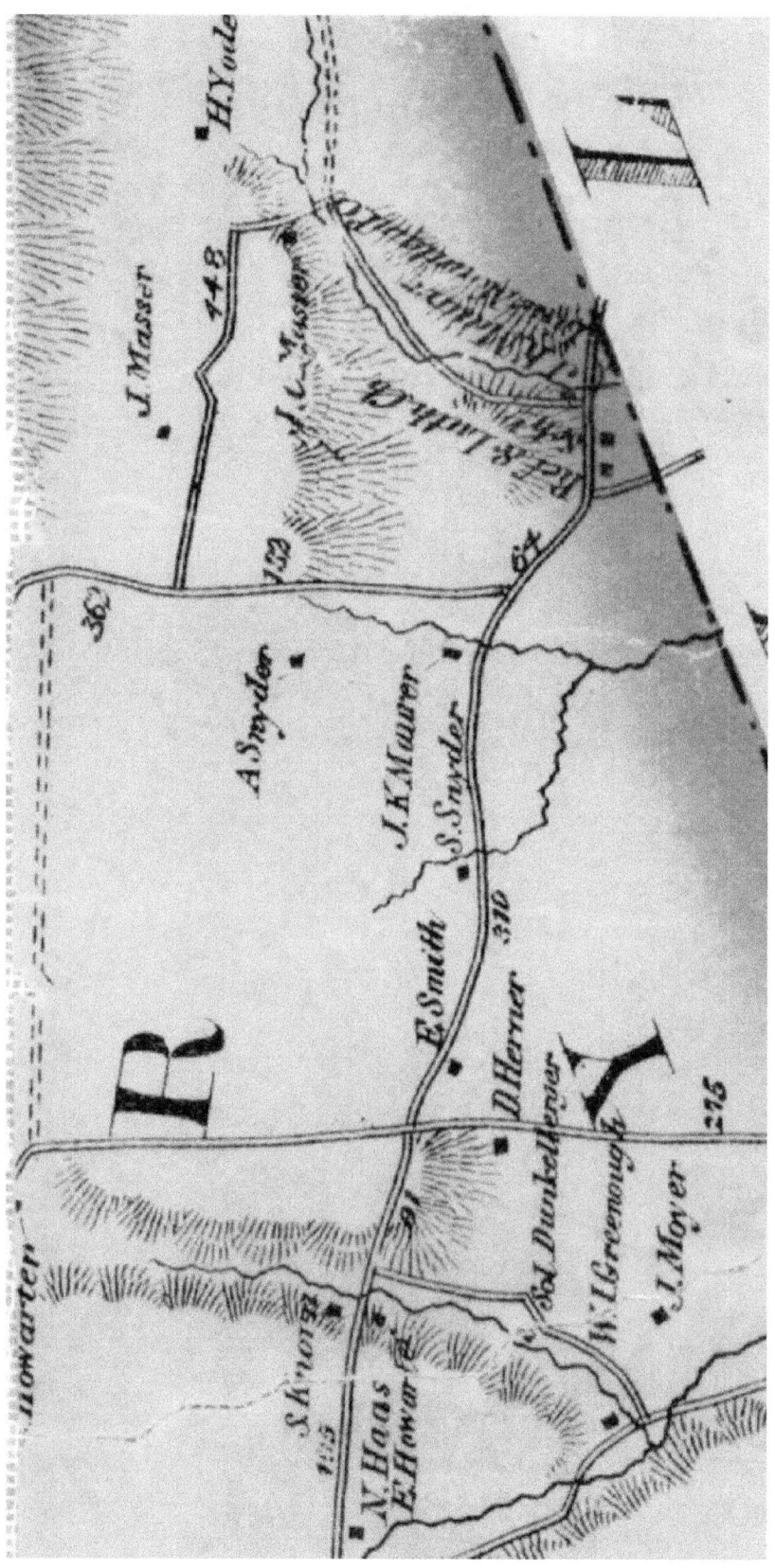

Appendix

Pennsylvania SS.   By the Proprietaries.

(Seal)

Whereas during the life of our late Father William Penn Esq[ui]r[e] as well by himself as by his Commissioners of Property Orders were given to the Surveyor General to survey or cause to be surveyed to and for his & our own use & behoof the tenth part of all such Lands as sh[oul]d be from time to time survey'd & laid out in the several Counties of o[ur] Province, And Whereas notw[ith]standing the said Orders given as [afo]resaid they were not executed as r[eq]uired but were too much neglected to[our] [o]ur great loss and disappointment, [The]se [a]re to authorize and require you for the time to come to survey [or] [ca]use to be surveyed for our own [so]le per use and behoof the quantity of Five hundred acres out of every Township or Tract of Five thousand acres of land which shall be here[af]ter surveyed within our said [Prov]ince & make returns from time [to] time into our Secretary's Office for which this shall be our sufficient Warrant. Witness J[a]mes Hamilton Esq[r] Lieutenant Governor of the said Province wh[o h]i[s] pursuance & by virtue of certain [po]wers and Authorities to him for this purpose (inter alia) granted [by] said Proprietaries hath [here]unto set his Hand and caused the seal of the Land Office to b[e affi]xed at Philadelphia this Twenty [eigh]th Day of November Anno Domini 1748.

                               James Hamilton

To Nicholas Scull Surveyor General.

IN TESTIMONY that the above is a copy of the original remaining on file in the Department of Internal Affairs of Pennsylvania, made conformably to an Act of Assembly approved the 16th day of February, 1883, I have hereunto set my Hand and caused the Seal of said Department to be affixed at Harrisburg, this fifth day of July 1910.

                                Henry Houck
                                Secretary of Internal Affairs.

Pennsylvania ss.

By Virtue of a Warrant Dated the 25 day of November 1748 I have caused to be Surveyed on the 29th day of October 1749 to the use of the Honourable the Proprietaries a Certain Tract of Land Situate on Stind Creek beyond the Blue Mountains in the County of Lancaster. Beginning at a Stone and from thence extending by Vacant Land the Six Courses and Distances next following Vizt. North twenty Degrees East Four hundred and twelve perches, North seventy Degrees West Four hundred and eighty perches, South one hundred and thirty five Perches, South fifteen Degrees West One hundred and Seventy Perches, South Eleven degrees West Sixty eight Perches, and South sixty five Degrees, fifteen Minutes East four hundred and eight perches to the place of Beginning Containing One Thousand Acres and the usual allowance of six Acres & Cent for Roads &c. Returned in to the Secretarys Office the Second Day of January Anno Domini 1755.

(now Berks County)

Pennsylvania ss.

By virtue of a warrant dated the 26 day of November, 1748 I have caused to be surveyed on the 29th day of October 1749 to the use of the Honourable the Proprietaries a certain tract of land situate on Kind Creek beyond the Blue Mountains in the County of Lancaster. Beginning at a stone and from thence extending by vacant land the six courses and distances next following vizt North twenty degrees east four hundred and twelve perches, north seventy degrees west four hundred and eighty perches, south one hundred and thirty five Perches, south fifteen degrees west one hundred and seventy perches, South eleven degrees west sixty eight perches, and south sixty five degrees fifteen minutes east four hundred and eight perches to the place of Beginning Containing one thousand acres and the usual allowance of six acres ♁ Cent for roads &c⍺ Returned into the Secretarys office the second day of January Anno Domini 1755. now Berks County.

IN TESTIMONY that the above is a copy of the original remaining on file in the Department of Internal Affairs of Pennsylvania, made conformably to an Act of Assembly approved the 16th day of February, 1888, I have hereunto set my Hand and caused the Seal of said Department to be affixed at Harrisburg, this eighth day of April 1910.

Henry Houck
Secretary of Internal Affairs.

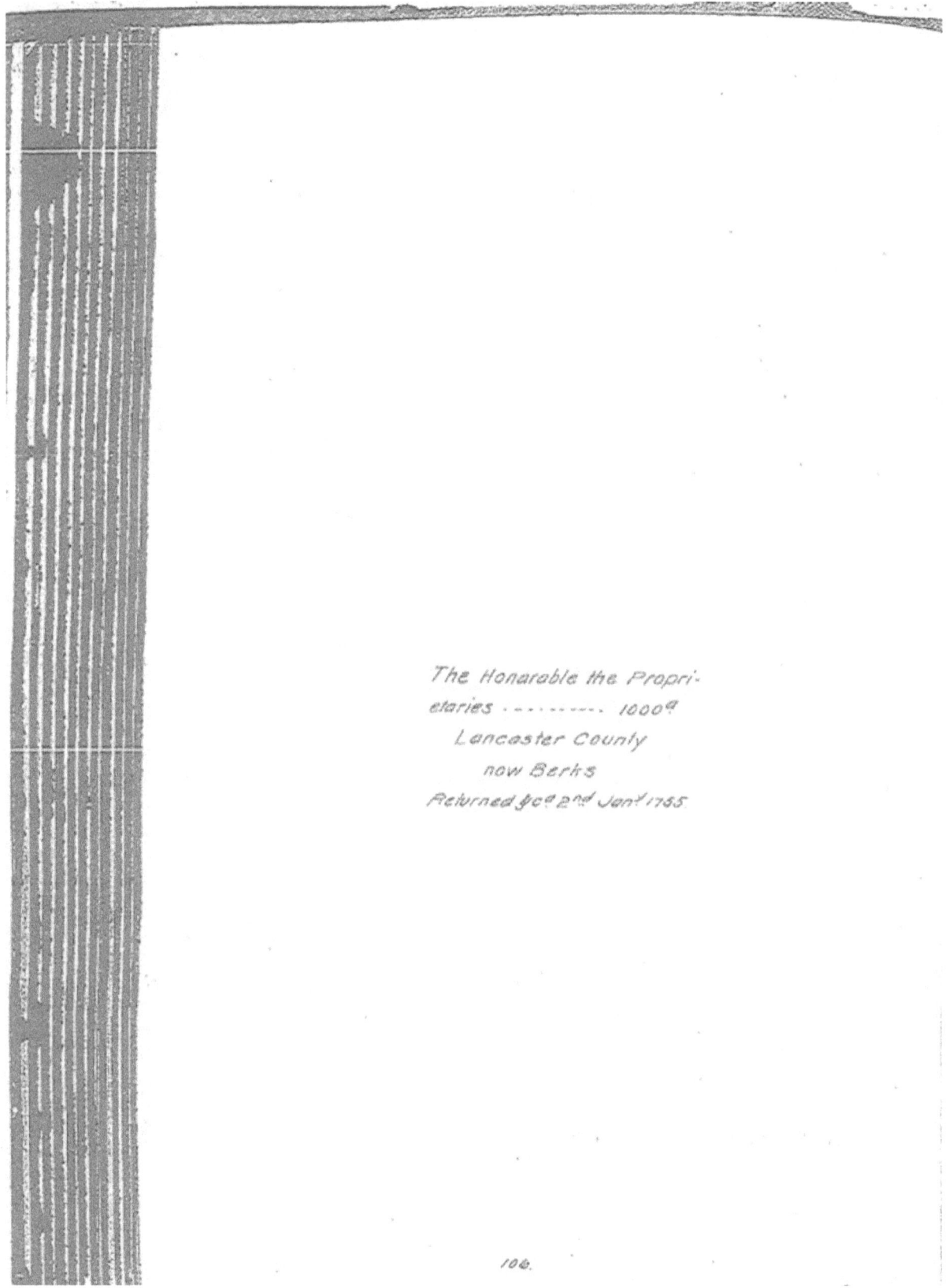

Appendix

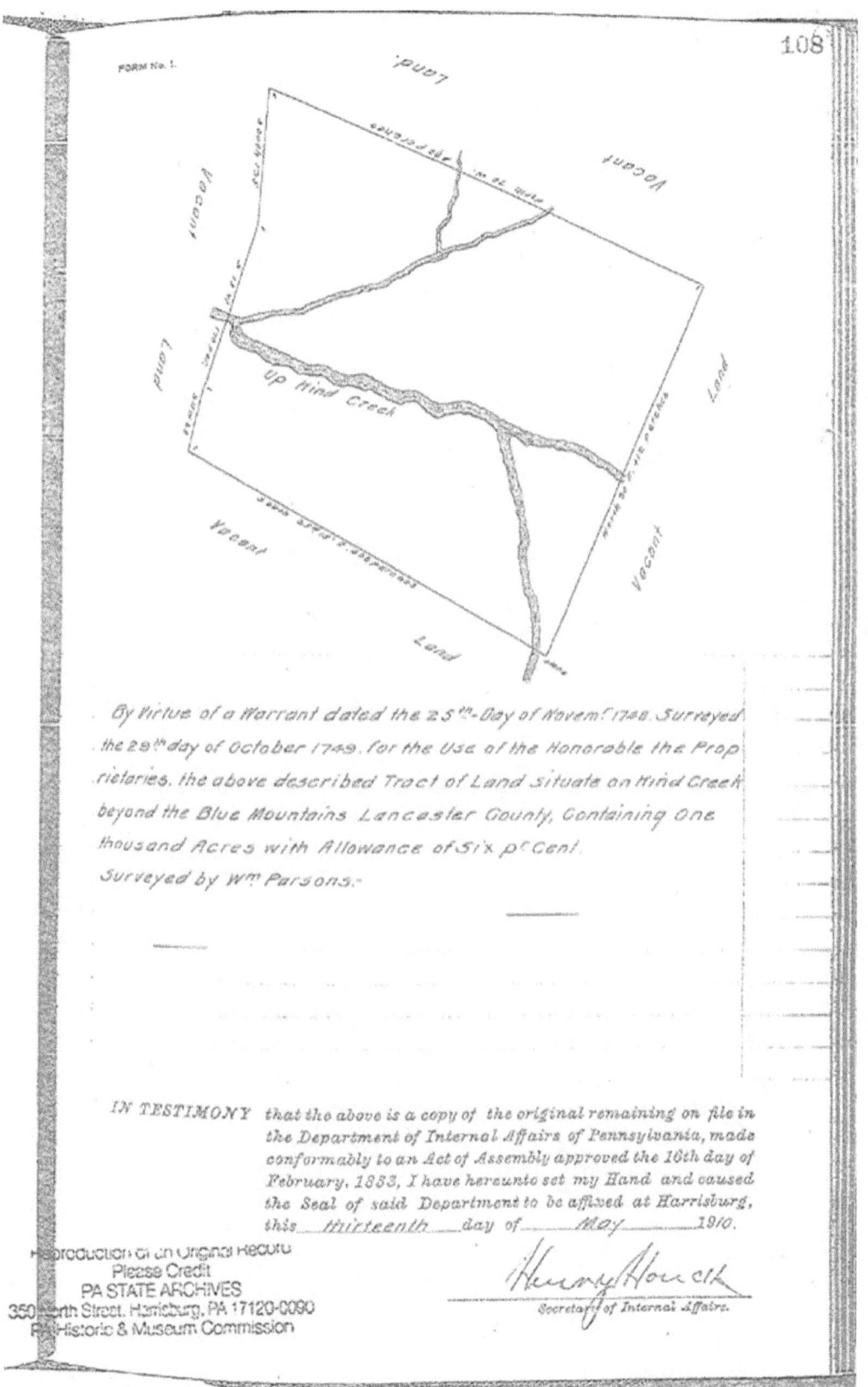

By Virtue of a Warrant dated the 25th Day of Novemr 1748, Surveyed the 29th day of October 1749, for the Use of the Honorable the Proprietaries, the above described Tract of Land Situate on Hind Creek beyond the Blue Mountains Lancaster County, Containing One thousand Acres with Allowance of Six p Cent.
Surveyed by Wm Parsons."

IN TESTIMONY that the above is a copy of the original remaining on file in the Department of Internal Affairs of Pennsylvania, made conformably to an Act of Assembly approved the 18th day of February, 1833, I have hereunto set my Hand and caused the Seal of said Department to be affixed at Harrisburg, this thirteenth day of May 1910.

Henry Houck
Secretary of Internal Affairs.

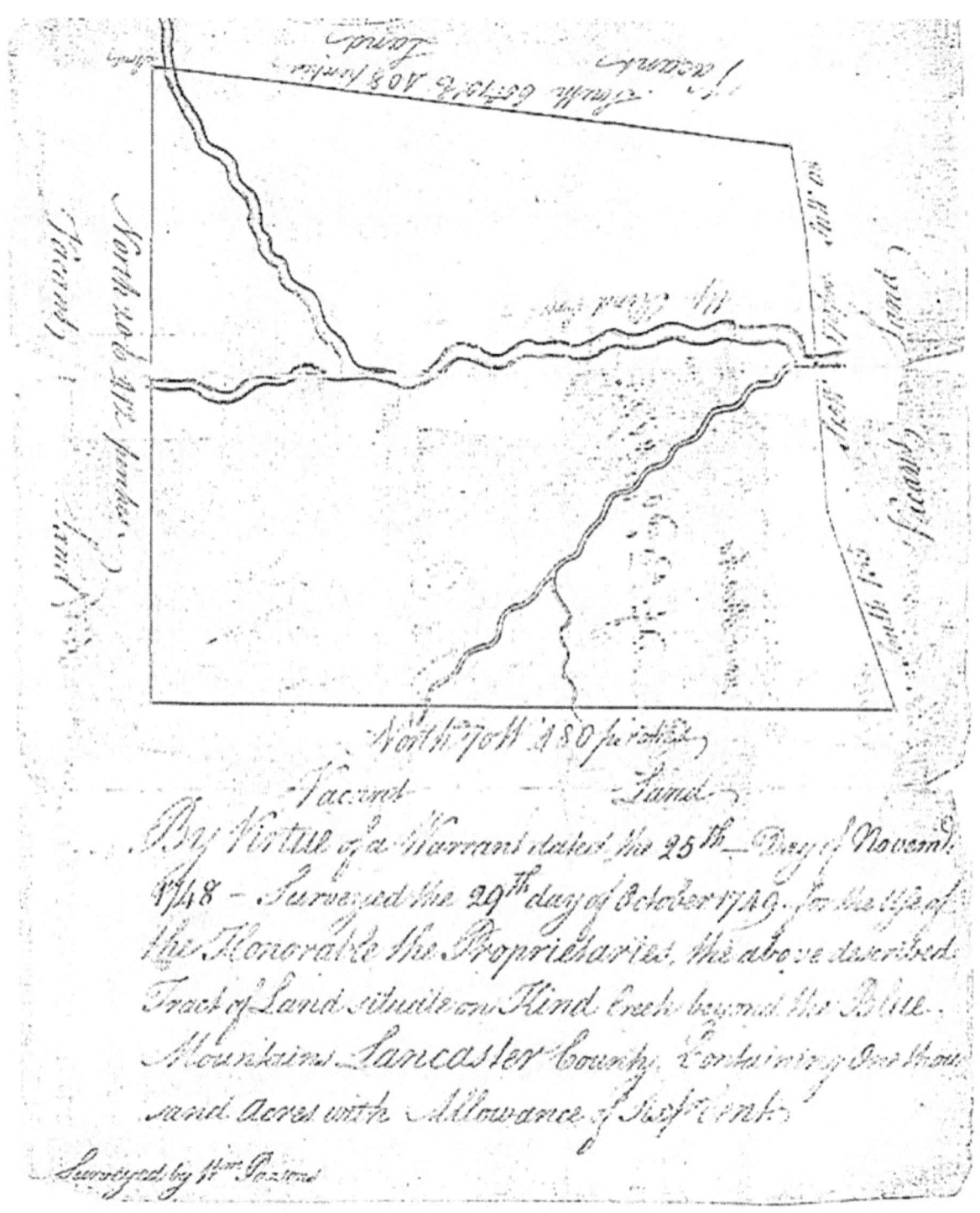

Appendix

Early Troutman Warrants, Surveys, and Patents of the Mahantongo Valley

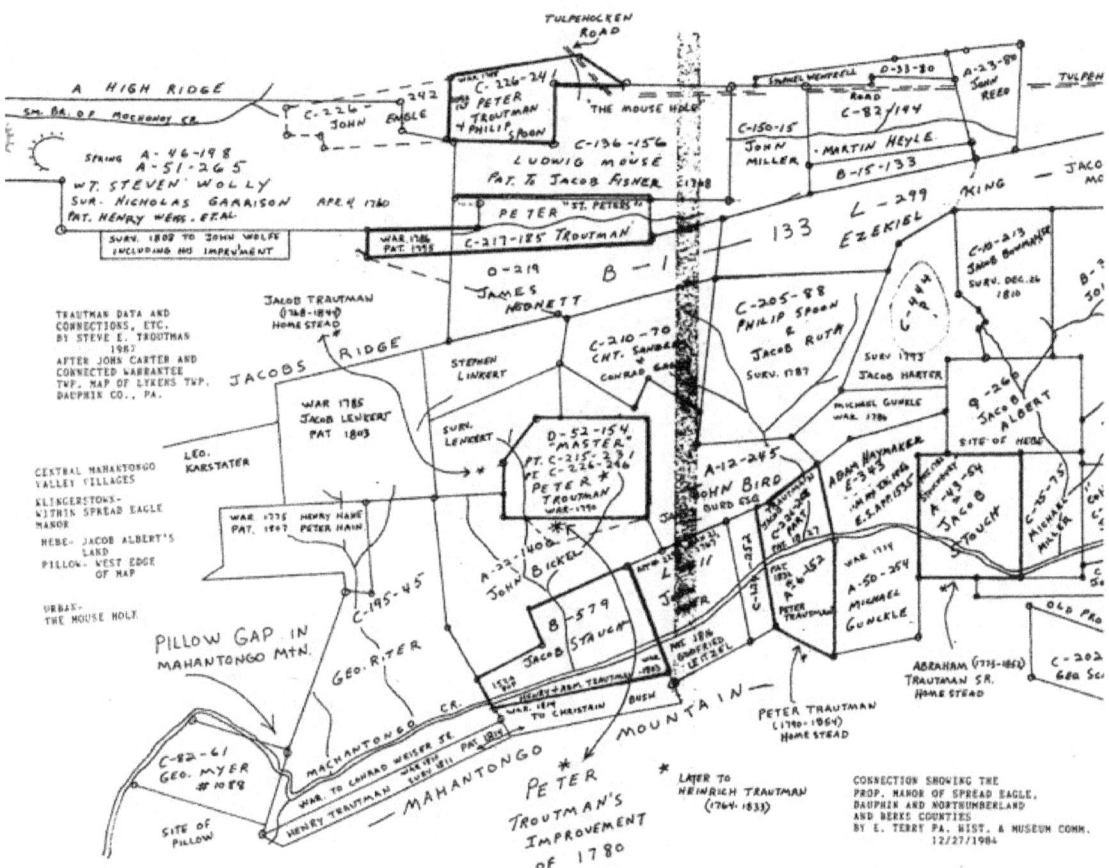

Peter Trautman (1738/40–1809) A-6; C-226-241; C-217-185; D-52-154

"The Trautman-Troutman Family History", published in 1997, by Steve E. Troutman

Early Troutman Warrants, Surveys, and Patents of the Mahantongo Valley

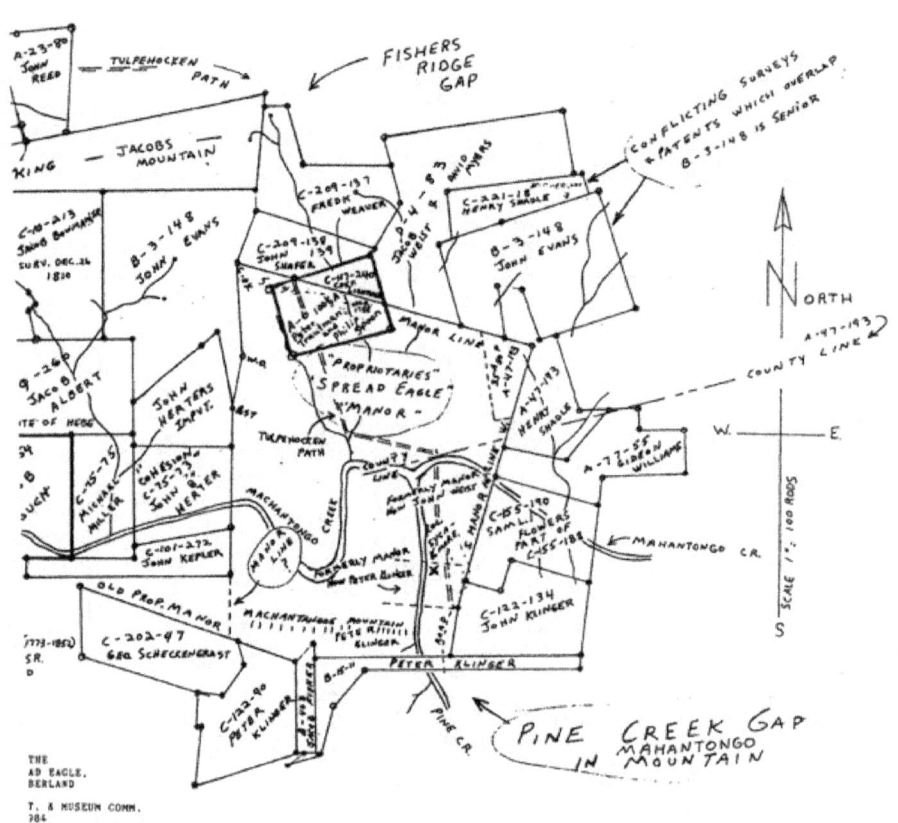

Heinrich and Abraham Trautman B-579

Abraham Trautman A-43-54

Peter Trautman (1790-1854) A-6-152

Jacob Trautman C-226-268

"The Trautman-Troutman Family History", published in 1997, by Steve E. Troutman

Warrant Description and Survey Draft for Robert Clark, Mahntongo Valley Pioneer

Robert Clark's pioneer land was the land on both sides of Mahantongo Creek near the old Klingerstown school house. This diagram describes the land on the warrant to Robert Clark. Note the Spread Eagle Manor line is the western boundary of the warranted land. This land is located west of Benigna's vineyard, east of Klingerstown. The land south of Robert Clark's warrant belonged to John Klinger. Two streams found on Mahantongo Mountain are identified on the survey being located in the hollows of the mountain south of the old school house. Robert Clark's warrant, C-155-190, is the same land surveyed earlier to Samuel Flower and William Witman.

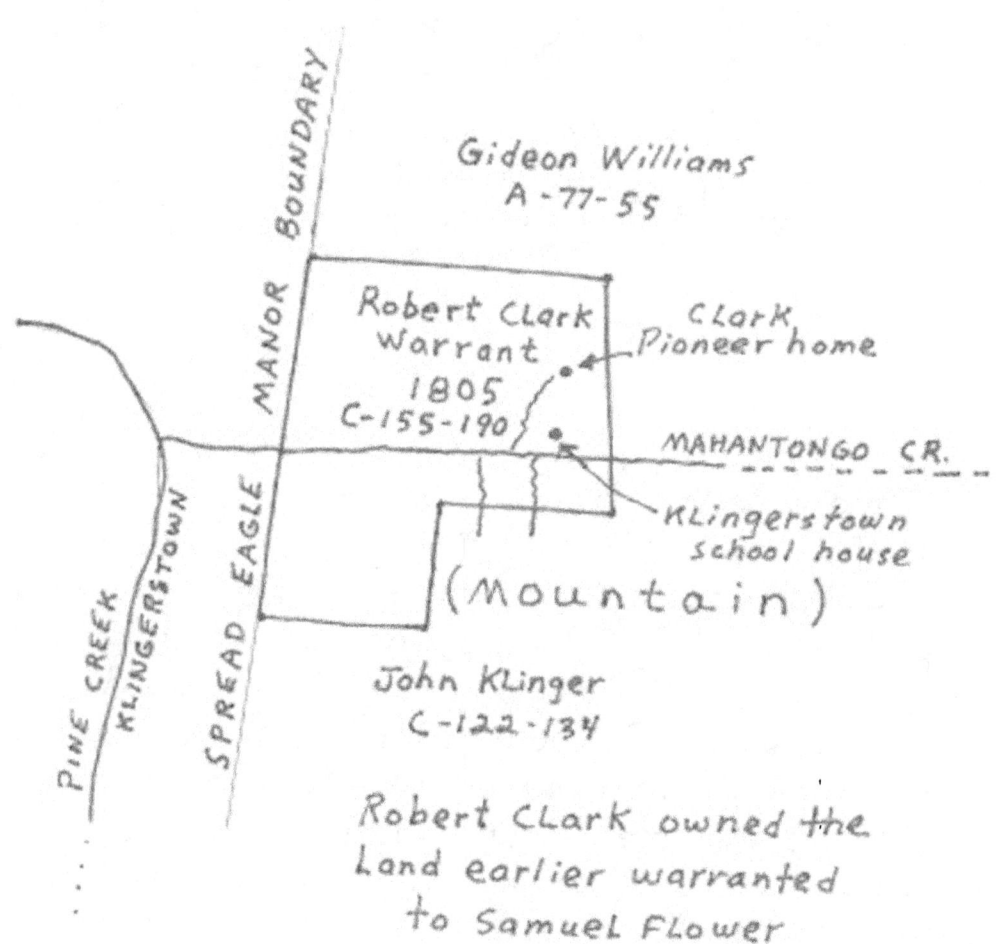

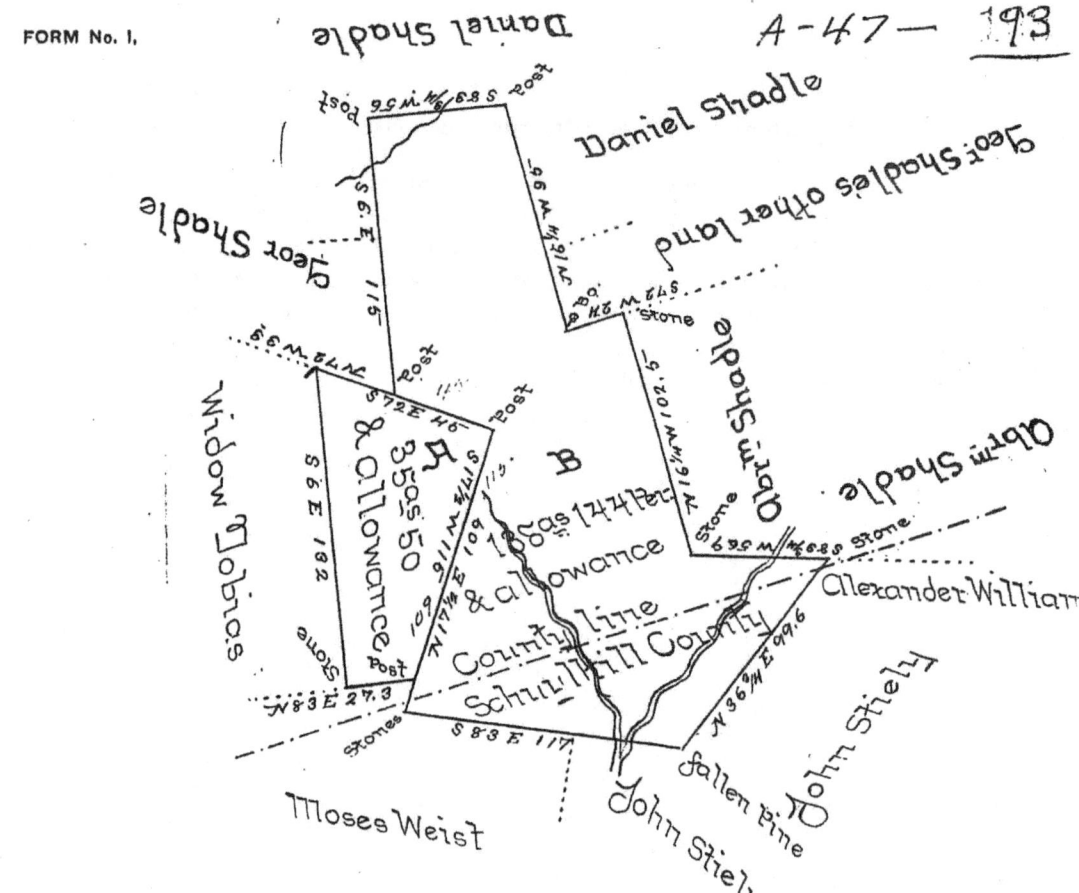

Resurveyed the first day of September A.D. 1852 at the request of George Shadle. Letter (A) is a part of what is called Manor of Spread Eagle land containing thirty five acres & fifty perches and allowance of 6 per cent &c and (B) is the same which was Surveyed unto Henry Shadle in pursuance of a warrant dated the 11th day of April 1817 Surveyd the 20th day of May 1817 by Jacob Rockefeller D.S. The above draught B represents the Original courses & distances as near as it could be assertained. Situate partly in Schuylkill and partly in Northumberland County containing one hundred and thirty eight acres one hundred and forty four perches & allowance &c.

Jo. Porter Brawley Esqr.
Surveyor General

Saml Young C.S.

570

Appendix

Families who Migrated from the Mahantongo Valley to Jefferson, Armstrong, and Clarion Counties

The History of the Mahantongo Valley, by Carrie Haas Troutman, was published in 1935 in the *Joseph H. Zerby History of Pottsville and Schuylkill County Pennsylvania*. It was also published in the *Pottsville Republican* newspaper and the *Pottsville Morning Paper*. Her history can be found in the *Trautman/Troutman Family History*, Vol. II, by Steve E. Troutman. Carrie's narrative recounts the westward journey made by Mahantongo Valley families to Red Bank, PA. They left in covered wagons. It took more than three weeks to make the trip to Red Bank. This area, named for the Red Bank River, is located south of Brookville, near the junction of Jefferson, Armstrong, and Clarion counties. Family wagon train names included Yoder, Haas, Brosius, Troutman, Klinger, Maurer, Snyder, Schlagel, Buffington, Kuntzelman, Hepler, and Reiner.

Donna (Mowrey) Ward of 795 North Fourth Street, Mifflinburg, has identified additional families who participated in this westward migration. Donna is from Jefferson County. Additional families who migrated westward include the names Thomas, Mertz, Dinger, Reitz, Shaffer, Geist, and Byerly. Donna's Mowrey family reunion was held close to North Freedom. A 1924 Mowrey Reunion picture includes a Mulatto young Enty boy in the front row. Donna's great great grandfather Isaac Shaffer was married to Christena Geist from Leck Kill, PA. They left the Rough and Ready area with the wagon train. Isaac Shaffer's name can be found on page 274 of this book. Isaac is named as an adjoining land owner to William Simmy Sr. in 1834. It has been established by census records that the Tobias Enty family lived near Isaac Shaffer and William Simmy Sr. in the Mahantongo Valley. Donna Ward has identified the later residence of Isaac Shaffer in Jefferson County. Isaac settled on Little Sandy Creek, which is a tributary of the Red Bank River, north of the Village of Worthville. *The 1878 Atlas of Jefferson County* shows the Isaac Shaffer residence and the Enty residences on page 112 (Ringold Township) and page 127 (Beaver Township). The Entys lived on both sides of Little Sandy Creek where they continued to be neighbors to Isaac Shaffer in Jefferson County, as they had been next door neighbors in Schuylkill County. Isaac Shaffer and the Entys must have travelled west together.

Enty cemeteries were established as family plots. These cemeteries are recorded in *Tombstone Hoppin, Cemetery Inscriptions of Jefferson County, PA*, by Patricia Steele of Brookville, PA. She records the George Enty cemetery between Pansy and Ringold, and the Peter Enty cemetery located northeast of the George Enty cemetery. Nine Enty graves are identified. They include **Abram**, died 1890, age 78y 5m 2d; **Amey**, w/o Abm., died 1880, 70y 8m 20d: **George**, (no dates), CO. H, 43, USCI (Civil War veteran); **Margaret Ann**, w/o George (1837-1866); **Peter Enty** (12-15-1874); **Harriet**, w/o Peter (2-10-1896); **Benj.** died (10-21-1914).

The Jefferson County Pennsylvania History records the name Thomas as early settlers in this area. The Bethlehem Lutheran Church in Ohl, PA was established in 1830-1833 when a small group of Germans migrated from the eastern part of the state (Snowdale and Rough and Ready) and settled in Beaver Township. Emanuel Thomas placed the corner stone. The Thomas family was originally from Snowdale, and Rough and Ready area. The log church and cemetery was on land donated by George Berkhouse Sr. also from Snowdale and Rough and Ready area. Many of Donna Ward's ancestors are buried here, including Isaac Shaffer, died 4-16-1868, age 69y 2m 16d, married

Christena Geist Shaffer, died 5-25-1884, age 81y 7m 1d. The Shaffers and the Geists were originally from Leck Kill in Northumberland County and the Rough and Ready area in Schuylkill County at the time of their migration.

Pioneer Colored Settlers in Jefferson County, PA

Pioneer colored settlers are named in the book, *Jefferson County Pennsylvania, Her Pioneers and People, 1800-1915*, by William James McKnight, M.D., of Brookville, PA. The pioneer colored settler in this wilderness was Fudge Van Camp. He was jet-black, fine featured and thin lipped. Fudge Van Camp was born a slave, but purchased his freedom after he grew to manhood. ... Van Camp's real name was Enos Fudge. His owner's name was Avas Van Camp. Fudge was hired by his master to the Patriot Army of the Revolution to drive team, and by playing the violin to soldiers and in other ways he accumulated five hundred dollars, which he presented to his master, who in consideration of this gave him his freedom.

Fudge came to Port Barnett (Jefferson County) from Easton, Northumberland County, PA, in the winter of 1801, and traveled this distance on foot. .... His wool was white as the wool of a sheep and his face was black as charcoal, and yet he was married to a white woman. In the company of Stephen Roll and August Shultz they made the trip to Jefferson County. The last 33 miles of unbroken wilderness were the most difficult. They were foolish enough to start the last part of their journey without anything to eat on the way. After they started it snowed all day in this wilderness until the snow was 2 feet deep. Van Camp was a large and powerful man. He undertook to break the road for the other two, but hunger and cold overcame him when within a mile of Barnett's, and this last mile, he had to make on his hands and knees. He reached Barnett's at midnight, half frozen, and so exhausted as to be scarcely able to tell of the condition of his two companions. A rescue party of four or five men was at once started. Roll was met a few rods from the house, making his way on hands and knees. Shultz was found some two miles further, almost frozen. He lost several toes and eventually died from this exposure. Roll and Van Camp lived to be old men. ... Being pleased with the country, Fudge Van Camp returned to Easton only to migrate here with his four children, bringing his effects on two horses. He brought apple seeds with him and planted them on his farm, this being the first effort to raise fruit in this wilderness. Some of the trees are still living. Fudge Van Camp married a white woman. She died in Easton. Fudge Van Camp was the only colored person living in Jefferson County as late as 1810. He was a fiddler and a great fighter, and was the orchestra for all the early frolics. Van Camp died about the year 1835 and is buried in the old graveyard in Brookville.

The family of Fudge Van Camp consisted of two sons and two daughters, Richard and Enos, Susan and Sarah. Susan married Charles Southerland, and Sarah married William Douglas, who was a hunter. Richard married Ruth Stiles, a white woman, and left the county; he was the great grandfather of Tom and Tobias Enty. Some Enty men served in the Civil War from Jefferson County. They include Privates Peter B. Enty and Peter F. Enty, both died in service, killed at New Market Heights, Virginia, with Company H, Sixth United States Colored Troops. Edward Enty (colored) is named in 1841 on the assessment list of Porter Township, Jefferson County.

www.ingramcontent.com/pod-product-compliance
Lightning Source LLC
Chambersburg PA
CBHW082107230426
43671CB00015B/2627